DacEasy Accounting 3.0

Quick Start and Reference Guide

Gia L. Rozells and Monica B. Hempel

COMPUTE! Books

Greensboro, North Carolina
Radnor, Pennsylvania

Editor: Robert Bixby
Cover design by Anthony Jacobson

Printed in the United States of America

10 9 8 7 6 5 4 3 2 1

Library of Congress Cataloging-in-Publication Data
Rozells, Gia L.
    DAC-easy accounting 3.0 quick start and reference guide/Gia L.
Rozells and Monica B. Hempel.
        p.   cm.
    Includes index.
    ISBN 0-87455-158-7
    1. Dac Easy accounting (Computer program)   2. Accounting—Data
processing.   I. Hempel, Monica B.   II. Title.   III. Title: DacEasy
accounting 3.0 quick start and reference guide.
    HF5679.R685   1989
    657'.028'55369—dc19   88-63148
                                                                      CIP

COMPUTE! Books, Post Office Box 5406, Greensboro, North Carolina 27403, (919) 275-9809, is a Capital Cities/ABC, Inc. company and is not associated with any manufacturer of personal computers. *DacEasy* and *DacEasy Accounting* are trademarks of Dac Software, Inc. IBM, IBM PC, and PC-DOS are registered trademarks of International Business Machines Corporation. Microsoft and MS-DOS are registered trademarks of Microsoft Corporation.

Contents

Foreword

Since 1985 almost half a million businesses like yours have chosen *DacEasy Accounting* as the program to manage their business. Virtually every type of business imaginable uses *DacEasy Accounting* and in more than 20 countries in 10 languages.

Here's your key to successful accounting. With *DacEasy Accounting 3.0 Quick Start and Reference Guide* and the *DacEasy Accounting* package, you can tame those nagging accounting problems. Following the easy step-by-step procedures included here, you'll be able to create your own personalized accounting system. *DacEasy Accounting* isn't like other accounting packages you may have tried. It's fast and friendly. It's operated through menus and provides such necessary features as a check-printing facility and automatic updating of accounts payable and receivable.

Authors Rozells and Hempel haven't written a substitute for the *DacEasy Accounting* manual: *DacEasy Accounting 3.0 Quick Start and Reference Guide* teaches this best-selling accounting package by providing examples and exercises, allowing you to practice each important action as you read about it.

DacEasy Accounting 3.0 Quick Start and Reference Guide provides an overview of your PC and of *DacEasy*. The early chapters concern basic organization of *DacEasy Accounting* and simple exercises that will take you from beginning-level through advanced concepts.

If you're new to *DacEasy Accounting*, but have had experience using other accounting packages on your computer, this book quickly relates the basic accounting concepts with which you're already familiar, so you can rapidly move on to the sample exercises that teach advanced uses of *DacEasy Accounting*.

Here are some things you'll find in this book: An overview of how your PC works; how to set up *DacEasy Accounting* for your system; and sample exercises that teach the features of *DacEasy*. You'll also learn to enter purchase order and accounts payable transactions, including entering and printing purchase orders, entering payments and adjustments, and so on; complete Billing, Accounts Receivable, and Inventory transactions, including entering and printing invoices, entering and printing checks, entering cash receipts, creating inventory count sheets, and so on; use *DacEasy*'s accounting journals; and operate the Reports, End of Period Routines, and Forecasting operations. Plus, you'll become familiar with *DacEasy*'s default system settings and file management.

Noted authors Gia L. Rozells and Monica B. Hempel walk you through each procedure, explaining every step in detail. You won't need an advanced accounting degree or extensive knowledge of your PC to follow their explanations. *DacEasy Accounting 3.0 Quick Start and Reference Guide* is all you'll need to get a usable accounting procedure going. And later, as your business grows, you'll grow with it by using the reference chapters to incorporate more elaborate and useful procedures in your accounting routine.

Kevin Howe
President and CEO
Dac Software, Inc.
October, 1988

Introduction

Welcome to *DacEasy Accounting 3.0 Quick Start and Reference Guide*, the fast-track handbook to using Dac Software's powerful new accounting program for your IBM PC or compatible computer.

This book will rapidly teach you how to use every major feature of *DacEasy Accounting*, Version 3.0. And, instead of simply listing the commands and functions, *DacEasy Accounting 3.0 Quick Start and Reference Guide* lets you learn through practical examples and exercises. This way, you can practice each important action as you read about it.

This book is organized and written to assist a variety of readers. Those of you who are new in the PC world, the *DacEasy* world, or both will use *DacEasy Accounting 3.0 Quick Start and Reference Guide* to gain an overview of your PC and of *DacEasy*. The first chapter shows you the basic organization of *DacEasy Accounting* and the second leads you right into sample exercises that will take you from beginning-level through advanced concepts. Once you've learned *DacEasy*, you'll be able to use this book as a handy reference manual.

For those who have used a PC and other accounting programs, but are new to *DacEasy*, this book quickly relates the basic accounting concepts with which you're already familiar and allows you to jump quickly into the sample exercises that teach advanced uses of *DacEasy Accounting*.

Later, when you're more familiar with the package, this book will still be valued as an essential reference guide.

Those who have already used *DacEasy Accounting* a little bit, but want to really get to work without necessarily studying the *DacEasy Accounting* manual can skim the first chapter and jump right into the sample exercises. When the exercises are clear to you, use this book as a reference guide for future work.

DacEasy Accounting 3.0 Quick Start and Reference Guide is divided into eight chapters.

Chapter 1 gives you an overview of how your PC works and how to set up *DacEasy Accounting* for your system.

Chapter 2 jumps directly into sample exercises that teach you all the major features of *DacEasy* by building an accounting system for Dr. Humane's Small Animal Hospital. You'll set up the necessary accounting files so various transactions can be performed and printed later.

Chapter 3 teaches you how to enter purchase order and accounts payable transactions, including entering and printing purchase orders, entering payments and adjustments, and so on.

Chapter 4 covers the areas of *DacEasy*'s Billing, Accounts Receivable, and Inventory transactions, including entering and printing invoices, entering and printing checks, entering cash receipts, creating inventory count sheets, and so on.

Chapter 5 teaches you how to utilize *DacEasy*'s accounting journals. It also covers posting operations.

Chapter 6 teaches you how to operate the Reports operations, including the Trial Balance and the Balance Sheet/Income Statements.

Chapter 7 covers the End-of-Period and Forecasting operations.

Chapter 8 reviews *DacEasy*'s menus. You can use this chapter to familiarize yourself with *DacEasy*'s menu options as well as for quick reference purposes.

Chapter 9 summarizes *DacEasy*'s default system settings, which are now accessed through the Options menu as opposed to the File Utilities menu (F3 Function key) used in version 2.0.

Chapter 10 covers file management topics. You'll learn how DOS interacts with you, your computer, and *DacEasy* programs.

Using This Book

DacEasy Accounting 3.0 Quick Start and Reference Guide uses clear, simple language and many illustrations to teach you what you need to know. It's the quickest way to get up and running with *DacEasy*. And, though the chapters are made to be studied in order, they are each self-contained so you can skip around if you like.

You may have noticed when you bought *DacEasy Accounting* that it comes with one manual by Dac Software, titled *DacEasy Accounting Version 3.0*. This manual fully explains all of *Dac Easy*'s commands—there are eight major operation menus that branch off into some 115 submenus. *DacEasy Accounting 3.0 Quick Start and Reference Guide* purposely avoids addressing each and every command. Instead it focuses only on the commands you need to know for a quick start, and then takes you straight through to advanced techniques. Later, as is suggested occasionally in this book, you may want to refer to the other text to approach extremely advanced applications.

The tutorials in this book are based on version 3.0 of *DacEasy Accounting* and run on the IBM PC or compatible with two disk drives (or one disk drive and a hard disk) and a color or monochrome monitor. The program requires 256K of memory, MS-DOS or PC-DOS 2.0 or higher, and an 80-column printer (if you want hardcopy output of your information), which in compressed mode, can print 132 columns.

One advantage of *DacEasy* is that it isn't copy-protected, which lets you make multiple backup copies or lets you install it on your hard disk.

Version 3.0

Version 2.0 introduced these advantages:

- Easy to install and operate.
- Allows you to convert from a floppy disk system to a hard disk system if more memory is needed.
- Provides complete integration between seven primary accounting modules—General Ledger, Accounts Receivable, Accounts Payable, Purchasing Orders, Billing, Inventory, and Budgeting. Data entered once is automatically posted (recorded) to the other modules.
- Contains a sample Chart of Accounts, Income Statements, and Balance Sheets that are revisable so they can meet the criteria of your business.
- Provides context-sensitive help screens.
- Contains special billing system for service-oriented business, built-in financial ratioing capabilities, and forecasting routines.
- Provides the potential to run over 700 different reports.
- Uses function keys to speed up applications.
- Provides both batch and online processing.
- Maintains more than one open period.
- Provides password protection.
- Includes on-demand invoices option for point-of-sale transactions.

3

Version 3.0 also includes these features, in addition to the following high points:

• New user interface using a *pull-down* menu system organized by functional area instead of journal type. Version 2.0's main menu has been replaced by a horizontal *Opening menu.*
• An added Tax Id. Number Field and a Tax Table Code field for both the Customer and Vendor Files.
• Changed journal access, posting procedures, reports, and periodic closing operations using specific pull-down options.
• Eliminated the use of the File Utilities (F3) function key. All default system settings are now accessed through the Options pull-down selection.

Converting Version 2.0 to Version 3.0 Files

DacEasy gives you the ability to convert your version 2.0 data files to version 3.0 data files. To do this, go to the directory that holds the *DacEasy* program files. At the prompt, type *deau* and press the Enter key. Select option 2 (Run Convert Routine) and press the Enter key. Follow the instructions displayed on the screen to convert your *DacEasy* data files.

Chapter 1
DacEasy Fundamentals

DacEasy is designed to make the most of your PC by utilizing all of its power. And, although the computer has to be very complex to run a powerful accounting program like *DacEasy*, the program is actually surprisingly simple to use.

You don't have to be a computer whiz or a "power user" to learn and use *DacEasy Accounting*, any more than you would have to be an expert on automobile mechanics to drive.

However, if you'd like to learn more, this chapter is written for you. You'll learn about the PC's hardware—the keyboard and disk drives—and about the commands you need to run *DacEasy*. Of course, if you already understand the workings of computers, and you've installed the *DacEasy Accounting* program as explained later in this section, you may want to skip this chapter and head right into learning *DacEasy* in Chapter 2.

DacEasy Accounting

In all businesses, an accounting system is the most critical financial tool in the office. Business managers and owners need accurate financial information to make good business decisions. Inaccurate accounting records or records that are difficult to understand often lead a business into failure and bankruptcy. Thus, it's extremely important that managers and owners—or anyone involved in making financial decisions—understand accounting terms and accounting practices. Understanding the language of business accounting helps people make better business decisions.

Until the dawn of the PC, accounting records were done manually. It was a tedious, time-consuming, yet important task. There's a great margin for error when recording and reporting financial data is done by hand. Fortunately for modern-day business people, powerful electronic accounting programs are available that can save time and improve accuracy of business data and accounting practices. *DacEasy*'s accounting program is capable of meeting the accounting needs of offices and businesses both large and small. And, whether you've ever used an automated accounting system, you'll find *DacEasy*'s accounting system simple and easy to understand.

For those who aren't familiar with accounting systems, the following section is a brief explanation of the basic concepts of *DacEasy*. After this quick accounting primer, the chapter goes on to explain general *DacEasy* concepts and specific methods.

What is an Accounting System?

Automated accounting systems are bookkeeping and financial planning tools made more powerful by your computer. Planning for automated accounting is similar to planning for manual accounting. Planning any accounting system consists of two steps:

- Setting goals: Deciding what is to be recorded and reported
- Establishing procedures: Deciding steps to be followed in carrying out the goals

Accuracy is equally important in both manual and automated accounting. Results in any accounting system can only be as accurate as the data put into the system. For example, if an accountant records an amount of $35.60 instead of $36.50, data on financial statements for any system will be incorrect.

There are four phases of automated accounting:

- Input
- Processing
- Storage
- Output

Data put into a computer is called *input*. Input may be data on receipts, checks, and other business forms.

Working with data according to precise instructions is called *processing*. Posting transaction data to general ledger accounts is an example of the processing phase.

Filing or holding data until needed is called *storage*. Keeping data in general ledger accounts until needed is an example of the storage phase.

Information produced by a computer is called *output*. Examples of output are information about assets, liabilities, capital, revenue, and expenses reported on financial statements. Output can also be printed on forms such as checks.

DacEasy's accounting system is set up like a traditional paper accounting system using general ledgers, financial statements, customer, vendor and service files, and so forth.

Also like a traditional accounting system, *DacEasy Accounting* lets you do daily bookkeeping chores and create reports. In addition, *DacEasy Accounting* allows you to forecast information such as financial budgets, sales quotas, inventory usage, and so on, because it has the ability to gather and save three years' worth of historical information in each of the following files:

- Chart of Accounts
- Customer File
- Products File
- Services File
- Vendor File

DacEasy's unique forecasting capability lets you "see the future" by allowing you to perform "what if" scenarios. (For example, what would your profit be if your customer's spending increased by 15 percent?)

Accounting Definitions

DacEasy's accounting system is one of the most complete packages on the market today. It is purposely designed for people who don't have in-depth knowledge of accounting principles; however, some of the operations require that you understand a few basic accounting terms and concepts.

If you're an accounting novice, this section defines some of these basic accounting terms and concepts so you'll have a better understanding of what *DacEasy Accounting* is all about.

Account Balance   The difference between the totals of amounts in an account's debit and credit columns.

Accounting Equation   An equation (Assets = Liabilities + Capital) showing the relationship among assets, liabilities, and capital.

Accounts Payable   Amounts you owe others. When you make a payment, your accounts payable is reduced.

Accounts Receivable   Amounts others owe you. When a payment is made to you, the amount is credited toward the amount they owe you, and your accounts receivable amount is reduced.

Assets   Anything of value owned by a business and used to conduct its activities, such as cash, equipment, and supplies. Assets may be used to pay debts.

Balance Sheet   A financial statement that reports assets, liabilities, and capital on a specific date.

Budget   A forecast and plan for coordinating income and expenses.

Capital   The value of an owner's equity.

Chart of Accounts   A list of account titles and numbers showing the location of each account in a ledger.

Contra Account   An account that reduces a related account on financial statements. Contra accounts are used to avoid losing control over the original value of an asset account. Using a contra account lets you know the original value as well as the accumulated depreciation.

Credit   An entry in an account showing money received.

Customer   A person or business to whom merchandise or services are sold.

Data   Details or factual information.

Debit   An entry in an account showing money paid out or owed.

Depreciation   Fixed assets (building, office equipment, cars, and so forth) transferred to an expense account due to the loss of value.

Double-Entry Accounting   The recording of debit and credit parts of a transaction. The assumption that each transaction affects at least one other account by decreasing the amount in one and increasing the amount in another.

Entry   Each item recorded in a journal.

Equity   The value of property or of an interest in it in excess of claims against it.

Expense   A decrease in capital resulting from the operation of a business.

Fiscal Period   The length of time for which a business analyzes financial information.

Income Statement   A financial statement showing the revenue and expenses for a fiscal period.

Interest   An amount paid for the use of money. Banks and other lending institutions generally charge interest on money borrowed by their customers.

Inventory   An itemized list showing the value of assets and goods on hand.

Invoice   A form describing the merchandise or supplies sold, the quantity, and the price.

Journal   A form for recording accounting information in chronological order.

Ledger   A ledger that contains all accounts needed to prepare financial statements.

Liabilities   Amounts owed by a business (debts).

Posting   Transferring information from journal entries to ledger accounts.

Proving Cash   Determining that the amount of cash on hand agrees with accounting records.

Purchase Order   A form describing the merchandise or supplies to be purchased, the quantity, and the price.

Revenue   An increase in capital resulting from the operation of a business.

Sorting   A list grouping data in a certain place or order, that is, alphabetically, numerically, territorially, or by some other system.

Transaction   A normal business activity that changes assets, liabilities, or an owner's equity.

Vendor   A business from which merchandise or supplies are purchased.

The Accounting Equation

An equation showing the relationship among assets, liabilities, and capital is called an *accounting equation*. Most often, an accounting equation is written as:

Assets = Liabilities + Capital

For example, let's say you're starting a new accounting system for a business. First, you must prepare a list of the business' assets and liabilities for the beginning of a particular fiscal year.

What is Owned (Assets)	What is Owed (Liabilities)
Cash on hand or in bank	2,000.00
ABC Supply Company	250.00
Supplies	900.00
Smith Company	275.00
Prepaid Insurance	250.00
Total Owned	3,150.00
Total Owed	525.00

These total amounts are placed in the accounting equation.

Assets = **Liabilities + Capital**
$3,150.00 = $525.00 + x

To calculate the equity (capital), you must subtract the liabilities from the assets (3,150.00 − 525.00 = 2,625.00). The equity, 2,625.00, is placed in the accounting equation.

Assets = **Liabilities + Capital**
$3,150.00 = $525.00 + 2,625.00

An accounting equation must be in balance to be accurate. That is, the total of amounts on the equation's left side must equal the total of amounts on the right side. In the example above, the left side total, 3,150.00, equals the right side total, 3,150.00

The Double-Entry Accounting Theory

The theory of double-entry accounting is "for every debit there is a corresponding credit." To help you understand this expression, review the following example.

Accounting transactions are recorded by entering *applications* of funds (debits) and *sources* of funds (credits). For instance, let's say you owe $100.00 to your car insurance company and you pay them by check. You've *applied* $100.00 toward the purchase for the car insurance and used your bank checking account as the *source* of the money. This transaction is recorded as follows.

Car Insurance Account (Debit)	Bank Checking Account (Credit)
$100.00	($100.00)

The Chart of Accounts

DacEasy's accounting program furnishes you with a built-in Chart of Accounts. This chart gives you five main categories of accounts:

1 Assets
2 Liabilities
3 Stockholder's Equity

4 Revenues
5 Total Expenses

Each of these account titles contain subaccounts relating to it. All accounts and subaccounts have levels that give you various degrees of detailed information. For example, Account #3 provides Stockholder's Equity information. Account #3 also contains these subaccounts: Capital Stock (Account #31), Retained Earnings (Account #32), and Current Earnings (Account #33). All accounts and subaccounts have specific levels assigned to them as indicated by the *Level* column within the Chart of Accounts. The higher the level, the more detailed the information; thus, they're called *Detail accounts*. Accounts that receive information from these detail accounts are called *General accounts*.

Stockholder's Equity (Account #3) is considered a general account and is assigned as a Level 1 account; Capital Stock (Account #31) is also considered a general account; however, it's assigned as a level 2 account. Common Stock (Account #3101) is also a general account, but is assigned as a level 3 account.

Par Value (Account #31011) and Surplus (Account #31012) are detail accounts and are both assigned as level 4 accounts. The detail accounts receive transactions (in the form of debits and credits) directly. These detail accounts must pass their information on to a higher priority account (or another way to look at it would be that the detail accounts pass information to accounts with lower numbers). The Par Value and Surplus accounts pass information to Common Stock (level 3). Common Stock will, in turn, pass its information to Capital Stock (level 2), and Capital Stock will pass its information to Stockholder's Equity (level 1). The higher the level number, the more detailed information it contains. Level 1 accounts don't pass information to other general accounts. They retain all the information entered "down-line" from them.

It isn't mandatory that you use the Chart of Accounts provided, but a good suggestion is to follow its design. If you're a beginner, it's recommended that you use *DacEasy*'s Chart of Accounts as a starting point. The examples in upcoming chapters use the Chart of Accounts provided in *DacEasy*'s program. NOTE: Accounts can be added to or deleted from the Chart of Accounts.

PC's Basic Hardware

While working with *DacEasy* and practicing this manual's tutorials, it helps to understand these PC basics:

Disks

Floppy disks, usually just called *disks*, are thin magnetic media used to record and play back computer data much like (though much more complicated than) cassette tapes or record albums. The disks you use on your PC are 5¼ inches in diameter. They're enclosed in square plastic covers that are somewhat flexible; thus they're given the name floppy disks. Keep disks in their envelopes, stored upright in a cool location. Keep them safe from heat, dust, and magnetic fields. Also, be sure to write on their labels with felt pens only—ball points could damage them.

Finally, you may leave the disks in the drive when turning off the computer, but don't take them out while the red light indicates that the computer is currently reading them.

The little-understood hard disk drive is also a magnetic disk, but is much larger and denser than a floppy disk. In fact, even small hard disks can hold more data than some 25 floppies. The hard disk is in a box inside the computer Central Processing Unit (CPU) of your computer.

Knowing Your Disk Drive Names

The PC identifies your computer's disk drives by single-letter names. You need to know these names to handle many *DacEasy* file management operations. If your computer has two disk drives set side by side or on top of one another, one is drive A: and the other is drive B:. Insert disks into each and type *DIR A:*. The drive whose light comes on is drive A:.

If your computer has a hard disk, it's known as C:. When you open, close, or store a *DacEasy* file, you tell *DacEasy* what disk to store it on by identifying the drive in which the disk is currently placed.

Your PC Keyboard

If your computer is an IBM or compatible, its keyboard probably looks something like the one in Figure 1-1. As you can see, it's a little like a standard typewriter keyboard, but with more keys.

The keys on your keyboard are split into four specialized groups: function keys, typewriter keys, control keys, and the numeric keypad. The white keys in the center work just like the standard typewriter's keys. On keyboards similar to the keyboards that came with IBM PCs and PC-XTs, there are additional

Figure 1-1. A Typical PC Keyboard

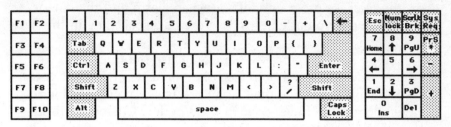

keys for backslash (\\) and double bar (|) positioned between the left Shift key and the Z key.

If you are a trained touch typist, you'll have to train yourself not to hit the backslash key when you're trying to reach the Shift key.

How to Use the Typewriter Keys

In addition to the usual typewriter keys, your computer keyboard uses the following symbols:

[ ]   The left and right square brackets
{ }   The left and right braces (or curved brackets)
`   The accent mark (like a backward apostrophe)
~   The tilde
< >   The less-than and greater-than signs

How to Use the Control Keys

The gray keys marked Shift, Ctrl, Alt, Enter, and Esc are control keys. They're used in combination with other keys to enter commands to the computer. Each key is labeled with its specific use.

If you press the Shift key and type a letter, the letter is entered in uppercase.

Use the Enter key just as you would a Return key on a standard typewriter. However, rather than pressing Enter at the end of each line as on a typewriter, in *DacEasy* you only need to press Enter when you want to leave a particular field. Data just typed in the current field will be accepted once the Enter key is depressed; the cursor moves on to the next field. *DacEasy* will also automatically move the cursor back to the first field of your file after the last field has been saved by pressing the Enter key.

Use the Backspace key to delete the previous character; how-ever, the *DacEasy* program will sound an alarm and the cursor will not move if you attempt to use the backspace key in the first position of a field.

To type in all uppercase characters, use the Caps Lock key the same way you use a Shift Lock key on a typewriter. If you press the Shift key while the Caps Lock is set, you'll be able to type temporarily in lowercase. In the Vendor, Customer, Prod-ucts, and Accounts files, the *DacEasy* program will automatically convert all codes or ID numbers into uppercase even if you used lowercase when you entered the information. In other alphabetic fields (names, addresses, and so on) the case you enter will re-main unchanged. Although *DacEasy* accepts both uppercase and lowercase responses, it's a good idea to keep Caps Lock turned off. Most keyboards have a light indicating when Caps Lock is on.

Use the Control (Ctrl) and Alternate (Alt) keys in combina-tion with other keys to give the computer commands. For exam-ple, you would press Ctrl-X to remove any entries on the current screen and return to the first field of the screen. If you press Alt-D in files where line-by-line entries are made, an entire line will be deleted.

Using the Numeric Keypad

The white keys on the right side of the keyboard are the numeric keypad. These keys work just like a calculator and are most use-ful when you need to enter many numbers in your files. Notice, however, that to use them to enter numbers you must press the gray Num Lock key. This is necessary because these keys func-tion as cursor-control keys when Num Lock isn't on.

The cursor is the flashing mark—usually an underline—on your screen that shows where your typing will be entered. The 2, 4, 6, and 8 keys are marked with directional arrows. When Num Lock is off, use these keys to move the cursor on the screen. Moving the cursor won't erase the text on the screen.

In *DacEasy* these keys are also used to move from one field to another within the files.

Notice that the white keys in the corners of the keypad are labeled Home, End, PgUp, and PgDn. You can use them rather than the other arrows to move farther in the document. For in-stance, if you press the Home key, you'll move the cursor to the beginning of a field. If you press Shift-Home, you'll move to the first field of the document. The action of the other keys are covered in full a little later in this text.

The final keys in the keypad are Ins (Insert) and Del (Delete), which are used to insert or remove text from your document. For example, if you press the Del key, you'll delete the character at the current cursor position.

Using the Function Keys

The gray keys labeled F1 through F10 on the left side of the keyboard are called *function keys.* They're used in *DacEasy Accounting* to give the computer special commands, such as requesting the Help menu, deleting selected text, or recording (saving) a document.

For instance, pressing F1 brings up *DacEasy's* Help menu. Any function keys available for use within an accounting file will appear on the status line at the bottom of the screen. This way, you can take full advantage of the options available to you. The following three function keys are always available:

Key	Function
F1	Help
F4	Change Date
F10	Process

The *DacEasy* Environment

DacEasy is organized to make the best use of your PC and your time. You can choose one of two ways to manage the program: You can select options from the opening menu by entering the first letter of your choice and pressing Enter, or you can select options from the opening menu by using the cursor-control keys, and pressing Enter. If you opt for the second alternative, pressing Home will take you to the first menu item displayed on the screen, and pressing End will take you to the last menu item.

All submenu items have a corresponding number in front of the option. To choose the desired item, either type the number and press Enter or use the cursor-control, Home, or End keys to move the cursor to the desired item; then press Enter.

The Home, End, Ins, Del, and Backspace keys all perform other functions when you're working in any of the following files:

General Ledger, Accounts Receivable, Accounts Payable, Products File, and Services File.

Anytime you're editing or adding records to these files, pressing the up-arrow key positions the cursor on the previous field. The down-arrow key positions the cursor on the next field. Pressing Ctrl-Home simultaneously positions the cursor on the first field of the file; pressing Ctrl-End positions the cursor on the last field of the file.

These keys also serve different functions *within* a field. Pressing Ctrl-left arrow positions the cursor one character to the left; pressing Ctrl-right arrow positions the cursor one character to the right. Pressing Home or End while within a field moves the cursor to the beginning or end of the field, respectively.

You can quickly insert data within a field: Press the Ins key and then type the new information. To exit the insert mode, press Ins again when you've finished inserting data.

There are three ways to erase unwanted data:

• Press Del to erase the character the cursor is currently on.
• Press Backspace to erase the character currently left of the cursor.
• Press Alt-D simultaneously to erase an entire line.

The last delete function (Alt-D) only works in areas where line-by-line entries are made (called data-entry routines). Examples of data entry routines include general ledger transactions, purchase orders, and financial statement formats.

DacEasy Menus

DacEasy uses an opening menu and submenus that keep you constantly informed of the possible operations you can perform. The one shown in Figure 1-2, for example, lists the routines you can select from the opening menu. Once a routine is selected, a submenu appears, giving you an even more detailed choice of the routine you wish to perform.

The Function Keys

The function keys, ranging from F1 to F10 on most keyboards, and F1 to F12 on others, provide additional operations and functions. These keys are usually located in two columns at the left end of the keyboard (as shown in Figure 1-1), or in a single row along the top of the keyboard.

Figure 1-2. The *DacEasy* Main Menu

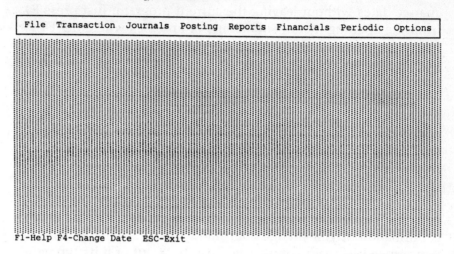

```
File  Transaction  Journals  Posting  Reports  Financials  Periodic  Options
```

```
F1-Help F4-Change Date  ESC-Exit
```

- **Getting Help (F1).** *DacEasy* provides assistance instantly if you're confused or need additional information. To display the Help Function, press F1. A *help window* appears, displaying information pertinent to what you're doing at the moment. This is known as *context-sensitive help*.

For example, if you press F1 while using a menu, information on the highlighted menu item will be described. In the same way, if you press F1 while using the Customer File Maintenance worksheet, all your customer file options will be described.

When you want to exit the Help mode, press any key and you'll return to the program. Note: The F1 (Help) key is available in all *DacEasy* operations.

The F2 Function Key. *DacEasy*'s F2 key has a variety of functions. Specific functions available in a given accounting operation are displayed on the status line at the bottom of your screen. For example, from within the General Ledger Transaction Entry worksheet, the F2 key allows you to automatically set up a new line item placing the difference in the appropriate debit or credit field (differences account). F2 lets you center text from within the Company Name Table operation.

The F2 key also has a function in the Customer File Maintenance and Vendor File Maintenance operations, but here pressing the F2 key enters the appropriate tax rates.

The F3 Function Key. Version 3.0 of *DacEasy Accounting* doesn't utilize this function key.

Changing the Date (F4). *DacEasy* makes it very easy to change dates without leaving the current program. Just press F4 from the opening menu, submenus, or any files where the F4 option is displayed on the status line, and instructions on changing the date will appear. Note: The F4 (Change Date) key is available in all *DacEasy* operations.

Showing the Balance on an Invoice (F5). *DacEasy*'s program enables you to see the balance of a particular invoice before and after payment by pressing the F5 key. There are only two areas where this key works: The first is in the Accounts Receivable module (when entering Cash Receipts), and the second is Accounts Payable (when entering payments).

Deleting Records (F6). *DacEasy*'s F6 function key allows you to delete records. A warning will appear on the screen asking for confirmation; if you change your mind about deleting a file, or if you pressed F6 inadvertently, you can back out of it by typing *N* (for *No*) in answer to the prompt.

Setting Up Beginning Balances (F7). *DacEasy*'s F7 key permits you to set up the beginning balances for the following files: Customers' File, Products' File, and Vendors' File.

Sorting Data (F8). *DacEasy* lets you sort data in Cash Receipts and Enter Payments routines simply by pressing F8.

Automatic Entry (F9). Use *DacEasy*'s F9 function key for automatic application of payments in the Cash Receipts and Enter Payments routines.

Pressing F9 will also save you keystrokes and assure first-time accuracy when entering transactions in the General Ledger, Accounts Receivable, and Accounts Payable files. After you've keyed in the final account number of the transaction, press F9 and the correct amount will automatically be placed in the Debit or Credit column.

Saving Data (F10). To save (record) all the information you've entered, simply press F10. If you forget to enter any mandatory information, *DacEasy* will display a message on the screen asking you to fill in the empty field. Note: The F10 (Process) key is available in all *DacEasy* operations.

Getting Started

Before you can use *DacEasy*, you need to install it into your computer system. Follow the directions suited to your configuration.

Before you proceed, however, format some new data disks on which to save your *DacEasy* files using these steps:

- Load DOS in your computer.
- At the DOS prompt (usually A> or C>), type FORMAT A: (or B:).
- When prompted, put the disk to be formatted (prepared to accept data) in the appropriate drive (A: or B:).
- Press Enter.

Remember that formatting a disk removes all information on the disk. Use new disks for this purpose or disks that contain information you're sure you won't mind losing.

Backing Up DacEasy's Program Disks

Before loading or otherwise working with *DacEasy*, make backup copies of your original *DacEasy* disks. Then, use the copies to work with and store the originals in a safe place.

Before copying your two *DacEasy* disks, prepare some blank, formatted disks as described in the previous section. Then, follow these steps:

- Load DOS. If the A> prompt isn't displayed, type A: (to switch to drive A:) and press any key.
- Insert the first *DacEasy* disk in drive A: and one of the formatted disks in drive B:.
- Type Copy A:*.* B: and press Enter. All files on the program disk will be copied to the disk in drive B:.
- Take out the finished disk and label it. Store the original.
- Repeat this process for the second disk.
- Store all the originals.

If you're working with a system that only has a single floppy drive, follow these instructions:

- Load DOS. If the A> prompt isn't displayed, type A: (to switch to drive A:) and press any key.
- Insert the first *DacEasy* disk in drive A:.
- Type Copy A:*.* B: and press Enter.
- Shortly you'll be prompted to change disks. Take the *DacEasy* disk out of drive A: and insert the backup disk in drive A:.

- Keep switching disks as the computer prompts you until all files on the program disk are copied to the disk in drive B:.
- Take out the finished disk and label it. Store the original.
- Repeat this process for the second disk.
- Store all the originals.

Installing *DacEasy* on Your Floppy Disk System

Before using *DacEasy* for the first time on your system, follow these steps to install it on your system:

- Load DOS in your computer. It's important that you enter the actual date and time at the prompts unless your computer automatically performs this function.
- Format two blank disks. Label the first disk Program-1. Label the second disk Program-2.
- Remove the DOS disk from drive A: and replace it with the *DacEasy* Disk-1 disk (Install/Program).
- Type A: to make drive A: the active drive and type *INSTALL*. Press Enter.
- Remove Disk-1 from drive A: and replace it with Disk-2. To continue, press any key.
- At the prompt, remove Disk-2 from drive A: and replace it with Disk-1. Press Enter.
- The screen in Figure 1-3 will appear.
- At the prompt, type *F* to indicate that you're installing *DacEasy* on a floppy disk system. At this time, *DacEasy* searches your

Figure 1-3. The *DacEasy* Installation Screen

```
                        DAC-EASY INSTALLATION


                    WELCOME TO DAC-EASY ACCOUNTING!

   This routine is used to install Dac-Easy onto your hard disk or to create
   working copies of your program files if you are using a dual-floppy system.
   This process will also configure your hardware to take full advantage of
   Dac-Easy's features.

   If you are installing Dac-Easy for a floppy drive system, you will need two
   blank formatted diskettes (in addition to the disks found in your Dac-Easy
   Accounting Package).  Label these disks PROGRAM-1 and PROGRAM-2.  If you do
   not have these disks ready, press ESC to exit this routine.  Use the FORMAT
   command to prepare the blank disks (see your DOS manual for more information
   on FORMAT).



          Is Dac-Easy to be installed on a Floppy or Hard Disk (F/H)?
```

DOS program for a file named CONFIG.SYS as indicated in Figure 1-4. If it doesn't exist, *DacEasy* will automatically create it; if it does exist, *DacEasy* may modify it according to its required file and buffer settings.

- You have one of two options at this point. If no prompt appears at the bottom of the screen, the CONFIG.SYS file exists and is correct. Simply press Enter to move to the next step. If a prompt appears at the bottom of the screen, replace the Install disk in drive A: with the DOS disk. Press Enter. You must wait a few moments so the computer can either create or modify the CONFIG.SYS file on your DOS disk.

- Once this procedure is completed, the DOS disk is removed from drive A: and replaced with the Install (*DacEasy* Disk-1) disk.

- Next, insert the blank, formatted disk labeled Program-1 into drive B:. Press Enter.

- *DacEasy* will copy the files on *DacEasy* Disk-1 to the Program-1 disk in drive B:. When this procedure is completed, the following message will appear on the screen: Replace the disk in drive A: with *DacEasy* Disk-2. Replace the disk in drive B: with the blank disk labeled "Program-2."

- Follow the instructions on the screen; then press Enter. It takes several minutes for your computer to copy the files from the *DacEasy* Disk-2 disk to the Program-2 disk in drive B:.

- Once this procedure is completed, all the disks are removed from their respective drives.

Figure 1-4. Buffer and File Requirements

```
                        DAC-EASY INSTALLATION

 For maximum performance, Dac-Easy requires that the following two statements
 exist in the CONFIG.SYS file of the boot (DOS) disk:

    FILES=20
    BUFFERS=16

 If the CONFIG.SYS file does not exist, it will be created at this time.  If
 CONFIG.SYS exists but these statements are either not found or do not have
 the minimum settings, the file will be modified accordingly (no other
 statements will be changed).




```

Press <─┘ to continue, ESC to exit.

- If the CONFIG.SYS file is either created or modified during the installation of *DacEasy*, your computer, monitor, and printer must be turned off at this point. Wait one minute before turning everything on again.

Installing *DacEasy* on Your Hard Disk System

Before using *DacEasy* for the first time, follow these steps to install it on your hard disk system:

- Make sure DOS is contained in the hard disk. It's important that you enter the actual date and time at the DOS prompts unless your computer automatically performs this function.
- Place the *DacEasy* Disk-1 (Install/Program) disk into drive A:.
- At the C> prompt, type A: to set drive A: as the active drive and press Enter.
- Type *INSTALL* and press Enter.
- Remove Disk-1 from drive A: and replace it with Disk-2. To continue, press any key.
- At the prompt, remove Disk-2 from drive A: and replace it with Disk-1. Press Enter.
- The screen in Figure 1-3 will appear.
- At the prompt, type *H* to indicate that you're installing *DacEasy* on a hard disk system. At this time, *DacEasy* searches your DOS program for a file named CONFIG.SYS as indicated in Figure 1-4. If it doesn't exist, *DacEasy* will automatically create it; if it does exist, *DacEasy* may modify it according to its required file and buffer settings. Once this procedure is completed, the screen in Figure 1-5 will appear.

To create a new file path, follow these steps:

- Press Enter to accept the file path name that already appears on the screen.
- If you don't want to use this path name, type the name you do want; then press Enter. The message, *Directory does not exist, would you like to create it (Y/N)?* will appear on the bottom of the screen.

To create the *DacEasy* program files directory:

- Type *Y*. The *DacEasy* program files will be copied from the *DacEasy* Disk-1 disk in drive A: to the program files directory on

Figure 1-5. Locating *DacEasy* on Your Path

```
                         DAC-EASY INSTALLATION

The Dac-Easy Program files will now be copied to your hard disk.  Specify
the path name for the directory where you would like the program files
stored.  If the path name does not exist, the system will create it for you.

Enter path name: C:\DEA3
```

the hard disk. At the prompt, follow these steps:

• Remove the *DacEasy* Disk-1 disk in drive A: and replace it with the *DacEasy* Disk-2 disk. Press Enter. The program files on Disk-2 will be copied onto your hard disk. Once this procedure is completed, the following message appears on the screen: *The installation process has been successfully completed. Thank you for using* DacEasy Accounting.

• Remove the *DacEasy* Disk-2 disk from drive A:. Store all disks in a safe place.

Note: You'll need to restart your computer if the CONFIG.SYS file was either created or changed during the installation process.

DacEasy Accounting version 3.0 includes a file named READ.ME on one of the disks. The most significant, up-to-date information regarding the correct operation of your new software is located in this file. To read the information contained in this file, place the disk that contains the READ.ME file into drive A:. At the DOS prompt, type *TYPE READ.ME* and press Enter.

Starting an Accounting System

There is no better way to learn *DacEasy*'s accounting program than by sitting down in front of your computer and experimenting with it. At this point, and through the rest of this book, there are examples where you're able to do just that. At the same time, you'll be creating, updating, and maintaining an accounting system for a fictional company named "Dr. Humane's Small Animal Hospital." You may wish to use your own business name.

Defining Your Accounting Files

The next step in *DacEasy*'s installation process is defining your accounting files. This procedure

1. Lets you verify if there is adequate space for all your files if you're using a floppy drive system.
2. Reserves the appropriate amount of space so your accounting data won't interfere or conflict with other programs if you have a hard disk system.

Floppy Drive Systems

Here are step-by-step instructions for defining your accounting files on a floppy disk system:

- Place the Program-1 disk in drive A: and a formatted disk labeled *DacEasy Accounting Data* in drive B:.
- Type *DEA3* at the A> prompt, and press Enter. The *DacEasy* copyright date will appear on the screen.
- Remove the Program-1 disk from drive A: and insert the Program-2 disk. To continue, press any key. (This procedure must be executed each time you load *DacEasy* into your computer.)
- Next you must choose the disk drive and subdirectory where you want your accounting files stored.
- Press Enter to select the default directory. It's recommended, but not mandatory, that you use *DacEasy*'s built-in Chart of Accounts. To use the Chart of Accounts, follow these steps:
- Type *Y* and press Enter.
- Replace the Program-2 disk from drive A: with the Install disk. To continue, press any key. *DacEasy* will copy the Chart of Accounts. The message *Copy Chart of Accounts* will appear during this procedure.
- Remove the Install disk from drive A: and insert the Program-2 disk.
- Type *Y* and press Enter. If you're using *DacEasy*'s Chart of Accounts, the first question on the screen is already filled in. Answer the last four questions displayed on the screen. When entering the numbers, take into consideration a 20 percent growth factor.

Sample. Dr. Humane currently has 500 customers. Taking into consideration a 20 percent growth margin,

- Type 600 in the column beside the second question and press Enter. The cursor will move down one question. Dr. Humane currently has 10 vendors. To add a 20 percent growth factor to that amount:
- Type 12 in the column beside the third question and press Enter.
- In the next space, type 100 and press Enter.
- Answer the last question by typing 15. Press Enter.

At this point, *DacEasy* calculates how much space will be required to set up the system files and how much disk space is available to your computer. Once these calculations have been made, *DacEasy* displays a prompt asking for confirmation of the numbers you just entered. Type *N* if you want to change any of these numbers, or type *Y* to save them.

When you type *Y*, *DacEasy* begins the initialization of files and creates a file named DEA.CIA. Your accounting files will be located in this file.

Tip: If the DEA.CIA file is ever accidentally deleted, go to the DOS prompt, type *DEA3*, press the space bar, and type the drive and/or path of your data files. Press Enter. You may then access these files. (The drive and/or path name is created during the installation procedure and stored as a subdirectory within the directory storing your *DacEasy* program.

- If, after running this routine, your computer takes you back to the beginning, this means you don't have enough available disk space in your computer. You must either add a higher capacity disk drive or a hard disk. Once you do this, repeat the steps in the exercise above. During the initialization of the files, *DacEasy* will display a message prompting you to insert your Install/Program disk in drive A:.
- Remove the Program-2 disk from drive A: and insert the Install/Program disk. To continue, press any key. *DacEasy* will copy the Chart of Accounts. The message *Copy Chart of Accounts* will appear during this procedure.
- Remove the Install/Program disk from drive A: and insert the Program-2 disk. To continue, press any key. After *DacEasy*

Figure 1-6. Entering Your Company Name

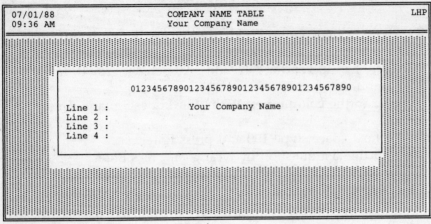

```
07/01/88                  COMPANY NAME TABLE                      LHP
09:36 AM                  Your Company Name
```

```
                    01234567890123456789012345678901234567890
        Line 1 :              Your Company Name
        Line 2 :
        Line 3 :
        Line 4 :
```

```
F1-Help F2-Center  F10-Process  ESC-Exit
```

completes the initialization of data files procedure, the screen in
Figure 1-6 will appear.

The Company Name Table within *DacEasy*'s File Creation and
Maintenance menu lets you enter your company's name and address. Four lines of forty characters each are available. For identification purposes, the first line you enter will be displayed at the
top of most of the files you'll be using. To enter a company
name, follow these steps:

- On Line 1, type *Dr. Humane's Small Animal Hospital*, press F2 to
  center the line, and then press Enter.
- On Line 2, type *555 East Meadows Lane*, press F2; then press
  Enter.
- On Line 3, type *San Diego, CA 92122*, press F2; then press
  Enter.
- On Line 4, type *(619) 555-3636*, press F2; then press Enter. The
  screen should resemble the one in Figure 1-7.

When you finish typing the last entry, the cursor will move
to the Opening menu.

Hard Drive Systems

Here are the steps for setting up your accounting system on a
hard drive:

Figure 1-7. Example Company Name

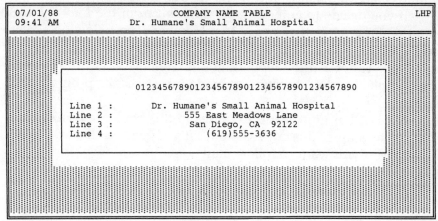

```
07/01/88                    COMPANY NAME TABLE                        LHP
09:41 AM              Dr. Humane's Small Animal Hospital


                   01234567890123456789012345678901234567890
         Line 1 :       Dr. Humane's Small Animal Hospital
         Line 2 :           555 East Meadows Lane
         Line 3 :           San Diego, CA  92122
         Line 4 :             (619)555-3636




F1-Help F2-Center  F10-Process  ESC-Exit
```

• At the C> prompt, type *CD DEA3* (or the name of the subdirectory that contains your *DacEasy* program files), and press Enter.
• Type *DEA3* and press Enter to display the screen in Figure 1-8.

Next, follow the instructions found in the rectangle at the lower half of your screen. You may use the directory name *DacEasy* has provided or you may create your own name using

Figure 1-8. The Installation Screen for Hard Disks

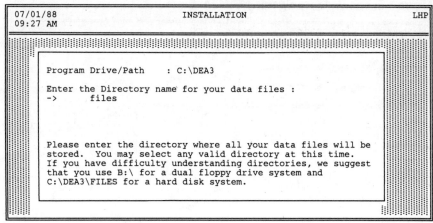

```
07/01/88                      INSTALLATION                            LHP
09:27 AM


    Program Drive/Path     : C:\DEA3

    Enter the Directory name for your data files :
    ->      files




    Please enter the directory where all your data files will be
    stored.  You may select any valid directory at this time.
    If you have difficulty understanding directories, we suggest
    that you use B:\ for a dual floppy drive system and
    C:\DEA3\FILES for a hard disk system.


F1-Help F10-Process  ESC-Exit
```

up to eight alphanumeric characters (letters and numbers). Press Enter when the name is the way you want it.

If you decide to enter a name different from the *DacEasy* default, enter a name that's easy to remember. The following screen in Figure 1-9 will appear.

Type either *Y* or *N* depending on whether you want to use the sample Chart of Accounts provided in *DacEasy*'s program and press Enter.

Note: All examples and exercises in this book are based on *DacEasy*'s sample Chart of Accounts. It's suggested that you use this chart if you want to follow along.

- Type *Y* and press Enter to confirm that you want to use *DacEasy*'s sample Chart of Accounts. Next a prompt will appear in the middle of the screen.
- Place the *DacEasy* Program Disk-1 into drive A:. To continue, press any key. *DacEasy* will start copying the Chart of Accounts. Once this procedure is completed, the screen in Figure 1-10 will appear.

The *DacEasy* program will automatically fill in the blank for the first question. Next, answer the last four questions displayed on the screen. When entering the numbers, take into consideration a 20 percent growth factor.

Sample. Dr. Humane currently has 500 customers. Taking into consideration a 20 percent growth margin,

Figure 1-9. The *DacEasy* Opening Screen

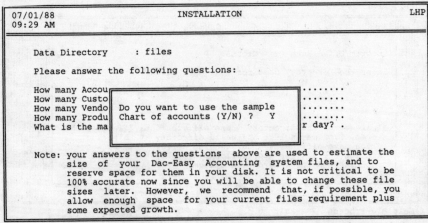

Figure 1-10. The Screen After the Chart of Accounts Is Copied

```
07/01/88                    INSTALLATION                      LHP
09:29 AM


   Data Directory      : files

   Please answer the following questions:

   How many Accounts in your chart of Accounts? ............. 275
   How many Customers do you have? ......................... 0
   How many Vendors do you have? ........................... 0
   How many Products and/or Services do you have? .......... 0
   What is the maximum number of Invoices you have per day? . 0


   Note: your answers to the questions  above are used to estimate the
         size  of  your  Dac-Easy Accounting system files, and to
         reserve space for them in your disk. It is not critical to be
         100% accurate now since you will be able to change these file
         sizes  later.  However,  we  recommend  that, if possible, you
         allow  enough  space  for your current files requirement plus
         some expected growth.

F1-Help F10-Process  ESC-Exit
```

- Type 600 in the column beside the second question and press Enter. The cursor will move down one question. Dr. Humane currently has 10 vendors. To add a 20 percent growth factor to that amount:
- Type 12 in the column beside the third question and press Enter.
- In the next space, type 100 and press Enter.
- Answer the last question by typing 15. Press Enter.

Your screen should look like the one displayed in Figure 1-11.

At this point, *DacEasy* calculates how much space will be required to set up the system files and how much available disk space your computer has. Once these calculations have been made, *DacEasy* displays a prompt asking for confirmation of the numbers you just entered.

Type *N* if you want to change any of the numbers shown, or type *Y* to save them.

When you type *Y*, *DacEasy* begins the initialization of files and creates a file named DEA.CIA. Your accounting files will be located in this file.

Tip: If the DEA.CIA file is ever accidentally deleted, go to the DOS prompt, type *DEA3*, press the space bar, and type the drive and/or path of your data files. Press Enter. You may then access these files. (The drive and/or path name is created during the in-

Figure 1-11. Prompt to Start Creating Files

```
07/01/88                    INSTALLATION                        LHP
09:29 AM

    Data Directory    : files

    Please answer the following questions:

    How many Accou|                                    | 275
    How many Custo|                                    | 600
    How many Vendo|                                    | 12
    How many Produ|START CREATING YOUR FILES NOW (Y/N) ?| 100
    What is the ma|                                    | 15


       Total Space Required -->        513,370
       Total Space Available ->     10,172,416

```

F1-Help F10-Process ESC-Exit

stallation procedure and stored as a subdirectory within the directory storing your *DacEasy* program. For example, in the installation procedures completed above, the path name FILES was
created.

• Type *Y* and press Enter. The numbers on your screen may
differ from the ones displayed in Figure 1-11 because your
screen will show the actual disk space available in your
computer.

   Note: If after running this routine, your computer takes you
back to the beginning, this means you don't have enough available disk space in your computer. You must either add a higher
capacity disk drive or an additional hard disk. Once you do this,
repeat the steps in the exercise above.

   When the initialization procedure is complete, the screen in
Figure 1-6 will appear. The Company Name Table within
DacEasy's File Creation and Maintenance menu lets you enter
your company's name and address. Four lines are available and
up to 40 characters per line can be entered. For identification purposes, the first line you enter will be displayed at the top of most
of the files you'll be using. To enter a company name, follow
these steps:

• On Line 1, type *Dr. Humane's Small Animal Hospital*, press F2 to
center the line, and then press Enter.

- On Line 2, type *555 East Meadows Lane,* press F2; then press Enter.
- On Line 3, type *San Diego, CA 92122,* press F2; then press Enter.
- On Line 4, type *(619)555-3636,* press F2; then press Enter. The screen should resemble the one in Figure 1-7.

Once you finish typing the last entry, the cursor will move to the Opening menu.

Exiting *DacEasy* from the Opening Menu

At this point, you may either exit *DacEasy* or continue working. To exit *DacEasy:*

- Press Esc. The prompt *Do you want to exit (Y/N)? Y* will appear.
- If you decide you want to remain in the program, type *N* at the prompt; otherwise just press Enter.

Loading *DacEasy*

Now that you've made backups and installed *DacEasy* on your system, you're ready to load and run *DacEasy.* Follow the steps appropriate for your system as follows.

Floppy Drive Systems

If you have a floppy drive system, insert the DOS Disk in drive A:, turn on your computer, and enter the date and time at the appropriate prompts.

Next, insert the *DacEasy* Program-1 Disk in drive A: and the *DacEasy Accounting* Data Disk in drive B:. At the A> prompt, type *DEA3* and press Enter. *DacEasy's* copyright date will appear on the screen; then the Opening menu will be displayed.

Hard Disk Systems

If you have a hard disk system, the C> prompt will appear after you've turned on the computer and DOS has been initialized. Make sure you've entered the date and time at the appropriate prompts. At the C> prompt, type *CD\DEA3* and press Enter (or type the subdirectory name you're using for this program). At the next C> prompt, type *DEA3* and press Enter. *DacEasy's* copyright date will appear on the screen; then the Opening menu will be displayed. You're now ready to work with the *DacEasy* Accounting Program.

Using *DacEasy*'s Menus

DacEasy's menus are simple to use. They all branch off from the Opening menu. To view a submenu from the Opening menu, use the arrow keys to select an operation or enter the number next to the desired operation. Thus, you can select an operation from a submenu two different ways:

• The first way is to use the up-arrow and down-arrow keys on the right side of the computer. Use these direction keys to highlight the command you want, and then press Enter.
• The second way is to press the number next to the menu item you want: Press 3 to select the Tax Table operation from within the Options menu, press 5 to select Billing from within the Transaction menu, and so on. If you want to return to a previous menu, press Esc. When you press Esc from the Opening menu, you'll exit the *DacEasy* program.

To exit any menu (except the Opening menu), select Esc and you'll return to the previous screen. If you want to know what a specific menu command does, highlight that item and press F1 (Help Key). A help window will appear, explaining the high-lighted menu item.

Exiting *DacEasy*

After saving the files you've been working on, you can quit the *DacEasy* program and return to DOS by selecting Esc-Exit from the Opening menu. Type *Y* to exit *DacEasy*. The DOS prompt will be displayed on your screen.

A Quick Walk Through *DacEasy Accounting*

As mentioned earlier, there's no better way to become familiar with *DacEasy* than by sitting in front of your computer and exper-imenting with the program. This chapter takes a close look at some of the basic features you'll need to know to enter, save, retrieve, and print your files. Once you become acquainted with these basic, but important functions, you'll be able to apply them when you create a sample accounting system in the next chapter.

Entering the Program

As you know, *DacEasy* must be loaded into your computer's memory before you can work with it.

If you're using a floppy-based system, your *DacEasy* Program-1 Disk should be placed in drive A: and your *DacEasy* Accounting Data Disk should be placed in drive B:. The screen should also be displaying the A> prompt. Type *DEA3* and press Enter.

If you're using a hard disk, the C> prompt should be displayed. Type *CD\DEA3* to enter the specific directory that holds your *DacEasy* files. Next, type *DEA3* and press Enter.

DacEasy will be entered into your computer's memory and the copyright date will appear on the screen; then the Opening menu will be displayed.

Assigning a Password

In some instances you may want to protect your work from unauthorized access.

To accomplish this, *DacEasy* allows you to assign up to five passwords with a maximum of eight characters each. Before a file with a password can be retrieved, the correct password must be supplied.

To assign a password or passwords, go to the Options menu and press Enter. Next, press 6 to display the password table. The screen in Figure 1-12 will appear. Type the desired password be-

Figure 1-12. The Password Screen

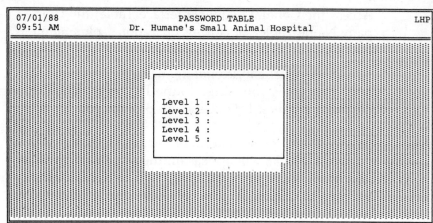

```
07/01/88                    PASSWORD TABLE                        LHP
09:51 AM          Dr. Humane's Small Animal Hospital




                        Level 1 :
                        Level 2 :
                        Level 3 :
                        Level 4 :
                        Level 5 :




F1-Help   ESC-Exit
```

side each of the levels. You can use up to eight characters for each of the five levels. Press Enter after each password. The cursor will then move to the next level. After all the appropriate passwords have been entered, press Esc.

The five levels are explained below.

Level	Access
1	Access the Accounts Receivable entry, transaction journal, and cash receipts operations.

Access the Accounts Payable transaction entry, transaction journal, and payments journal, purchase order status, and sales journal operations.

2   Access the General Ledger transaction entry, journal report, and activity report operations.

Access all Accounts Receivable, Accounts Payable, and Inventory report operations, the File Status operation, plus the Level 1 menu operations.

3   Access the Chart of Accounts maintenance operation, the customer, product, service, vendor, purchase order code, and statement text maintenance operations, plus the menu operations from Levels 1 and 2.

Also lets you work with the Price Assignment/Entry operation, all posting operations, as well as the Tax Table, the File Rehash operation, and defaults maintenance operations.

Financial statements can also be created at this level.

4   Access the General Ledger Interface Table, the Company Name Table, all closing operations, plus menu operations from Levels 1, 2 and 3.

5   Access any *DacEasy Accounting* menu and accounting area, plus gives you access to the Password menu. If a file has a password, *DacEasy* will prompt you for it.

Type the password and press Enter. For security reasons, as you type the password, blocks will appear on the screen rather than the password itself. Make sure you type the password accurately because *DacEasy* will display an error message and abort the command if the password is incorrect. If this happens, press any key. The Opening menu will appear and you can try again.

Printing

You can use *DacEasy* to perform many printing options, such as printing checks, inventory count sheets, invoices, purchase orders, or reports.

For instance, to print a check or checks (Figure 1-13):

- Select the Accounts Payable menu option from the Transaction menu (3). The Accounts Payable menu will be displayed.
- Press 4 to select the Print Checks option. Enter the information at the four prompts by typing the appropriate data.
- Next, a message will appear on the screen asking you to place the forms (checks) in your printer and press any key when you're ready to align your continuous form checks.

DacEasy always voids the first check (it will appear in the Accounts Payable Payments Journal as a voided check). *DacEasy* also allows you to reprint checks. Once in a while your printer may jam, or you may find an error on a check that's been printed. If this occurs, select *Y* from the Reprint Checks prompt, enter the check numbers that need to be reprinted, and *DacEasy* will automatically reprint the checks and generate a complete audit trail, voiding the previous checks and creating the new check numbers.

Special Keys

DacEasy uses many of the keys on your keyboard in special ways, but there are two of particular importance that you'll use constantly.

The Esc key. The Esc key in *DacEasy*'s program is a handy tool that allows you to change your mind, exit the current operation, and return to the previous menu. *DacEasy* automatically incapacitates the Esc key during some critically important processes so your data will be protected. The Esc key also works within *DacEasy*'s menus. Suppose you select a menu command that displays a prompt. If you decide not to carry out the command, press Esc and the command is canceled.

Esc will also exit the current menu and return you to a previous menu, OR if you are at the Opening menu, the prompt to exit the *DacEasy* program will appear.

The End key. The End key moves the cursor to the corners of a current field of data or, when used in conjunction with the Ctrl key, moves the cursor to the last field in your file.

Sorting Features

DacEasy provides several ways to sort information. For instance, if you want to print customer labels for a special mailing, the Accounts Receivable Customer Labels operation lets you sort by customer code, customer name, department, salesperson, or zip code.

Once they're sorted, simply choose the print customer labels option. The following summarizes the operations with sorting capabilities and how they can be sorted.

Operation	Fields to Sort
Accounts Receivable Statements, Aging Report, Forecasting, Customer Directory, and Customer Labels operations	Code, name, department, salesperson, or zip code
Accounts Payable Statements, Aging Report, Vendor Directory, or Vendor Labels operations	Code, name, type, territory, or zip code
Inventory Reports (also known as Product Reports), such as Product Listing, Product Price List, Product Activity Report, Product Alert Report, and Inventory Statistical Reports operations	Inventory #, description, department, bin (location), or vendor
Service Reports and Service Statistical Reports provide complete analysis of your service billing	Service # description, or department

Figure 1-13. DacEasy Can Print Checks for You

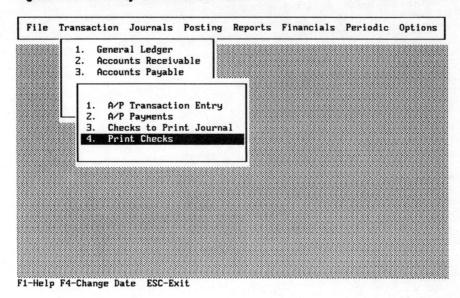

Chapter 2

Setting Up *DacEasy's* Accounting Files

The previous chapter gave you an overview of *DacEasy*'s features and how to use some of them. In this chapter, you'll be able to use some of these features firsthand by following step-by-step procedures to set up and create the accounting files needed to use *DacEasy*'s accounting program. You'll create an accounting system for a fictitious company named Dr. Humane's Small Animal Hospital, introduced in the previous chapter.

Before beginning the tutorial, you need to know how to invoke the commands described in this book. You will access options through the Opening menu and submenus; to choose the Transaction menu from the Opening menu, you must highlight that option using the arrow keys, then press Enter. To access an option in any submenu, press the number corresponding to it or highlight it with the arrow keys to select it. Then press Enter.

To choose the Company Id. option from the Options menu, highlight the Options menu from the Opening menu and press Enter. The Options menu will appear. Next, type 2 or move your cursor to Company Id. to highlight it, then press Enter to select it. That's all there is to it.

Starting the Program

If you have a floppy drive system, insert the DOS Disk in Drive A:, turn on your computer, and enter the date and time at the appropriate prompts. Next, insert the *DacEasy* Program-1 Disk in Drive A: and the *DacEasy* Accounting Data Disk in Drive B:. At the A> prompt, type *DEA3* and press Enter.

DacEasy's copyright will appear on the screen; then the Opening menu will be displayed.

If you have a hard disk system, the C> prompt will appear after you've turned on the computer and DOS has been initialized. Make sure you've entered the date and time at the appropriate prompts. At the C> prompt, type *CD/DEA3* and press Enter. (If DEA3 isn't the subdirectory where you've stored the program, type the subdirectory name you're using.)

At the next C> prompt, type *DEA3* and press Enter. *DacEasy*'s copyright will appear on the screen. Then the Opening menu will be displayed.

You're now ready to work with the *DacEasy* Accounting Program.

Initializing Your Accounting Files

The *DacEasy* Accounting program uses seven accounting *modules*. *DacEasy* named these accounting functions modules because, even though they are independent units, they're used together to constitute the total accounting system. These modules, or accounting functions, are:

- General Ledger
- Accounts Receivable
- Accounts Payable
- Inventory
- Billing
- Purchase Order
- Forecasting (Budgeting)

These modules *interface*, which means they communicate with each other. Figure 2-1 illustrates how *DacEasy*'s accounting modules interface.

This interfacing feature is a type of multilevel accounting. Through multilevel accounting, any transaction you enter not only creates or updates a particular accounting function, it also creates or updates all related accounts.

For instance, let's say you create a purchase order to buy products needed for your business. Once those products are received, redisplay the appropriate purchase order and enter the actual quantities received. Once this information is saved (processed), not only do you have an updated purchase order, but the applicable vendor file, the inventory quantities on hand, amounts, back-order information, and historical information are also automatically updated.

The illustration in Figure 2-2 shows how the Purchase Order Module interfaces with other files.

In order to enjoy the full benefits of *DacEasy Accounting*, all of these modules must be initialized or *set up*.

Figure 2-1. How the Modules Interface

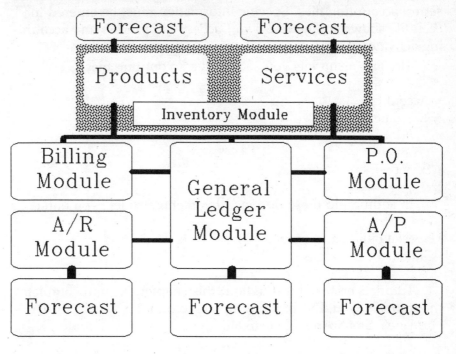

Figure 2-2. How the Purchase Order Module Interfaces with Other Files

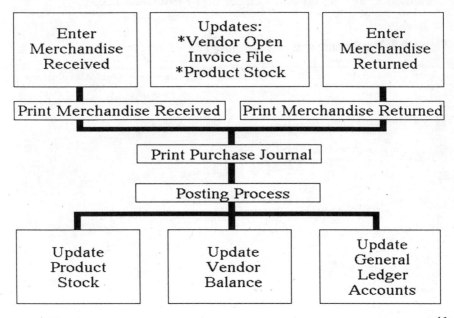

The File option on the *DacEasy* Opening menu allows you to set up accounting files. Specific information must be entered in each file shown in Figure 2-3 so *DacEasy* can process any accounting activities.

The File menu lets you set up five accounting files:

- Accounts
- Customers
- Vendors
- Products
- Services

In addition to these options, this menu also lets you enter

- Special billing and purchase order codes
- Statement messages

Tutorials are used throughout this chapter. As you complete the tutorials, you'll be building up an accounting system for Dr. Humane's Small Animal Hospital.

Setting Up *DacEasy*'s General Ledger

DacEasy's General Ledger includes a Chart of Accounts, Financial Statements, and a General Ledger (G/L) Interface Table.

Figure 2-3. The Components of a *DacEasy* File

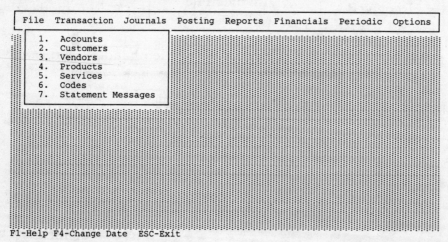

These files are automatically created by *DacEasy* if you choose to use the built-in Chart of Accounts provided in this program. You may disregard the following section that describes how to set up these files. (You can move on to the section in this chapter on setting up the Tax Rates Table, and continue from there.)

If you want to set up your own Chart of Accounts, Financial Statements and G/L Interface Table, or just review the procedures, continue from this point.

What is a General Ledger?. A group of accounts is called a *ledger*. A ledger that contains all accounts needed to prepare financial statements (reports) is called a general ledger.

What is a Chart of Accounts?

A name given to an account is called an *account title*. A number given to an account is called an *account number*. A list of account titles and account numbers showing the location of each account in a ledger is called a *chart of accounts*.

DacEasy's Chart of Accounts. Chapter 1 describes *DacEasy's* Chart of Accounts and how five main accounts (Assets, Liabilities, Stockholder's Equity, Revenues and Total Expenses) relate to different levels of subaccounts. You can review the section in Chapter 1 before proceeding, or if you're familiar with it, continue here.

Setting Up a Chart of Accounts

The File menu gives you the option to set up a Chart of Accounts. To select this option from within the File menu simply press 1 (Accounts) and the screen in Figure 2-4 will appear. You may now enter the appropriate information in each field.

Note: For the best results, follow the same layout as *DacEasy's* built-in Chart of Accounts. You may want to review this sample before planning your own.

To help you complete this account file, a brief description of each field and an example of how to enter data in each field is explained below.

Account Number. An account number identifies your account. You can enter up to six alphanumeric characters within this field. Note: If an account number already exists within the Chart of Accounts, its information will appear on the screen once the number is entered.

Figure 2-4. The Opening Screen of the Chart of Accounts

```
 07/01/88                  ACCOUNTS FILE MAINTENANCE                      LHP
 09:07 AM             Dr. Humane's Small Animal Hospital
 ─────────────────────────────────────────────────────────────────────────
 Account Number           :
 Account Name             :
 General or Detail (G/D)  :
 Account Level (1-5)      :
 General Account          :
 Previous Balance         :        0.00
 This Period Balance      :        0.00
 Current Balance          :        0.00


 ═══════════════════════ HISTORICAL INFORMATION ═══════════════════════
                          BALANCE            VARIANCE      % CHANGE

 Year before last     :        0.00
 Last Year            :        0.00            0.00          0.00
 Current YTD          :        0.00            0.00          0.00
 Forecast at end year :        0.00            0.00          0.00
 ─────────────────────────────────────────────────────────────────────────
```

F1-Help F6-Delete F7-Update Balance F10-Process ESC-exit

1. Type 11073 and press Enter.
   Account Name. This field identifies the name of the account.
   You can enter up to 20 alphanumeric characters to describe the
   account.
2. Type *Merchandise Inventory.* Press Enter.
   General or Detail (G/D). This field indicates whether the account is a general (G) account or a detail (D) account. Detail
   accounts receive transactions directly and are always below
   general accounts in the Chart of Accounts. General accounts
   receive information from other general accounts below them or
   from detail accounts. Enter G or D in this field.
3. Type *D* and press Enter.
   Account Level (1–5). This field requires the level of the account. The higher the account level, the more detailed it is.
   Level 1 accounts must be created first.
4. Type 4 and press Enter.
   General Account Number. Every account has a general account where information is passed on (except Level 1 accounts). In this field, enter the account number that should
   receive any transactions from this account. If this account is a
   level 1 account, enter a 1 in this field.
5. Type 1107 and press Enter. Note: If you haven't created a general account number, this field cannot be completed. It's important to create General Accounts first.
   Previous Balance, This Period Balance, and Current Balance.
   DacEasy automatically creates and updates these fields.

Selecting an Account Type

Once the data in the Accounts File Maintenance operation is entered, *DacEasy* prompts you to select the Account Type. To select an account type, press the letter that corresponds to it. Note: If you're adding an account to the existing Chart of Accounts, this message will not appear.

Saving your account. The final step in completing this operation is saving or recording it. Simply press the F10 (Process) function key. A blank Account File will appear on the screen after *DacEasy* has saved the one you just finished. You can continue adding accounts or press Esc to return to the File menu.

6. Press F10, then press Enter.

Entering the Account Balance

Version 3.0 of *DacEasy Accounting* has added a convenient feature to the Account File Maintenance operation. This feature lets you enter account balances from the Account File Maintenance screen at the time you're setting up the individual accounts.

To enter an account balance, follow these steps:

7. Type 11073 and press Enter. The account you just entered and saved will appear on the screen. You'll notice an option that reads *F7 - Update Balance* on the status line at the bottom of the screen.

8. Press F7. The screen in Figure 2-5 will appear.

When the amount field is entered (remember that credit entries should be preceded with a minus sign), press the F10 (Process) function key. Both the Account Balance and General Ledger Transaction file are updated.

When account balances are entered during this set-up procedure, *DacEasy* automatically goes to the G/L Transaction file and enters *SU* (set-up) in the code field. It also enters the month and day this account is processed, plus the debit or credit amount for this account, and a debit or credit to the Differences account (The G/L Transaction file and the Differences account are explained in greater detail later.)

Because of this automatic updating, your general ledger should never be out of balance.

Figure 2-5. Update Balance Screen

```
07/01/88              ACCOUNTS FILE MAINTENANCE                  LHP
09:15 AM           Dr. Humane's Small Animal Hospital

Account Number        : 11073
Account Name          : Merchandise Invntry
General or Detail (G/D) : D
Account Level (1-5)┌──────────────────────────────────────┐
General Account    │       UPDATE ACCOUNT BALANCES        │
Previous Balance   │                                      │
This Period Balance│ Account Number   : 11073             │
Current Balance    │                                      │
                   │ Amount           :         .         │
                   └──────────────────────────────────────┘
                   ══════════ HISTORICAL INFORMATION ══════════
                            BALANCE        VARIANCE    % CHANGE

Year before last    :        0.00
Last Year           :        0.00          0.00         0.00
Current YTD         :        0.00          0.00         0.00
Forecast at end year :       0.00          0.00         0.00
```

F1-Help F6-Delete F7-Update Balance F10-Process ESC-exit

Important note: It's extremely important to check the accuracy of your work before pressing F10. Once you process your work, any error you find must be corrected by entering an adjustment through the General Ledger Transaction Entry operation. Since this procedure is used only while setting up the account file, *DacEasy* won't let you delete or correct an entry after it's been processed (only additions can be entered).

Since the example above was entered for sample purposes only, let's delete it at this time.

9. Press Esc to return to the previous screen.
10. To delete account 11073, press the F6 (Delete) function key. At the confirmation prompt, press Enter to accept the default (Y).
11. To return to the Opening menu, press Esc twice.

What are Financial Statements?

Financial Statements are reports prepared from the Chart of Accounts file. The Balance Sheet and Income Statement are two examples of financial statements. The Balance Sheet reports the financial condition of a business; an Income Statement reports a business' financial progress.

Creating Customized Statements

If you're using *DacEasy*'s built-in Chart of Accounts, the financial statements format is automatically created. Once sufficient information is entered in the program and is updated as data, it can be printed by selecting the Print Financial Reports option 2 from the Reports menu.

Note: Procedures on how to generate and print financial statements are explained later in this manual.

If you're not using *DacEasy's* Chart of Accounts, you'll have to create your own financial statements.

To create a report format, or edit one that already exists, select the Financial Statement Generator (Option 5) from within the Financials menu. (See Figure 2-6)

Next, press 1 to select the Edit Financial Reports option. The screen in Figure 2-7 will appear.

Virtually any type of report can be created. The data for reports is obtained from the Chart of Accounts file.

As you can see, four custom statements are available:

• Balance Sheet (BAL)
• Income Statement (INC)
• Financial Ratio Statement 1 (RA1)
• Financial Ratio Statement 2 (RA2)

The Financial Ratio Statements provide data illustrating the difference between current assets and current liabilities.

Specialized reports, such as Arithmetic and Geometric ratios, can also be created through *DacEasy*.

Figure 2-6. The Financial Statement Generator Menu

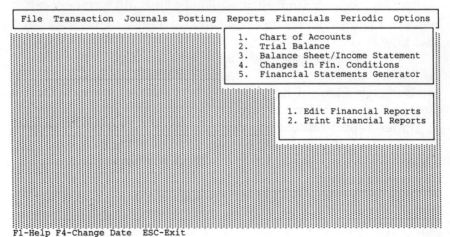

```
 File  Transaction  Journals  Posting  Reports  Financials  Periodic  Options

                                         1.  Chart of Accounts
                                         2.  Trial Balance
                                         3.  Balance Sheet/Income Statement
                                         4.  Changes in Fin. Conditions
                                         5.  Financial Statements Generator


                                            1. Edit Financial Reports
                                            2. Print Financial Reports




F1-Help F4-Change Date  ESC-Exit
```

Figure 2-7. The Edit Financial Reports Screen

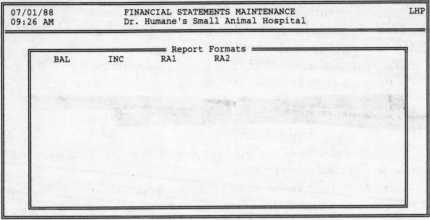

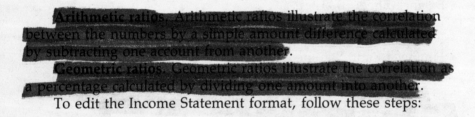

To edit the Income Statement format, follow these steps:

1. Press the right-arrow key once.
2. Press the F2 (Edit) function key.

The screen in Figure 2-8 will appear.

DacEasy reports are formatted line by line and numbers can be totaled within the report. You can also add or delete a line at a later time.

To help you complete this file, a brief description of each field is provided below. Note: Because the tutorials in this manual use *DacEasy*'s Chart of Accounts, no hands-on samples are incorporated in the following example.

Enter Report Name. This field identifies the report. You can use up to four alphanumeric characters to describe it. If you enter a code that already exists, its information will appear and can be reviewed or revised.

Print (Y/N). This field gives you the option of printing the current line in the report. *DacEasy* automatically prints each line unless you enter an *N* in this field. You would also enter *N* if you

Figure 2-8. Editing the Income Statement

```
07/01/88                                                              LHP
09:30 AM              Dr. Humane's Small Animal Hospital

  Enter Report Name : INC

  Print                              Amount Amount To        Lines
  (Y/N) Acct.# Description           From   1   2   3   %    99=pg.

    Y           * Income Statement * 0                        C
    Y                                0
    N     4     Revenues             99                  +
    Y              GROSS MARGIN:     0                        C
    Y                                0
    Y              Department 01     0                        C
    Y                                0
    Y    4101    Sales               99     +
    Y    4201    Returns             99     +             -
    Y            Net Sales           1                        1
    Y    5101    Cost of Goods Sold  99     -             -
    Y            Gross Margin Dept.01 1                       1
```

F1-Help ALT I-Insert ALT D-Delete ALT P-Print F10-Process ESC-exit

were using the line for calculation purposes only. Note: All calculations are still performed whether or not this line is printed.

Account #. This field is optional. Enter the appropriate account number from your Chart of Accounts. You can skip this field by pressing Enter or the right-arrow key if you don't want to use account data.

Description. This field automatically displays the account name that corresponds with the account number entered in the previous field. Note: You can revise this field using up to 20 characters to describe the account. The account name in the Chart of Accounts won't be affected.

Amount From. The number 99 is automatically inserted in this field if a valid account was entered in the Account # field. The number 99 means the information to be printed on this line has an account balance. Five other special codes can also be entered within this field:

1. To print a description only, enter 0 in this field.
2. To print the total from Accumulator 1, enter 1.
3. To print the total from Accumulator 2, enter 2.
4. To print the total from Accumulator 3, enter 3.
5. To compute and print a ratio using two Accumulator columns, press /.

Accumulators are columns in the Amount To field (which follows). Special codes that tell the system how to compute and

49

print financial reports are entered in these columns. An explanation of ratios appears later in this chapter.

Amount To. This field has four columns (Accumulators): 1, 2, 3, and %. An Accumulator is a temporary storage area, like a piece of scratch paper you might keep at hand to write down important values for later reference, or like a calculator's memory function. The first three columns are used to

- Store information to the Accumulator
- Add to the Accumulator
- Subtract from the Accumulator
- Read from the Accumulator
- Use the Accumulator in ratio computations
- Clear the Accumulator

The following codes can be used in these columns:

+	Add the amount from the current line to the Accumulator
−	Subtract the amount from the current line from the Accumulator
0	Clear the Accumulator, press 0

If you enter a slash (/) in the Amount From column, enter one of these codes in the appropriate column:

N	Use the Accumulator as the numerator (top value) in division (ratio) computations
D	Use the Accumulator as the denominator (bottom value) in division computations, press D.

The % column (Accumulator) stores an amount that is used as the base (root) in the computation of percentages throughout reports.

Lines 99=pg. This field allows you to enter special format instructions.

Format	Text in Lines 99=pg
Single spacing between lines	1
Double spacing between lines	2

New page	99
Single line under the amount fields	–
Double lines under amount fields	=
Center a description on the report	C

What is a ratio? A ratio is the number resulting from the division of one number by another. *DacEasy Accounting* version 3.0 provides the capability to perform division within the report design operation. This enables you to enter information for ratio analysis.

To perform division computations, the following operations are necessary:

- The numerator (top value) for the division computation must be entered for accumulation in one of the 3 AMOUNT TO columns.
- The denominator (bottom value) for the division computation must be entered for accumulation in another AMOUNT TO column.
- A / (slash) must be entered in the AMOUNT FROM field on the line where you want the computation executed.
- An *N* must be entered in the AMOUNT TO column holding the numerator.
- A *D* must be entered in the AMOUNT TO column holding the denominator.

To assist you in the format of reports, *DacEasy* also provides these keys:

- To add a new line at the cursor, press Alt-I.
- To delete the line at the cursor, press Alt-D.
- To print a copy of the report that is currently onscreen, press Alt-P.
- To save your work and exit the operation, press the F10 function key or the Esc key.

Exiting the format operation. To exit the format operation, press Esc. At the exit prompt, press Enter to accept the default *(Y)*.

Printing Financial Statements

To print a financial statement(s), follow these steps:

1. Go to the Financial Statements Generator submenu from the Financials menu.
2. Choose option 2 (Print Financial Reports). Press Enter.
3. Press the F2 (Select) function key to indicate which report(s) you want printed. An asterisk will appear at each of the reports to be printed. To remove an asterisk, press the F3 (Unselect) function key.

The message *Include Account Numbers (Y/N)? Y* will appear on the screen. This prompt gives you the option of printing your reports with or without account numbers.

When you're finished reviewing this operation, press Esc until you return to the Opening menu.

DacEasy's MDUL G/L Interface Table

DacEasy uses a General Ledger (G/L) Interface Table to control the integration between each accounting module. Account numbers taken from your Chart of Accounts are entered in each of the fields in this file (Figure 2-9). These numbers are used when the general ledger is posted.

If you're using *DacEasy*'s sample Chart of Accounts, the account numbers are automatically entered; however, if you've created your own, this table must be completed.

Setting Up DacEasy's Tax Rates Table

DacEasy Accounting Version 3.0 features a tax rate table. You can enter up to ten different sales tax rates that are connected to the Accounts Receivable files through the sales tax rate field.

This feature comes in handy for businesses that sell to customers located in geographic areas where sales tax rates differ.

Before your customer and vendor files can be created, this table must be completed.

Figure 2-9. General Ledger Interface Table

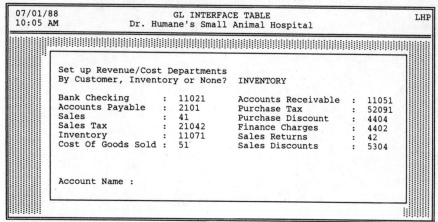

```
07/01/88                      GL INTERFACE TABLE                    LHP
10:05 AM                Dr. Humane's Small Animal Hospital

        Set up Revenue/Cost Departments
        By Customer, Inventory or None?   INVENTORY

        Bank Checking        :  11021    Accounts Receivable  :  11051
        Accounts Payable     :  2101     Purchase Tax         :  52091
        Sales                :  41       Purchase Discount    :  4404
        Sales Tax            :  21042    Finance Charges      :  4402
        Inventory            :  11071    Sales Returns        :  42
        Cost Of Goods Sold   :  51       Sales Discounts      :  5304


        Account Name :
```

F1-Help ESC-Exit <SPACE>-USE THE SPACE BAR TO SELECT ANSWER

To complete the Tax Rates Table, follow these steps:

1. Highlight the Options menu and press Enter.
2. Press 3 to select the Tax Table operation.

The screen in Figure 2-10 will appear.

3. Type 6 in the first field. Press Enter.
4. Type 6.5 in the second field. Press Enter.
5. Type 7 in the third field. Press Enter.

After all applicable tax rates are entered, press the F10 (Process) function key to record your entries.

6. Press F10.

The cursor will move back to the Options menu.

Using the Message File

DacEasy provides a special message file where you can store up to 40 messages. Some messages that might be used include:
Check discount with supervisor or *Check last payment date.* Each message can contain text up to 39 characters. Once messages have been created and stored, they can easily be assigned to both

Figure 2-10. The Tax Rates Table

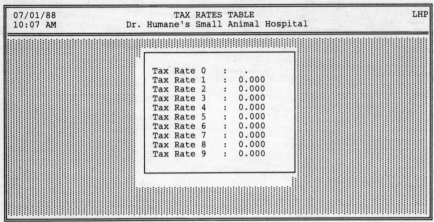

```
07/01/88                    TAX RATES TABLE                        LHP
10:07 AM              Dr. Humane's Small Animal Hospital


                    Tax Rate 0   :    .
                    Tax Rate 1   :   0.000
                    Tax Rate 2   :   0.000
                    Tax Rate 3   :   0.000
                    Tax Rate 4   :   0.000
                    Tax Rate 5   :   0.000
                    Tax Rate 6   :   0.000
                    Tax Rate 7   :   0.000
                    Tax Rate 8   :   0.000
                    Tax Rate 9   :   0.000




F1-Help F10-Process  ESC-Exit
```

customer and vendor files (there's a message code field within these files).

A message will be displayed to an employee when an account containing a message is accessed. These messages will never be seen by your customers.

Other areas where messages are useful are within the purchase order and billing operations. Messages entered in these operations can later be printed on purchase order forms or invoices. Messages used in the purchase order and billing operations *can* be seen by customers. This is a good way to communicate special messages to the customer. For example, if you want to remind a customer about a special discount, you may print a message that reads: *Five percent discount given for all referrals.*

To create messages in the Message File, use these steps:

1. Select 7 (Defaults) from the Options menu. Next, press 5 (Messages). A Special Messages Table will appear on your screen (Figure 2-11).

As you can see, *DacEasy* has provided four messages. Sixteen messages can be displayed on the screen at one time. To look at any messages not on the current screen, press Enter or the arrow keys and the screen will scroll. To see the last message in this Table, press Ctrl-End.

Figure 2-11. Special Messages Table

```
07/01/88                      SPECIAL MESSAGES TABLE                        LHP
10:11 AM                   Dr. Humane's Small Animal Hospital

    Msg. No.      Message

       1          Check Credit Available
       2          Ask P.O. Number
       3          Check Discount with Manager
       4          Thank You Very Much for your Business
       5
       6
       7
       8
       9
      10
      11
      12
      13
      14
      15
      16
```

F1-Help F10-Process   ESC-Exit

2. With the cursor positioned at message number 5, type *Sr. Citizen Discount* and press Enter.
3. At message number 6 type *Ask for price if buying in volume.* Press Enter.
4. At message number 7 type *Slow paying Customer.* Press the down-arrow key.
5. At message number 8 type *We appreciate your patronage.* Press the down-arrow key.
6. At message number 9 type *Send reminder notice in January.* Press Enter.
7. At message number 10 type *Send reminder notice in February.* Press Enter.

Messages can be edited very easily by moving the cursor to the desired field. Press Ctrl-Home to move the cursor to the first message; press Ctrl-End to move to the last message.

For example, to change message number 5:

1. Press Ctrl-Home. The cursor will move to message number 1.
2. Press the down arrow until the cursor is positioned on the message number 5 field.
3. Type *15% Sr. Citizen Discount.* Press Enter.

You can see how simple this is. And messages can prove to be very valuable to your business.

Figure 2-12. Edited Special Messages

```
07/01/88                    SPECIAL MESSAGES TABLE                    LHP
10:11 AM                 Dr. Humane's Small Animal Hospital

    Msg. No.      Message
    ━━━━━━━━━━━━━━━━━━━━━━━━━━━━━━━━━━━━━━━━━━━━━━━━━━━━━━━━━━━━━
       1          Check Credit Available
       2          Ask P.O. Number
       3          Check Discount with Manager
       4          Thank You Very Much for your Business
       5          15% Sr. Citizen Discount.
       6          Ask for price if buying in volume.
       7          Slow paying Customer.
       8          We appreciate your patronage.
       9          Send reminder notice in January.
      10          Send reminder notice in February.
      11
      12
      13
      14
      15
      16

F1-Help F10-Process   ESC-Exit
```

Your screen should look like Figure 2-12.

The last step is to save your messages. After you've finished setting up your Message Table, simply press the F10 (Process) function key. The messages will be saved; then press Esc, and the cursor will return to the Options menu.

Using the Statement Texts File

DacEasy provides another feature similar to the Message File. This feature lets you print tailored messages on your customers' monthly statements based on their present balance and the age of the balance. There are five categories for which statement messages can be utilized:

Inactive
Current Balance
Late 1–30 Days
Late 31–60 Days
Late Over 60 Days

For example, a customer who is always up-to-date with payments might receive a message reading: *We appreciate the promptness of your payments. Thank you for allowing us to serve you.* A customer whose balance is 1–30 days late might receive a message like *We appreciate your business, but your payment is past due.*

Figure 2-13. Customer's Statement Texts

```
07/01/88                   CUSTOMER'S STATEMENT TEXTS                LHP
10:15 AM                Dr. Humane's Small Animal Hospital

   Inactive         Line 1    Thank you for your past business, we
                    Line 2    hope we can be of service in the future

   Current Bal.     Line 1    Thank you for your business, it is nice
                    Line 2     to have such a prompt paying customer

   Due 1-30 Days    Line 1    Thank you for your business, but it
                    Line 2    seems that your payment is past due

   Due 31-60 Days   Line 1    Thank you for your business, but your
                    Line 2          payment is seriously past due

   Due Over 60      Line 1    Your payment will be turned over to our
                    Line 2    legal department if not paid immediately

F1-Help F2-Center  F10-Process  ESC-Exit
```

To create statement text messages, follow these steps:

1. Select 7 (Statement Messages) from the File menu. The Customer's Statement Texts Table will appear (Figure 2-13).

DacEasy has completed this operation for you; however, if you want to edit any statement messages, up to 40 characters of data can be entered on each line. The F2 function key can be used in this operation to center the message within a field.

Press the F10 (Process) function key to save your work, and return to the File menu.

Printing messages on your customers' monthly statements is valuable because it's a tactful way to get messages to your customers.

DacEasy's Costing System

In the business world, some type of costing method must be used to determine the cost of merchandise inventory. What is a costing system? During a physical inventory, quantities of merchandise on hand are counted; then purchase invoices or catalogs are used to find merchandise costs. These costs are recorded on inventory forms. The total *cost value* of that inventory is then figured.

A specific costing system (or method) allows a business to figure the total cost value of merchandise inventory. *DacEasy* automatically performs this function and provides three costing methods from which to choose:

- Average Cost
- Last Purchase Price
- Standard Cost

To determine which method is best-suited for your business, a definition of each follows.

Average Cost. This method calculates the cost value of merchandise by averaging the cost of beginning inventory plus the merchandise purchased to the cost of merchandise sold. (The ending inventory and cost of merchandise sold are priced at the same unit cost.) Every time a product is sold, *DacEasy* will determine the cost of that product using the calculated average cost. Note: *DacEasy* will automatically choose the Average Cost method if you don't select one yourself.

Last Purchase Price. This method calculates the cost value of merchandise by taking the last purchase price of a product and assigning it to the number of units sold. Businesses whose vendors frequently change prices prefer this method.

Standard Cost. This method calculates the cost value of merchandise based on a standard cost determined for a set period of time. Businesses that only change product prices once or twice a year, or whose prices fluctuate very little, prefer this method.

All three costing methods are acceptable accounting practices. However, a business should select one method and use it continually. Using the same costing method for all fiscal periods provides financial statements that can be compared with other fiscal year statements. If a costing method is changed, the difference in gross profit and net income will be affected. Note: Consult with an accountant or the IRS before changing costing methods.

Selecting a costing method. To select a costing method, follow these steps:

1. Type 7 from the Options menu to choose the Defaults submenu.
2. Type 1 to choose the Cost System option.

The screen in Figure 2-14 will appear.

Figure 2-14. The Define Cost System Screen

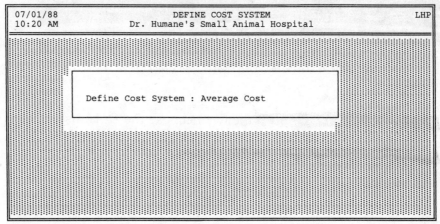

```
07/01/88                    DEFINE COST SYSTEM                        LHP
10:20 AM              Dr. Humane's Small Animal Hospital



            ┌─────────────────────────────────────────────┐
            │                                             │
            │   Define Cost System : Average Cost         │
            │                                             │
            └─────────────────────────────────────────────┘




F1-Help ESC-Exit   <SPACE>-USE THE SPACE BAR TO SELECT ANSWER
```

3. Press Enter to choose Average Cost.

    You'll then return to the Options menu.

Initializing Numbering Systems

Purchase Orders, invoices, and statements are identified by individual sequential numbering systems. *DacEasy's* Invoice/P.O. Numbers Table (Figure 2-15) lets you begin an automated num-

Figure 2-15. The Invoice/Purchase Order Numbers Screen

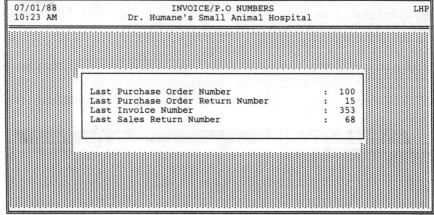

```
07/01/88                   INVOICE/P.O NUMBERS                        LHP
10:23 AM              Dr. Humane's Small Animal Hospital




        ┌──────────────────────────────────────────────────┐
        │  Last Purchase Order Number          :  100       │
        │  Last Purchase Order Return Number   :   15       │
        │  Last Invoice Number                 :  353       │
        │  Last Sales Return Number            :   68       │
        └──────────────────────────────────────────────────┘




F1-Help ESC-Exit
```

59

bering system by entering the next available number from your manual system. Any numbers from 00001 to 99999 can be entered. (When the number 99999 is reached, *DacEasy* starts the numbering from the beginning again.) This operation can be password-protected so unauthorized changes cannot be made.

To enter the numbers you want *DacEasy* to start with, follow these steps:

1. Select 7 from the Options menu to choose the Defaults sub-menu. Press Enter.
2. Select 2 (Invoice/P.O. Numbers option).

The cursor should be located at the field named Last Purchase Order Number.

3. Type 100 and press Enter.
4. Type 15 and press Enter.
5. Type 353 and press Enter.
6. Type 68 and press Enter.
7. Press Esc to return to the Options menu.

Note: This operation is unnecessary if you want your numbering system to begin with 00001, since *DacEasy* automatically starts the system using this number.

Purchase Order and Billing Codes

Businesses often purchase or sell items that aren't directly associated with merchandise. These include freight, packaging, insurance, and so on. These items are sometimes referred to as *noninventory items*. The charges connected with these items, however, are accountable and need to appear within your accounting system. That is, if your company orders new equipment, you'll need to pay for the equipment and the shipping charges. *DacEasy* specifically developed a billing and purchase order code system that lets you enter these noninventory items using miscellaneous codes.

You can create up to 20 special purchase order codes and 20 invoice (billing) codes. These codes must be set up before you try to use them in the Purchase Order or Billing operations. Each code requires an account name and its corresponding account number entered with it. When a transaction occurs, this account will receive the appropriate debit or credit in the general ledger.

Purchase Order Codes

If freight charges are incurred when a product is purchased, the Purchase Order code number that correlates with this item is entered in a specific field within a purchase order (entering purchase orders is explained in greater detail later in this manual). The description *Freight* will then appear on the purchase order, and the appropriate freight charges are entered. The freight charges appear as a debit (money you owe) in the general ledger once it's entered, printed, and posted under Merchandise Received.

Note: The General Ledger is not affected until the merchandise or service is actually received and entered in the Merchandise Received operation. Entering the charges in the Purchase Order operation alone doesn't affect the General Ledger.

If you return the merchandise, the freight charges appear as a credit (money you receive) in the General Ledger once the return is entered in the Purchase Order Return operation.

To enter Purchase Order Codes, follow these steps:

1. Press 6 from the File menu to select the Codes option.
2. Press 1 to select the Purchase Order Codes operation.

The screen in Figure 2-16 will appear.

Figure 2-16. The Purchase Order Codes Screen

```
07/          ****   PURCHASE ORDER CODES   ****                    LHP
10:
     Code No.        Description       Amount    Account No.  Taxable
     --------    --------------------  --------  -----------  -------
           1     Freight               0.00      52081          N
           2     Insurance             0.00      52082          N
           3     Packaging             0.00      52083          N
           4     Advertising Radio/TV  0.00      52191          Y
           5     Advertising Print     0.00      52192          Y
           6     Autos & Trucks        0.00      12011          Y
           7     Furniture & Fixtures  0.00      12021          Y
           8     Office Equipment      0.00      12031          Y
           9     Machinery & Equip.    0.00      12041          Y
          10     Other Fixed Assets    0.00      12061          Y
          11     Office Supplies       0.00      5211           Y
          12                           0.00
          13                           0.00
          14                           0.00
          15                           0.00
          16                           0.00


   F1-Help  F2-Toggle PO/Billing  F10-Process  ALT D-Delete  ESC-Exit
```

As you can see, *DacEasy* provides a comprehensive, thorough list for you. You can add additional data if necessary; otherwise, press Esc to return to the Files menu.

3. Press Esc.

Billing Codes

If freight charges are incurred when your company sells a product, the billing code that corresponds with this item is entered in a specific field within an invoice sent to the customer (entering invoices is explained in greater detail later in this book). The description *Freight* appears on the invoice and the appropriate charges are then entered. The freight charges appear as a credit (money you receive) in the General Ledger once the invoice is processed.

If merchandise is returned to you, the freight charges appear as a debit (money you owe) when the Sales Return operation is processed.

To enter codes in the Billing Table, follow these steps:

1. Press 6 from the File menu to select the Codes option.
2. Press 2 to select the Billing Codes operation.

The screen in Figure 2-17 will appear.

Figure 2-17. The Billing Codes Screen

```
07/                    ****  BILLING CODES  ****                    LHP
10:
       Code No.        Description      Amount    Account No.  Taxable
       --------    ---------------------  -----------  -----------  -------
          1        Freight               0.00        4301          N
          2        Insurance             0.00        4302          Y
          3        Packaging             0.00        4303          Y
          4        Surcharge             0.00        4304          Y
          5                              0.00
          6        Autos & Trucks        0.00       12011          Y
          7        Furniture & Fixtures  0.00       12021          Y
          8        Office Equipment      0.00       12031          Y
          9        Machinery & Equip.    0.00       12041          Y
         10        Other Fixed Assets    0.00       12061          Y
         11                              0.00
         12                              0.00
         13                              0.00
         14                              0.00
         15                              0.00
         16                              0.00
```

F1-Help F2-Toggle PO/Billing F10-Process ALT D-Delete ESC-Exit

As you can see, *DacEasy* has completed a comprehensive, thorough list for you. You can add additional data if necessary. Otherwise press Esc to return to the Files menu.

3. Press Esc.

Initializing Your Products File

Figuring out the size of inventory your company should maintain requires that you frequently analyze purchases, sales, and inventory records. A business may fail because too much or too little merchandise inventory is kept on hand, or the wrong product is kept on hand. *DacEasy*'s Products File lets you to keep your inventory under control.

Product-oriented businesses buy merchandise and supplies from vendors and then either use these products, or sell them to customers. For example, surgical equipment would be purchased and used by the business; flea sprays, pet vitamins, leashes, and so on would be purchased by the business and then resold to customers). These products become part of that business's inventory. Inventory is an itemized list showing the value of goods on hand. Use *DacEasy*'s Products File to enter that inventory.

Dr. Humane's Small Animal Hospital purchases merchandise from several different vendors. Some merchandise is used directly by the hospital and some is resold to customers. All merchandise purchased becomes part of the animal hospital's inventory and must be recorded in a Products (Inventory) File.

DacEasy's Product File allows you to enter data which, in turn, is used to obtain a variety of information, including finding out which products sell quickly or which generate the most profits. Product catalogs with encoded costs (prices converted into a code) can be printed as can inventory count sheets that might be needed during physical inventories.

To enter inventory into the Products File, follow these steps:

1. Press 4 (Products) from within the File menu. The Product File Maintenance document will appear on the screen (Figure 2-18).

The cursor should be positioned at the Product Code field. The product code identifies the product. You can use up to 13 characters to enter this code. (*DacEasy* takes into consideration the possible use of the Universal Product Code (UPC) or European

Figure 2-18. Product File Maintenance Screen

```
┌──────────────────────────────────────────────────────────────────────┐
│ 07/01/88                  PRODUCT FILE MAINTENANCE                  LHP │
│ 10:36 AM            Dr. Humane's Small Animal Hospital                  │
│  Product Code   :              Description :                            │
│  Measure        :              Fraction    :   0          Dept.   :     │
│  Bin            :              Vendor      :                            │
│  Sales Price    :       0.000  Taxable(Y/N): Y                          │
│  Last Sale Date:     /  /      Minimum     :   0          Reorder :   0  │
│  Last Purch. Date :  /  /  Lst.Purch.Price :   0.000                    │
│  Std. Cost      :       0.000  Avg. Cost   :   0.000                    │
│  On Hand   Units :        0.000 Dollars    :       0.000                │
│  Committed Units :        0.000                                         │
│  On Order  Units :        0.000                                         │
│ ═══════════════════════════ STATISTICAL INFORMATION ═══════════════════ │
│                 Yr.Bef.Lst Last Year This Year  Forecast  Variance   %  │
│  Units Purch. :     0         0        0          0         0      0.0  │
│  $ Purchase   :     0         0        0          0         0      0.0  │
│  Units Sold   :     0         0        0          0         0      0.0  │
│  $ Sales      :     0         0        0          0         0      0.0  │
│  $ Cost       :     0         0        0          0         0      0.0  │
│  $ Profit     :     0         0        0          0         0      0.0  │
│  Times Turn   :   0.0       0.0      0.0        0.0       0.0      0.0  │
│  Gross Return :     0         0        0          0         0      0.0  │
└──────────────────────────────────────────────────────────────────────┘
 F1-Help   F6-Delete   F7-Enter Stock   F10-Process   ESC-exit
```

code). If you previously entered this code, its product information will automatically appear and can be edited.

2. Type 0038188 and press Enter.
   The cursor will move to the Description field. You can use up to 20 characters to identify the product name.
3. Type *Flea Powder* and press Enter.
   The cursor will move to the Measure field. You can use up to four characters to describe the units of measure for a product (for instance, case, doz, or 6pk).
4. Type *Case* and press Enter.
   Fraction field. This field is necessary and cannot remain at 0. Any number from 1 to 1000 can be entered. This number defines the breakdown of the measure field above. For example, if a case of flea powder contains 36 cans, and you sell it by the case, 1 would be entered in the fraction field. If you sell each can individually, 36 would be entered in the fraction field. If you purchase three cases and 12 cans, enter 3.12. *DacEasy* knows the 12 is a fraction of a complete case (12/36). This feature will alleviate problems when buying or selling products in unusual quantities because *DacEasy* will easily keep track of the units you have on hand.
5. Type 36 and press Enter.
   Department field. This field is used if you want to departmentalize by Inventory. The department number is entered in

this field if you've set up revenue and cost departments in your G/L Interface table. You can use up to five digits. The department number must correspond to the general ledger account that will be used when grouping revenues and costs created by this stock.

If you don't want to departmentalize (and you're using *DacEasy*'s sample Chart of Accounts) type 01 in this field. By entering 01, you leave the option of departmentalizing open just in case you change your mind later).

6. Type 01 and press Enter.
   The cursor will move to the Bin field. You can use up to four characters to enter the location of the product.
7. Type 0001 and press Enter.
   The cursor will move to the Vendor Code field. You can use up to six characters to identify the vendor who supplies this product.
8. Type A001 and press Enter.
   Sales Price: The Sales Price field is used to enter the current price of the product. NOTE: When creating an invoice, this price may be overridden.
9. Type 5.00 and press Enter.
   Next, the Taxable field is entered. If the product is taxable, press Enter to select *Y* (the default); if not, enter *N* and press Enter.
10. Press Enter (*Y* will appear in this field).
    Last Sales Date: *DacEasy* will automatically maintain this field.

Minimum field. Use this field to enter the minimum balance of merchandise you want on hand. You can use up to six digits. If the merchandise balance reaches the minimum level, it appears on the Product Alert Report and additional merchandise should be reordered.

11. Type 10 and press Enter.
    Reorder field. Enter the desired quantity that will be reordered once the on-hand quantity reaches the Minimum level.
12. Type 72 and press Enter.
    Last Purchase Date and Last Purchase Price field: These fields are created and maintained by *DacEasy*.

The cursor should be located at the Standard Cost field. Enter the standard cost here if you choose to use the standard costing method. Leave this field blank if you've selected the average or last purchase price method.

13. Press Enter to leave this field blank.
    DacEasy allows you to enter any stock you may currently have on hand by pressing the F7 (Enter Stock) function key. Your screen will display a window asking you to *enter additional stock* (Figure 2-19).
14. Press F7.
15. Type 100 and press Enter at the Units field.
16. Type 5.00 and press Enter at the Unit Cost field.
    Once this information is entered, *DacEasy* automatically displays the total dollar amount.

Saving Your Work

To save the data entered in the Products File, simply press the F10 (Process) function key. *DacEasy* quickly saves the work, and a blank product record will appear. To return to the File menu, press Esc.

During the Process function, *DacEasy* not only saves your work, but also updates a transaction in the General Ledger (this maintains an audit trail and summarizes the inventory balance). The inventory account is debited and the Difference account is credited.

Your Products File should look like the one in Figure 2-20.

Figure 2-19. The Enter Additional Stock Box

```
07/01/88                  PRODUCT FILE MAINTENANCE                    LHP
10:36 AM              Dr. Humane's Small Animal Hospital
 Product Code  : 0038188       Description : Flea Powder
 Measure       : Case          Fraction    :   36       Dept.   : 01
 Bin           : 0001          Vendor      : A001
 Sales Price   :        5.000  Taxable(Y/N): Y
 Last Sale Date:  /  /          Minimum     :      10    Reorder :    72
 Last Purch. Date :  /  /  Lst.Purch.Price :     0.000
 Std. Cost        :     0.000   Avg. Cost  :     0.000
 On Hand   Units  :        0.000 Dollars   :        0.000
 Committed Units  :        0.000
 On Order  Units  :        0.000 ┌─ Enter Additional Stock : ──────────┐
═══════════════════ STATISTI │                                     │
                Yr.Bef.Lst Last│ Units     :            .            │   %
 Units Purch. :      0        │ Unit Cost :        0.000            │ 0.0
 $ Purchase   :      0        │ Dollars   :        0.00             │ 0.0
 Units Sold   :      0        └─────────────────────────────────────┘ 0.0
 $ Sales      :      0        0         0         0         0          0.0
 $ Cost       :      0        0         0         0         0          0.0
 $ Profit     :      0        0         0         0         0          0.0
 Times Turn   :    0.0      0.0       0.0       0.0       0.0          0.0
 Gross Return :      0        0         0         0         0          0.0
```

F1-Help F6-Delete F7-Enter Stock F10-Process ESC-exit

Figure 2-20. The Products File

```
07/01/88                    PRODUCT FILE MAINTENANCE                    LHP
10:36 AM              Dr. Humane's Small Animal Hospital
 Product Code  : 0038188        Description : Flea Powder
 Measure       : Case           Fraction   :   36       Dept.   : 01
 Bin           : 0001           Vendor     : A001
 Sales Price   :       5.000    Taxable(Y/N): Y
 Last Sale Date:                Minimum    :      10      Reorder :     72
 Last Purch. Date :         Lst.Purch.Price :     5.000
 Std. Cost     :       0.000     Avg. Cost :     5.000
 On Hand  Units :     100.000   Dollars    :      500.000
 Committed Units :      0.000
 On Order Units :       0.000
========================== STATISTICAL INFORMATION ======================
                 Yr.Bef.Lst Last Year This Year  Forecast  Variance     %
 Units Purch. :      0         0         0          0         0       0.0
 $ Purchase   :      0         0         0          0         0       0.0
 Units Sold   :      0         0         0          0         0       0.0
 $ Sales      :      0         0         0          0         0       0.0
 $ Cost       :      0         0         0          0         0       0.0
 $ Profit     :      0         0         0          0         0       0.0
 Times Turn   :    0.0       0.0       0.0        0.0         0       0.0
 Gross Return :      0         0         0          0         0       0.0
```

F1-Help F6-Delete F7-Enter Stock F10-Process ESC-exit

17. Press the F10 (Process) function key.
18. Press Esc to return to the File menu.

Now that you know how to set up inventory in the Product File, enter the following data:

Product Code: 2601
Desc.: Dog Food
Measure: Case
Fraction: 24
Dept.: 01
Bin: 0010
Vendor: A001
Sales Price: 1.00
Taxable: Y
Minimum: 24
Reorder: 96
Units: 110
Unit Cost: .80

Product Code: 2602
Desc.: Cat Food
Measure: Case
Fraction: 24
Dept.: 01
Bin: 0011
Vendor: A001
Sales Price: 1.00
Taxable: Y
Minimum: 24
Reorder: 96
Units: 150
Unit Cost: .60

Product Code: 4015
Desc.: Amoxicillin
Measure: Each
Fraction: 1
Dept.: 01
Bin: 0005
Vendor: G015
Sales Price: 10.00
Taxable: Y
Minimum: 10
Reorder: 25
Units: 45
Unit Cost: 5.00

Initializing Your Services File

Businesses that offer services (consultations, deliveries, examinations, and so on) need a file where important billing, pricing, and statistical information is kept. *DacEasy* provides this capability. A Services File, geared toward a service-oriented business, is available to enter and store this data. Utilizing this operation lets you control the services your business offers. Once information is entered, functions such as preparing and printing reports, statistical information, or invoices can be performed with ease. You'll have peace of mind knowing information won't be lost and billing procedures will be accurate.

To set up your Services File, follow these steps:

1. Type 5 from the File menu to select the Services option. The Service File Maintenance document will appear on the screen (Figure 2-21).

As you can see, very little data needs to be entered, yet this information will prove to be invaluable when you want to access various operations.

Your cursor should be highlighted at the Service Code field. You can use up to 13 alphanumeric characters to enter a service code. If the entered code already exists, its data will appear on the screen and can be reviewed or edited.

Figure 2-21. The Service File Maintenance Screen

```
07/01/88                   SERVICE FILE MAINTENANCE                    LHP
10:44 AM              Dr. Humane's Small Animal Hospital
 Service Code  :                   Description :
 Measure       :                   Fraction    :    0       Dept.   :

 Sales Price   :      0.000    Taxable(Y/N): Y
 Last Sale Date:     /  /



                      ═══════ STATISTICAL INFORMATION ═══════
                      Yr.Bef.Lst Last Year This Year  Forecast  Variance    %


 Units Sold    :          0          0         0          0          0     0.0
 $ Sales       :          0          0         0          0          0     0.0




F1-Help F6-Delete  F10-Process  ESC-Exit
```

2. Type S001 and press Enter.
   The cursor will move to the Description field. *DacEasy* lets
   you enter the type of service using up to 20 alphanumeric
   characters.
3. Type *Surgery*. Press Enter.
   Note: If this service is selected from the invoicing program,
   up to 50 characters can be used to describe the actual surgical
   service within the body of the invoice. For example, this service file describes S001 to be Surgery; however, in an invoice,
   this service could be entered in more detail (Abdominal Surgery, Exploratory Surgery, and so on).

The cursor should be highlighted at the Measure field. You
can use up to four characters to describe the unit of service. For
example, if a service is billed on an hourly basis, type *Hour* in the
Measure field.

4. Type *Hour* and press Enter.
   The cursor will move to the Fraction field. This field is used
   along with the Measure field. It tells *DacEasy* what the value
   of the Unit of Measure field is. For example, the value 60
   would be entered in the Fraction field if Hour is entered in
   the Measure field.
5. Type 60 and press Enter.
   Note: This unit value cannot be changed once it's entered
   unless the entire record is deleted (if no invoicing has occurred). The record can then be re-entered and the new Fraction value can be typed in.

Department field. This field is used if you've set up revenue
and cost departments by the Inventory option (for department
analysis) in the G/L Interface Table as explained earlier in this
chapter. You can enter up to five digits. The department number
you assigned when setting up these departments is entered in
this field and is used to match costs and revenues to the appropriate general ledger accounts.

The entire general account number entered in the G/L Interface Table does not have to be entered in this field. *DacEasy* automatically performs this for you when you post to the general
ledger. For example, the Sales Account # in the Chart of Ac-

counts is 41 and the departmental sales accounts are 4101 and 4102. The department number entered in this field will be automatically combined with the Sales Account # (41) when posted to the general ledger.

If you want to add more departments to the Chart of Accounts (see the section on setting up Revenue/Cost Centers discussed earlier in this chapter).

Note: This field can also be used for sorting purposes (for example, type of service, if you don't have departments. You can enter up to five characters to describe the service.)

If you don't want to departmentalize now, but think you may in the future (and you're using the sample Chart of Accounts), enter 01 in this field. This leaves the option open if you decide to departmentalize later.

6. Type 01 and press Enter.
   Sales Price field. Enter the price you would charge a customer for the service, using the same unit of measure entered in the Measure field. For example, if you enter 10.00 in the Sales Price field, *DacEasy* will compute it as $10.00 per hour.
7. Type 100.00 and press Enter.
   The cursor will move to the Taxable field. Most states don't place a tax on services; however, *DacEasy* has provided the default *Y* for this field. Type *N* to change this field to *No* if your business doesn't charge tax on services.
8. Type *N* and press Enter. The *N* will appear.
   DacEasy will automatically enter and update the Last Sales Date field whenever any accounting activity occurs.

If you have any statistical information, it can be entered now.

Saving Your Work

To save the information entered in this record, simply press the F10 (Process) function key. *DacEasy* quickly saves the work and another blank service record will appear on the screen. Additional services can be entered at this time, or you can return to the File menu by pressing Esc

9. Press F10.
10. Press Esc to return to the File menu.
    Your Services File should look like the one in Figure 2-22.

Figure 2-22. The Service File Maintenance Screen

```
07/01/88                    SERVICE FILE MAINTENANCE                    LHP
10:44 AM            Dr. Humane's Small Animal Hospital
 Service Code  : S001          Description : Surgery
 Measure       : Hour          Fraction   :   60      Dept.   : 01

 Sales Price   :    100.000    Taxable(Y/N): N
 Last Sale Date:   /  /




                      ══════ STATISTICAL INFORMATION ══════
                      Yr.Bef.Lst Last Year This Year  Forecast  Variance      %


 Units Sold   :                    0        0          0          0      0.0
 $ Sales      :          0         0        0          0          0      0.0



```
F1-Help F6-Delete F10-Process ESC-Exit

Now that you know how to set up the Services File, enter the following information:

Service Code: B005
Desc.: Boarding
Measure: Day
Fraction: 24
Dept.: 01
Sales Price: 10.00
Taxable: Y

Service Code: G006
Desc.: Grooming
Measure: Hour
Fraction: 60
Dept.: 01
Sales Price: 30.00
Taxable: Y

Service Code: E001
Desc.: Emergency
Measure: Each
Fraction: 1
Dept.: 01
Sales Price: 50.00
Taxable: Y

In the next section, you'll set up your Accounts Receivable files.

What Are Accounts Receivable?

Accounts receivable is an asset account that has normal debit balances. Accounts receivable accounts are increased by debits and decreased by credits. That is, accounts receivable shows how much customers owe you. When they make a payment, the amount is credited toward the amount they owe you, and your accounts receivable amount is reduced. A listing of customer accounts, account balances, and total amounts due from all customers is classified as accounts receivable and is outlined in an Accounts Receivable General Ledger.

DacEasy's automated Accounts Receivable module is a powerful managerial tool. Data you've entered are automatically compiled, thus allowing you to perform basic functions such as applying customer payments to specific invoices or to perform complex functions such as formulating sales quotas, tracking buying trends, sorting data for mailing purposes, and printing a variety of detailed reports. These options, plus the ability to forecast, are a tremendous benefit to every business. *DacEasy* delivers all of these right to your fingertips.

Initializing Your Customer Files

The next step is to set up your Accounts Receivable files. Once you enter all your customer information, *DacEasy*'s program will allow you to process customer payments to specific invoices, forecast cash flow, or print mailing labels or reports such as customer statements, aging reports, and sales reports. Not only do you have the data available to you, but up to three years of online history will automatically be accumulated on each customer.

To enter customer information, follow these steps:

1. Press 2 (Customers) from within the File menu. The Customer File Maintenance document will appear on the screen (Figure 2-23).

Enter the customer code number you have designated for your customer.

1. Type A001. Press Enter.
   Note: If you type a code for an existing customer, that customer's information will appear. You can edit or review an existing customer's file.

Next, using up to 30 characters for each line, type the Customer Name, Contact, and complete address. *DacEasy* takes into consideration the nine-digit zip code. If you know the last four digits of your customer's zip code, you may enter them; otherwise leave it blank.

Figure 2-23. The Customer File Maintenance Screen

```
07/01/88                 CUSTOMER FILE MAINTENANCE                   LHP
10:48 AM              Dr. Humane's Small Animal Hospital

  Customer Code :                    Type (O=Open B=Balance):   O
  Name          :                           Sales Person  :
  Contact       :                           G/L Department:
  Address       :                           Discount %    :    0.00
  City          :              State :      Discount Days :       0
  Zip Code      :          Tel :       -    Due days      :       0
  Tax Id. Number:                           Message Code  :
  Credit Limit    :        0.00    Previous Balance  :       0.00
  Credit Available :       0.00    This Period Bal.  :       0.00
                                   Current Balance   :       0.00
  Last Sale Date  :  / /         Last Payment Date :     / /
  Month Int. Rate :  0.00        Sales Tax Code    :    0 Rate:
 ═══════════════════════ STATISTICAL INFORMATION ══════════════════
               Yr.Bef.Lst Last Year This Year  Forecast  Variance     %

 # Invoices :        0          0        0          0         0       0.0
 $ Sales    :        0          0        0          0         0       0.0
 $ Costs    :        0          0        0          0         0       0.0
 $ Profit   :        0          0        0          0         0       0.0
```
F1-Help F2-Add Tax Rate F6-DELETE F7-Enter Invoice F10-Process ESC-exit

Position your cursor behind the Name field and

1. Type *Buffy Adams.* Press Enter.
2. At Contact, type *Mr. & Mrs. John Adams.* Press Enter.
3. At Address, type *66 Flamingo Street.* Press Enter.
4. At City, type *San Diego.* Press Enter.
5. At State, type *CA.* Press Enter.
6. At Zip Code, type *92101.* Press Enter.
7. At Tel., type *(619).* Press Enter. Type *5554664.* Press Enter.
   At this point, your screen should look like the one in Figure 2-24.

   Your cursor should be positioned behind the field marked *O=Open B=Bal.* The default entry is *O* (Open Invoice) which indicates to *DacEasy* that you want to track each outstanding invoice until its net balance is 0 and the end month process is run. If *B* (Balance Forward) is selected, *DacEasy* will maintain the transactions for the current month only. NOTE: A default item is a response that *DacEasy* anticipates for you in hopes of saving you time.
   To indicate the mode you want to utilize, follow these steps:

8. Press Enter. The *O* will appear and the cursor will move to the next line (Sales Person).
   The Sales Person field is used mainly for reporting functions.

Figure 2-24. The Filled-Out Customer File

```
07/01/88              CUSTOMER FILE MAINTENANCE                        LHP
10:48 AM            Dr. Humane's Small Animal Hospital
─────────────────────────────────────────────────────────────────────────
   Customer Code :   A001              Type (O=Open B=Balance):   O
   Name          :   Buffy Adams            Sales Person   :
   Contact       :   Mr. & Mrs. John Adams  G/L Department:
   Address       :   66 Flamingo Street      Discount %    :       0.00
   City          :   San Diego      State :  CA  Discount Days :         0
   Zip Code      :   92101-   Tel : (619)555-4664 Due days     :         0
   Tax Id. Number:                           Message Code  :
   Credit Limit    :          0.00  Previous Balance  :       0.00
   Credit Available :         0.00  This Period Bal.  :       0.00
                                    Current Balance   :       0.00
   Last Sale Date   :   / /         Last Payment Date :     / /
   Month Int. Rate  :   0.00        Sales Tax Code    :   0 Rate: 6.000
   ════════════════════════ STATISTICAL INFORMATION ════════════════════
               Yr.Bef.Lst Last Year This Year  Forecast  Variance     %

 # Invoices :        0          0        0         0         0        0.0
 $ Sales    :        0          0        0         0         0        0.0
 $ Costs    :        0          0        0         0         0        0.0
 $ Profit   :        0          0        0         0         0        0.0
```
F1-Help F2-Add Tax Rate F6-DELETE F7-Enter Invoice F10-Process ESC-exit

It can be utilized to sort and print reports that track sales, profits, and so on, by a specific salesperson's or employee's code or initials.

9. Type *IMH* in the Sales Person field and press Enter.
   G/L Department field. This field can be used in two ways.

- Use it to departmentalize customer accounts. If you enter a department number in this field, it merges with the Sales, Cost of Goods Sold, and Sales Return accounts in the General Ledger Interface Table. There, the department number is confirmed to make sure it exists. For example, if department 01 is entered in this field, and the Sales Returns account in the General Ledger Interface Table is 42, *DacEasy* will confirm that account 4201 exists. If it doesn't, an error message will be displayed.
- Use it to sort customer accounts. Sorting is effective when preparing and printing reports where you want to keep track of the type of customer you're serving (for instance, in Dr. Humane's practice, he tracks the type of animal—dog, cat, bird, or whatever—he examines, and uses the G/L Department field to sort that statistical information).

   In the G/L Department field:

10. Type DOG and press Enter.
    The Discount Fields. Any special discount terms you extend to your customers are entered in these fields. Once you enter

a specific discount amount, it will automatically become the default for future records you enter (however, it can be revised).

To enter your customer's discount terms, follow these steps:

11. Type 15.00 and press Enter (Discount %).
12. Type 30 and press Enter (Discount Days).
13. Type 30 and press Enter (Due Days).
    Your cursor should be positioned at the Tax I.D. Number field. This field is a feature added to *DacEasy Accounting* Version 3.0. You can enter up to 12 digits to identify your customer's tax number or social security number, or you can leave this field blank.
14. Press Enter to leave this field blank.
    Message Code. As explained earlier in this chapter, message codes can be useful.

In the Message Code field:

15. Type 5 and press Enter. (Message No. 5, which was stored in the Message Table earlier, will appear when working in the customer's file).
    Credit Limit. The cursor should be positioned at the Credit Limit field.
16. Type 500 and press Enter.
    The Credit Available field will be filled in automatically by *DacEasy*. Once you start working in your customer files, *DacEasy* will automatically update the Credit Available field by subtracting the Current Balance from Credit Limit.

Monthly Interest Rate. The cursor should be positioned at the Monthly Interest Rate field. If your business charges a monthly interest rate to customers, enter that information here; if not:

17. Press Enter to leave this field blank.
    Sales Tax Rate. *DacEasy* will automatically compute the sales tax for all taxable items established by the sales tax entered in this field. A number 0 through 9 is entered in this field. This number corresponds to the one you created during the Tax Rate Table operation earlier in this chapter.

18. Press Enter to select six percent.
19. Press the F10 (Process) function key to save your work. The next customer file screen will appear.
    To view the file you just saved, type the Customer Code and press Enter.
20. Type A001 and press Enter.
    At this point, you have completed the primary information needed for setting up a customer file.

Options Available When Report Is Finished

There are three options available now:

1. Exit the Customer File Maintenance document.
2. Enter any historical information you may have for your customer. This is not mandatory because *DacEasy* will perform this function automatically as transactions occur over time.
3. Enter the customer's current balance.
   To exit the Customer File Maintenance document, press Esc. You will return to the File menu.

   To enter historical information:

1. Move your cursor to the appropriate field and type the statistical information.
2. Go to the # Invoices field under the Last Year column. Type 3. Press Enter until the cursor moves directly under 3. At the $ Sales field, type 300. Press Enter until the cursor moves directly under 300. At $ Cost field, type 150 and press Enter. The $ Profit field is computed automatically.
   To enter the customer's current balance, press F7. The lower portion of the screen will display an area to enter either open invoices or balance forward entries (depending on what was entered when the customer file was created).

   How to Enter the Account Balance of Your Customer. The following section explains how to enter the customer account balance—both open invoice and balance forward modes use this procedure.

1. Position the cursor at the invoice # field. Up to eight alphanumeric characters can be entered in this field.

Tip: To avoid confusion during an audit, enter the same characters that appear on the original invoice sent by your vendor.

2. Type 13021 and press Enter.
   The cursor should be positioned at the Transaction Code field. There are three options identified with this field. One of three letters should be entered.

3. Enter *I* for an Invoice transaction; enter *D* for a Miscellaneous Debit transaction; or enter *C* for a Miscellaneous Credit transaction.

4. Type *I* and press Enter.
   The cursor will move to the Transaction Date field. The date you entered when you logged on to your computer will appear in this field. Press Enter if this is the correct date; otherwise, type the transaction date, then press Enter.

5. Type 063088 and press Enter.
   The cursor will move to the Amount Balance field. The invoice or balance forward amount should be entered here.

   Note: Enter a minus sign first if the balance is negative.

6. Type 25.00 and press Enter. Notice that *DacEasy* automatically fills in the This Period Bal. and Current Balance fields in the customer file and the Credit Available field is updated.
   The cursor will move to the Disc. Available Date. *DacEasy* will automatically compute this date using the information entered in the customer file. However, this date can be revised.

7. Press Enter.
   The cursor should be positioned on the Disc. Available Amount field. Again, this information is automatically computed by *DacEasy*. However, it can be revised.

8. Press Enter.
   As in the previous field, *DacEasy* will automatically enter this date, but it can be revised.

9. Press Enter.
   Reference Number is the last field in this procedure. *DacEasy* allows you to enter a reference number; if you don't have one, utilize *DacEasy*'s default word: *NONE*.

10. Press Enter. The word *NONE* will appear in the Reference Number field.

Saving Your Work

DacEasy's program makes it very easy to save your work, and it also provides a very valuable feature: It automatically updates all the files connected with the data you entered. For example, after carefully checking for the accuracy of the data you entered within the invoicing procedure, press the F10 (Process) function key. Not only will your work be saved, but also the Customer Balance, the Open Invoice file, and the General Ledger Transaction file will be updated at the same time. This saves you time and ensures the accuracy of all appropriate files. Both of these advantages are beneficial to any business.

To save your work:

1. Press F10 (Process).

   Your screen should look like the one in Figure 2-25.

   DacEasy will quickly process the information you entered in the account balance procedure and the cursor will appear at the beginning of the next blank customer file. If you don't want to enter any more customer information at this time, press Esc to go to the File Creation and Maintenance menu.

   Note: It's extremely important to check the accuracy of your work before pressing F10. Once you process your work, any error you find must be corrected by entering an adjustment through the accounts receivable transaction entry. Since this procedure is

Figure 2-25. The Processed Customer File Maintenance Screen

```
 07/01/88                   CUSTOMER FILE MAINTENANCE                    LHP
 10:48 AM               Dr. Humane's Small Animal Hospital

    Customer Code :   A001             Type (O=Open B=Balance):   O
    Name          :   Buffy Adams              Sales Person  :    IMH
    Contact       :   Mr. & Mrs. John Adams    G/L Department:    DOG
    Address       :   66 Flamingo Street       Discount %    :     15.00
    City          :   San Diego     State :  CA Discount Days :        30
    Zip Code      :   92101-    Tel : (619)555-4664 Due days   :        30
    Tax Id. Number:                            Message Code  :      5
    Credit Limit  :        500.00   Previous Balance  :        0.00
    Credit Available :     475.00   This Period Bal.  :       25.00
                                    Current Balance   :       25.00
    Last Sale Date :                Last Payment Date :
    Month Int. Rate :  0.00         Sales Tax Code    :    0 Rate:  6.000
 ======================= STATISTICAL INFORMATION=======================
              Yr.Bef.Lst Last Year This Year  Forecast  Variance     %

 # Invoices :        0        3        0         0         0        0.0
 $ Sales    :        0      300        0         0         0        0.0
 $ Costs    :        0      150        0         0         0        0.0
 $ Profit   :        0      150        0         0         0        0.0

 F1-Help  F2-Add Tax Rate  F6-DELETE  F7-Enter Invoice F10-Process  ESC-exit
```

used only while setting up the accounts receivable customer file, *DacEasy* won't let you delete or correct an entry after it has been processed (only additions can be entered).

Now that you know how to set up the Customer File, enter the following information:

Cust. Code: B016
Name: Champ
Contact: Bud Boswell
Address: 868 River Drive
            San Diego, CA 92117
Tel.: (619)555-0370
Sales Person: IMH
G/L Dept.: DOG
Discount Info.: None
Message Code: None
Credit Limit: 1,500.00
Sales Tax: 0 (6%)
Enter Invoices:
Invoice #: 202
Date: 6/2/88 Code: I
Amt. Bal.: 60

Cust. Code: R050
Name: Mittens
Contact: Frank Reynolds
Address: 44 So. Orange Ave.
            San Diego, CA 92133
Tel.: (619) 555-8331
Sales Person: IMH
G/L Dept.: CAT
Discount Info.: None
Message Code: 5
Credit Limit: 500.00
Sales Tax: 0 (6%)
Stats: Last Year
Invoices: 3
$ Sales: 125
$ Costs: 25

Cust. Code: S135
Name: Lady

Contact: Betsy Shaw
Address: 166 State Street, San Diego, CA 92103
Tel.: (619)555-2277
Sales Person: IMH   G/L Dept.: CAT
Discount %: 15.00   Discount Days: 30   Due Days: 30
Message Code: 5   Credit Limit: 500.00   Sales Tax: 6%
Stats: Last Year   Invoices: 4 $ Sales: $350.00
$ Costs: $125.00
Enter Invoices: Invoice #: 257   Code: I
Date: 6/25/88   Amt. Bal.: 25.00

The next section will explain how the Accounts Payable file is set up.

What Are Accounts Payable?

Accounts payable accounts are liability accounts and have normal credit balances. Liabilities are created when you receive merchandise or services from vendors. Accounts payable is increased by credits and decreased by debits. That is, Accounts Payable is the amount you owe others. When you make a payment, your accounts payable balance is reduced. For example, a listing of vendors and service companies and the total amount owed to them is classified as accounts payable and is outlined in an Accounts Payable General Ledger.

DacEasy's automated accounts payable module allows you to enter vendor invoices (whether or not they were purchased through a purchase order). A vendor can be a company that sells you merchandise or a company that provides you with a service (such as the telephone company, utilities company, bank, and so on). The data you enter will enable *DacEasy* to accomplish a variety of functions: compute payment due dates, retain payments, make partial payments, figure available discounts, and track any manual or computer checks that may be generated.

Also, *DacEasy* lets you reprint computer checks and, at the same time, voids the original checks. In addition to all these functions, *DacEasy* also generates important payable reports such as aging reports, statistical reports, as well as vendor directories, mailing labels, and so on.

Finally, one of the most valuable features *DacEasy* gives you is the ability to update several other areas of your accounting system (for instance, the General Ledger) when working within the

Accounts Payable program. Thus, a complete, accurate audit trail is automatically set up.

Initializing Your Vendor File

The next step is to set up your accounts payable files. After all your vendor information has been entered, the *DacEasy Accounting* program will permit you to control the amounts you owe to your vendors and issue payments quickly and easily.

To enter vendor information:

1. Select option 3 (Vendors) from within the File menu. The Vendor File Maintenance document will appear on the screen (Figure 2-26).

    Enter the Vendor Code Number you have designated for your customer.

2. Type A001 and press Enter.
    Note: If you enter a code for an existing vendor, that vendor's information will appear. You can edit or review any existing vendor file.

    Next, using up to 30 characters for each line, type the Vendor Name, Contact (if any), and complete address. *DacEasy* takes into consideration the nine-digit zip code. If you know the last

Figure 2-26. The Vendor File Maintenance Screen

```
07/01/88               VENDOR FILE MAINTENANCE                     LHP
11:01 AM             Dr. Humane's Small Animal Hospital
┌──────────────────────────────────────────────────────────────────┐
│  Vendor Code   :               Type (O=Open B=Balance):  O         │
│  Name          :                    Territory      :               │
│  Contact       :                    Type           :               │
│  Address       :                    Discount %     :       0.00     │
│  City          :            State :  Discount Days :        0       │
│  Zip Code      :        Tel :    -   Due days      :        0       │
│  Tax Id. Number:                    Message Code   :               │
│  Credit Limit     :      0.00   Previous Balance   :       0.00     │
│  Credit Available :      0.00   This Period Bal.   :       0.00     │
│                                 Current Balance    :       0.00     │
│  Last Purch. Date :   /  /       Last Payment Date :     /  /       │
│                                  Sales Tax Code    :   0 Rate:      │
│═══════════════════════ STATISTICAL INFORMATION═════════════════════│
│          Yr.Bef.Lst Last Year This Year  Forecast   Variance    %  │
│                                                                    │
│ # Invoices :      0         0        0         0        0     0.0  │
│ $ Purchases:      0         0        0         0        0     0.0  │
└──────────────────────────────────────────────────────────────────┘
F1-Help  F2-Add Tax Rate  F6-DELETE  F7-Enter Invoice F10-Process  ESC-exit
```

four digits of your vendor's zip code, you may enter them here; otherwise leave it blank.

Position your cursor behind Name and

3. Type *Ace Veterinary Supplies*. Press Enter.
4. At Contact, type *Mr. Lee Seller*. Press Enter.
5. At Address, type *511 North 6th Street*. Press Enter.
6. At City, type *La Mesa*. Press Enter.
7. At State, type *CA*. Press Enter.
8. At Zip Code, type *92040*. Press Enter.
9. At Tel, type *(619)*. Press Enter. Type *5550318*. Press Enter.

At this point, your screen should look like the one in Figure 2-27.

Your cursor should be positioned behind the field marked *O=Open B=Balance*. The default entry is *O* (Open Invoice) which indicates to *DacEasy* that you want to track each outstanding invoice. If *B* (Balance Forward) is selected, *DacEasy* will only track the current month's invoices.

To indicate the mode you want to use:

10. Press Enter. The *O* will appear, and the cursor will move to the next line (Territory).

The Territory field is used mainly for printing reports pertain-

Figure 2-27. The Vendor File Maintenance Screen with Vendor Information Entered

```
 07/01/88                VENDOR FILE MAINTENANCE                       LHP
 11:01 AM             Dr. Humane's Small Animal Hospital

   Vendor Code    :   A001            Type (O=Open B=Balance):   O
   Name           :   Ace Veterinary Supplies   Territory    :
   Contact        :   Mr. Lee Seller            Type         :
   Address        :   511 North 6th Street      Discount %   :      0.00
   City           :   La Mesaa        State :   CA Discount Days :      0
   Zip Code       :   92040-    Tel : (619)555-0318 Due days   :        0
   Tax Id. Number:                             Message Code :
   Credit Limit   :           0.00  Previous Balance  :        0.00
   Credit Available :         0.00  This Period Bal.  :        0.00
                                    Current Balance   :        0.00
   Last Purch. Date :   /  /        Last Payment Date :     /  /
                                    Sales Tax Code    :   0 Rate:  6.000
 ═════════════════════ STATISTICAL INFORMATION═════════════════════
              Yr.Bef.Lst Last Year This Year  Forecast  Variance      %

 # Invoices :        0         0         0         0         0      0.0
 $ Purchases:        0         0         0         0         0      0.0
```

F1-Help F2-Add Tax Rate F6-DELETE F7-Enter Invoice F10-Process ESC-exit

ing to specific territories. This field can be left blank if it's not applicable to your business.

11. Press Enter to leave this field blank.
    The Type field can be used for sorting reports (that is, vendor statistical reports). Up to four characters may be typed in this field, or it can be left blank.

12. Press Enter to leave this field blank.
    The terms your vendors extend should be entered in the Discount %, Discount Days, and Due Days fields. To help you save time, *DacEasy* will duplicate the preceding records entered in these fields; however, they can be revised.

13. Type 2.00 in the Discount % field. Press the down arrow.

14. Type 15 in the Discount Days field. Press the down arrow.

15. Type 30 in the Due Days field and press Enter.
    Your cursor should be positioned at the Tax Id. Number field. This field is a feature added to *DacEasy Accounting* Version 3.0.
    You can enter up to 12 digits to identify the vendor's Tax Id. or social security number, or you can leave this field blank.

16. Type 95-3078429 and press Enter.
    Message Code. Using messages in the Accounts Payable Vendor Files is just as advantageous as using them in the customer files. Special messages can be entered to inform employees of any circumstances that need to be brought to their attention. For example, if you're not sure whether a vendor offers a discount, you could enter a message code that correlates to a message that reads *Ask if discount available.*

Note: Vendors don't see these messages. They only appear on the computer screen to attract the employees' attention.

17. Type 2 and press Enter.
    The amount of credit the vendor has extended to you should be entered in the Credit Limit field.

18. Type 1500 and press Enter.
    DacEasy will automatically update the Credit Available field by subtracting the Current Balance from Credit Limit. The Current Balance field is also automatically updated by *DacEasy* every time Purchase Order or Accounts Payable transactions are posted (recorded).

Sales Tax Rate. Every time an invoice is entered, *DacEasy* will automatically compute the sales tax for all taxable items established by the sales tax rate entered in this field. A number 0 through 9 is entered in this field. This number corresponds to the one you created during the Tax Rate Table operation earlier in this chapter.

19. Press Enter to select 6.00%.
    You've now completed the primary information needed for a vendor file. Your screen should look like the one in Figure 2-28.

Up to three years of historical information can also be entered and automatically maintained within vendor files. If you choose not to enter any statistical information yourself, *DacEasy* will create it for you as it becomes available.

To enter statistical information, move your cursor to the appropriate field and type the total number of invoices and the total dollar amount of purchases accumulated within one year.

1. Move your cursor to the # of Invoices field under the column headed *Last Year*.
2. Type 12 and then continue pressing Enter until the cursor moves under the 12.

Figure 2-28. Completed Primary Information on Vendor File Maintenance Screen

```
07/01/88              VENDOR FILE MAINTENANCE                      LHP
11:01 AM            Dr. Humane's Small Animal Hospital

  Vendor Code    :   A001              Type (O=Open B=Balance):   O
  Name           :   Ace Veterinary Supplies    Territory    :
  Contact        :   Mr. Lee Seller             Type         :
  Address        :   511 North 6th Street       Discount %   :     2.00
  City           :   La Mesaa      State :  CA  Discount Days :      15
  Zip Code       :   92040-    Tel : (619)555-0318 Due days   :      30
  Tax Id. Number:    95-3078429             Message Code :   2
  Credit Limit     :       1500.00   Previous Balance  :    0.00
  Credit Available :       1500.00   This Period Bal.  :    0.00
                                     Current Balance   :    0.00
  Last Purch. Date :   /  /          Last Payment Date :    /  /
                                     Sales Tax Code   :   0 Rate: 6.000
============== STATISTICAL INFORMATION==============
                 Yr.Bef.Lst Last Year This Year  Forecast  Variance      %

# Invoices :                   0         0         0         0         0.0
$ Purchases:          0        0         0         0         0         0.0
```

F1-Help F2-Add Tax Rate F6-DELETE F7-Enter Invoice F10-Process ESC-exit

3. The cursor is in the $ Purchase field. Type 7000 and press Enter.

Entering Vendor Account Balances

This procedure is similar to the one used in the customer file because the same options—Open Invoice mode or Balance Forward mode—are accessed. You entered the option you wanted when the vendor file was created. Use the open invoice mode if you have the exact balance from each invoice.

Note: If you don't know exactly how much you owe a vendor, contact them and ask for that information.

Use the balance forward mode if you want *DacEasy* to manage the data after you initially enter the total current balance. Whether you choose the Open Invoice or the Balance Forward modes, the account balance is entered using the following procedure:

1. Press F7. The lower portion of the screen will display an area in which to enter either open invoices or balance forward entries (depending on what was entered when the vendor file was created). This procedure permits you to enter as many invoices as needed. However, only three entries at a time will appear on the screen. To view any entries not on the current screen, use the cursor movement keys.
Position the cursor at the Invoice # field. Up to eight alphanumeric characters can be entered in this field.

Tip: To avoid confusion during an audit, enter the same characters that appear on the original invoice.

2. Type H053669 and press Enter.
The cursor will move to the Transaction Code field. There are three options identified with this field. One of three letters should be entered here. Enter *I* for an Invoice transaction; enter *D* for a Miscellaneous Debit transaction, and enter *C* for a Miscellaneous Credit transaction.
3. Type *I* and press Enter.
The cursor will move to the Transaction Date field. The date you entered when you first logged on to your computer will appear here. Press Enter to keep the displayed date or type another date.

4. Press Enter to use the displayed date. The cursor will move to the Amount Balance field. The invoice or balance forward amount is entered here.
Note: Press the minus sign before the amount if it's a negative balance.
5. Type 125 and press Enter. Notice that *DacEasy* automatically updates the This Period Bal. and Current Balance fields.
The discount information will all be automatically computed by *DacEasy*; however, you can revise it if necessary.

Reference Number is the last field in this procedure. Enter a reference number if one is available. Otherwise use *DacEasy's* default word: *NONE*.

6. Press Enter.

Saving Your Work

DacEasy's program makes it very easy to save your work, and it also provides a valuable feature: It automatically updates all the files identified with the data you entered. For example, after carefully checking for the accuracy of the data within the invoicing procedure, press the F10 (Process) function key. Not only will your work be saved (recorded), but the Vendor Balance, the Open Invoice file, and the General Ledger transaction file will be updated at the same time. This attribute saves time and ensures the accuracy of all files involved. Both of these advantages are extremely beneficial to any business.
To save your work:

7. Press F10 (Process).
Your vendor file should look like the one in Figure 2-29.

DacEasy will quickly process the information entered in the account balance procedure, the current screen will clear, and another blank vendor file will appear. If you don't want to enter additional vendor information, press Esc to return to the File menu. To return to the file you just entered, type the Vendor's Code, then press Enter.
Note: It's important to check the accuracy of your work before pressing the F10 (Process) function key. Once you process the work, any error found must be corrected by entering an ad-

Figure 2·29. The Completed Vendor File Maintenance Screen

```
07/01/88                VENDOR FILE MAINTENANCE                        LHP
11:15 AM              Dr. Humane's Small Animal Hospital
   Vendor Code   :   A001              Type (O=Open B=Balance):   O
   Name          :   Ace Veterinary Supplies   Territory     :
   Contact       :   Mr. Lee Seller            Type          :
   Address       :   511 North 6th Street      Discount %    :       2.00
   City          :   La Mesa        State :  CA Discount Days :         15
   Zip Code      :   92040-     Tel :  619 555-0318 Due days  :         30
   Tax Id. Number:   95-3078429               Message Code   :    2
   Credit Limit     :        1500.00  Previous Balance  :       0.00
   Credit Available :        1375.00  This Period Bal.  :     125.00
                                      Current Balance   :     125.00
   Last Purch. Date :                 Last Payment Date :
                                      Sales Tax Code    :   0 Rate: 6.000
========================== STATISTICAL INFORMATION==========================
              Yr.Bef.Lst Last Year This Year  Forecast  Variance       %
 # Invoices :      0         12         0         0        0         0.0
 $ Purchases:      0       7000         0         0        0         0.0
```

F1-Help F2-Add Tax Rate F6-DELETE F7-Enter Invoice F10-Process ESC-exit

justment through the accounts payable transaction entry. Since this procedure is only used while setting up vendor files, *DacEasy* won't let you delete or correct any entry after it has been processed (only additions can be entered). Now that you know how to set up the Vendor File, enter the following information:

Vendor Code: G015
Name: Goodson's Drug Co.
Contact: Marjorie Miller
Address: 1606 Pearl Street
         San Diego, CA
Zip: 92110
Tel.: (619)555-4334
Type 02
Discount %: 3.00
Discount Days: 15
Due Days: 15
Message Code: 6
Tax ID: 95 8834521
Credit Limit: 2000.00
Stats: This Year
Invoices: 6
$ Purchases: 3,500.00
Enter Invoices:

Invoice #: H66300
Code: I
Amt. Balance: 500.00

Vendor Code: U008
Name: Utilities Co. of S.D.
Contact: Larry Brown
Address: 6222 Lakeshore Drive
         San Diego, CA
Zip: 92102
Tel.: (619)555-9165
Type 02
Discount %: 0
Discount Days: 0
Due Days: 7
Message Code: None
Tax ID: 95-9005445
Credit Limit: 0
Stats: This Year
Invoices: 5
$ Purchases: 1,250.00
Enter Invoices:
Invoice #: 23478
Code: I
Amt. Balance: 225.00

Chapter 3
A Detailed Look at Accounting Transactions

A normal business activity that changes assets, liabilities, or owner's equity is called a *transaction*. A transaction for the sale of goods or services results in an increase in *capital*. An increase in capital resulting from the operation of a business is called *revenue*. A transaction to pay for services results in a decrease in capital. A decrease in capital resulting from the operation of a business is called an *expense*. Business expenses are for items and services used to produce revenue.

Assets		=	Liabilities	+	Capital
Cash	Supplies	Prepaid Insurance	ABC Co.	Smith Co.	
+2,000.00					2,000.00 (Revenue)

Assets		=	Liabilities	+	Capital
Cash	Supplies	Prepaid Insurance	ABC Co.	Smith Co.	
			250.00		−250.00 (Expense)

Each transaction makes at least two changes on the accounting equation. For example, if you pay $10.00 cash for supplies, two asset items are changed (subtract $10.00 from the cash or checking account; add $10.00 to the supplies account). If you pay $50.00 toward your notes payable account, an asset and a liability item are changed (subtract $50.00 from the cash or checking account; subtract $50.00 from the notes payable account).

The tutorials that follow in this chapter (General Ledger, Purchase Order, and Accounts Payable Transactions) will show you, hands on, how transactions change your accounting equations.

DacEasy's General Ledger

A book containing accounts to which debits and credits are transferred in final form is called a *ledger*. A ledger that contains all accounts needed to prepare financial statements is known as a *general ledger*. A general ledger sorts and summarizes all information affecting income statement and balance sheet accounts.

DacEasy's General Ledger module has many unique features:

- It remains up-to-date by constantly observing all normal accounting activities in other modules, such as billing, purchasing, accounts receivable, accounts payable, and inventory.
- Only administrative activities such as amortization, depreciation, bad debt allowances, setting up account balances, and so on, need to be entered in the general ledger transaction operation.
- It keeps two months open and allows you to enter transactions within the general ledger for a new month so your accounting won't get behind while you're preparing to close the books for the previous month. When you're ready to close the books, it automatically performs the procedure for you.
- While in the year-end closing operation, it automatically closes out the revenue and expense accounts and updates historical files for each general ledger account.
- It allows you to print a range of general ledger journals, account activity detail reports, a trial balance, a chart of accounts, and financial statements.

Note: Before printing reports, statements, invoices, or purchase orders, you must set up printer parameters. To do this, see the chapter on *DacEasy*'s defaults (Chapter 8).

General Ledger Transactions

General Ledger transactions are entered through the General Ledger Transaction file illustrated in Figure 3-1.

To enter this file, choose option 1 from within the Transaction menu. Journal transactions from other modules can also be viewed, but *not revised*, from within this file. *DacEasy* prohibits editing these journals from this file to ensure that journals remain in balance. To view the transactions from another journal, enter its two-character code in the Journal field and the transaction date in the Transaction # field.

Figure 3-1. General Ledger Transaction Entry Screen

```
                        GENERAL LEDGER TRANSACTION ENTRY
  Journal.. :              Transaction #..:            Date..:

  Acct.#    Account Name           Description        Debit      Credit




















  Total Debits :                    |   Total Credits :
```
F1-Help F2-Difference F6-Delete F9-Auto Entry F10-Process ALT D-Delete line

Note: *DacEasy* assigned specific journal codes to be used when you want to review any transactions created through other modules.

A description of each journal's code and the type of transaction it displays is defined below.

If you want to see the summary of transactions created in the Purchasing Transaction operation, enter PO in the Journal field. The screen will display all Merchandise Returned and Purchase Order Returns transactions created from the Purchase Order posting process.

Billing Transaction. Enter *BI* in the Journal field. The screen will display all Invoices and Sales Returns transactions created from the Billing posting process.

Accounts Receivable Transaction. Enter *AR* in the journal field. All Transaction Entry, Cash Receipts, and Finance Charges *DacEasy* has generated in the Accounts Receivable operation will appear on the screen.

Accounts Payable menu. Enter *AP* in the Journal field. All transactions entered in the Transaction Entry file and the Accounts Payable Payments file will appear on the screen.

Inventory menu. Enter *IN* in the Journal field. All physical inventory adjustments created through the Post Physical Inventory (Adjustments) operation will appear on the screen.

If you're using the *DacEasy* Payroll program, the code PY can be entered in the journal field to display any transactions entered from *DacEasy* Payroll.

Another journal code, SU, should be entered in the Journal field when you enter transactions during set-up procedures— that is, when you're installing account balances. You must also post journal difference entries with this code. (This is defined in greater detail below).

You're not limited to the seven codes defined above. You can create your own codes if you want to use other types of journals. For example, you could create a separate journal for amortization and use the code AM. This lets you customize *DacEasy Accounting* for your own business needs.

What is the Journal Difference Account?

The Difference Account is a special utility account that *DacEasy* created to assist you while entering transactions. The Difference Account # is *D*. To activate this account, press the F2 (Difference) function key while in the General Ledger Transaction Entry operation.

The *D* account is used when debits and credits in a transaction don't balance. *DacEasy* won't let you leave a transaction when it's out of balance, but sometimes, due to unforeseen circumstances, it may be unavoidable. That's why a Difference Account was created. This account allows you to balance transactions temporarily so you may leave the transaction entry operation to correct the error in the appropriate account file. The following is an example of where the *D* account should be used.

Let's say you record an entry to an account that was never created in the Chart of Accounts. When you attempt to enter it, *DacEasy* displays an error message; however, if you press the F2 (Difference) function key, a new line item will automatically appear, showing the difference in the appropriate debit or credit field. You can then save your work by pressing the F10 (Process) function key, and go to the Account Maintenance file to create the account in the Chart of Accounts. Once this is done, you can go back into the General Ledger Transaction Entry operation where the *D* account was entered, and change the account number from *D* to the correct account.

Note: The correction doesn't have to be done immediately; however, it must be done before the posting procedure. If you attempt to post transactions before corrections are made and the *D* accounts haven't been deleted, *DacEasy* will abort the posting procedure, and allow you to correct the error before moving on.

The only *D* transactions allowed to be posted are the ones created in the SU journal during file setup.

Setting Up Account Balances

Once accounts are created, their account balances (also known as starting balances or set-up balances) must be entered in the General Ledger.

What are Account Balances?

When you create accounts, their balances (also known as *starting balances* or *set-up balances*) must be entered in the General Ledger. An account balance is the value of the account on the day you created it. All accounts created in the Chart of Accounts must have their current values, or balances, recorded. For instance, when the Petty Cash asset account is created, the actual amount of cash you have on hand is entered as the account balance. When the Mortgages Payable liability is created, the amount you currently owe is entered as the account balance.

Remember: Balances may be amounts you owe, have paid, or expect to earn.

As you know, only the detail accounts in the Chart of Accounts receive any type of transaction directly, so only the active detail accounts require account balances. *DacEasy* automatically transfers these balances to the higher level accounts (General accounts). *DacEasy* also automatically enters account balances for the Accounts Receivable, Accounts Payable, and Inventory modules, so there's no need to enter these balances. (These balances are set up when open invoices and/or current stock are entered in the maintenance files or when these accounts are posted.)

To enter account balances for Dr. Humane's Small Animal Hospital, follow these procedures:

1. Press 1 from the Transactions menu to choose the General Ledger submenu.

   The General Ledger Transaction Entry option displayed in Figure 3-1 will appear.

   The cursor should be positioned at the Journal field. This field identifies the journal for the transaction being entered. One of seven pre-assigned, two-character codes is entered here, or you can enter your own two-character code.

   Note: To review these codes, see the section on General Ledger Transactions discussed earlier in this chapter.

2. Type *SU* (Set-Up) and press Enter.

     The cursor will move to the Transaction # field. This field identifies the transaction being entered. You can use up to four characters to identify it. If you enter a transaction number that already exists within the journal you've selected, that transaction's data will appear.

3. Type 0001 and press Enter.

     Date field. *DacEasy* automatically displays the date you entered during logon procedures. You can change the date at this time or press Enter to accept it.

4. Press Enter.

     The cursor will move to the Acct. # field. The detail account number for each debit or credit entry is entered here.

5. Type 1101 and press Enter.

     The account name (Petty Cash) that corresponds to the account # entered in the previous field will automatically appear. The cursor will move to the Description field.

     Description field. You can enter up to 24 characters to describe the transaction.

6. Type *Set-Up Balance* and press Enter.

     Note: The description you enter will automatically appear as the default entry as you continue entering accounts; however, it can be revised. If it's revised, the new description becomes the default entry.

     Debit field. If the account you're entering is an asset or expense account, enter the balance in this field.

Figure 3-2. Entering a Value in the Debit Field

```
                        GENERAL LEDGER TRANSACTION ENTRY
  Journal.. :SU              Transaction #..:0001        Date..:07/01/88

  Acct.#    Account Name           Description          Debit       Credit

  1101    Petty Cash          Set-Up Balance          1500.00








  Total Debits :     1500.00      | Total Credits :       0.00
```

F1-Help F2-Difference F6-Delete F9-Auto Entry F10-Process ALT D-Delete line

Credit field. If the account you're entering is a liability, capital/equity, or revenue account, enter the balance in this field.

Note: If an asset or expense account has a negative balance, it should be entered in the credit field; if a liability, capital/equity, or revenue account has a negative balance, it should be entered in the debit field.

7. Move the cursor to the Debit field, type 1500, and press Enter. Your screen should look like the one in Figure 3-2.

8. Complete the account balance set-up procedure by entering the following information in the appropriate fields:

	Account	Debit	Credit
Assets:	12021	5,000	
	12031	60,000	
	13031	1,000	
	14013	200	

Liabilities:

	Account	Debit	Credit
	2102		10,000
	210411		250
	210416		100
	21042		2,000

Revenue:			
	4101		5,500
	4301		1,500

Expenses:			
	520111		10,000
	520112		6,000
	5211		500
	5217		250
	5218		125
	5401		80

Once you've entered the account balances, the difference between the debits and credits must be resolved. To resolve this difference:

9. Press the F2 (Difference) function key.

Saving Your Work

To save the account balances entered in this file, simply press the F10 (Process) function key. A blank Transaction Entry will appear. You may enter another transaction or press Esc to return to the General Ledger menu.

10. Press F10, then press Esc.

To see the account balance transaction you just created, follow steps 1 through 4 above. Your screen should look like the one in Figure 3-3.

As you can see, all the entries don't fit on one screen. To look at the rest of the entries, press the arrow keys until they appear.

Printing the General Ledger Journal Report

To print the General Ledger Journal Report that contains the account balance information, make sure you've set up printer parameters; then follow these steps:

1. Highlight the Journals Opening menu. Press Enter.
2. Press 1 to select the General Ledger Journals submenu. The screen in Figure 3-4 will appear.
3. Type *SU* in the Print Journal Code From field and press Enter.
4. Type *SU* in the Print Journal Code To field and press Enter.
5. Type 070188 in the Transaction Date From field. Press Enter.
6. Type 070188 in the Transaction Date To field. Press Enter.

The Initial Page field default is page 1. Press Enter to ac-

Figure 3-3. Sample Account Balance Transaction

```
                        GENERAL LEDGER TRANSACTION ENTRY
   Journal.. :SU             Transaction #..:0001         Date..:07/01/88

   Acct.#    Account Name          Description          Debit       Credit

   13031   Insurance            Set-Up Balance         1000.00
   14013   Utilities            Set-Up Balance          200.00
   2102    Notes Payable        Set-Up Balance                     10000.00
   210411  Federal Income W/H   Set-Up Balance                       250.00
   210416  State Income W/H     Set-Up Balance                       100.00
   21042   Sales Tax Payable    Set-Up Balance                      2000.00
   4101    Sales Dept. 01       Set-Up Balance                      5500.00
   4301    Freight              Set-Up Balance                      1500.00
   520111  Salaries             Set-Up Balance                     10000.00
   520112  Hourly               Set-Up Balance                      6000.00
   5211    Office Supplies      Set-Up Balance                       500.00
   5217    Licenses/Permits     Set-Up Balance                       250.00
   5218    Memships/Dues/Subscr Set-Up Balance                       125.00
   5401    Cash Short           Set-Up Balance                        80.00
   D       Journal Difference   Reconcile Trans. Differ.           31395.00

   Total Debits :    67700.00   |  Total Credits :   67700.00
```

F1-Help F2-Difference F6-Delete F9-Auto Entry F10-Process ALT D-Delete line

Figure 3-4. General Ledger Journal Report Screen

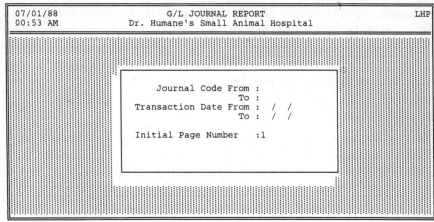

```
07/01/88                      G/L JOURNAL REPORT                        LHP
00:53 AM                 Dr. Humane's Small Animal Hospital


                      Journal Code From :
                                     To :
                      Transaction Date From :  / /
                                        To :  / /

                      Initial Page Number    :1
```

F1-Help ESC-Exit

cept this and begin printing or type in the appropriate page number and then press Enter.

7. Press Enter to begin printing the report as shown in Figure 3-5.

More on General Ledger Operations

Daily General Ledger account balances are usually not necessary. You only need balances of General Ledger accounts when finan-

Figure 3-5. The Journal Report

Date : 07/01/88
Time : 00:57 AM

Dr. Humane's Small Animal Hospital
555 East Meadows Lane
San Diego, CA 92122
(619)555-3636

Page no. 1

General Ledger Journal Report

Journal Trans.#	Date	Acct. #	Account Name	Description	Debits	Credits	Posted?
SU 0001	07/01/88	1101	Petty Cash	Set-Up Balance	1500.00		NO
		12021	Original Value	Set-Up Balance	5000.00		NO
		12031	Original Value	Set-Up Balance	60000.00		NO
		13031	Insurance	Set-Up Balance	1000.00		NO
		14013	Utilities	Set-Up Balance	200.00		NO
		2102	Notes Payable	Set-Up Balance		10000.00	NO
		210411	Federal Income W/H	Set-Up Balance		250.00	NO
		210416	State Income W/H	Set-Up Balance		100.00	NO
		21042	Sales Tax Payable	Set-Up Balance		2000.00	NO
		4101	Sales Dept. 01	Set-Up Balance		5500.00	NO
		4301	Freight	Set-Up Balance		1500.00	NO
		520111	Salaries	Set-Up Balance		10000.00	NO
		520112	Hourly	Set-Up Balance		6000.00	NO
		5211	Office Supplies	Set-Up Balance		500.00	NO
		5217	Licenses/Permits	Set-Up Balance		250.00	NO
		5218	Memships/Dues/Subscr	Set-Up Balance		125.00	NO
		5401	Cash Short	Set-Up Balance		80.00	NO
		D	Journal Difference	Reconcile Trans. Differ.		31395.00	NO
				TOTAL TRANSACTION :	67700.00	67700.00	
SU 0701	07/01/88	11051	Accts Rec'ble Module	Summ. Customer Setup	25.00		YES
		11071	Inventory - Module	Summ. Products Setup	500.00		YES
		D	Journal Difference	Summ. Vendor Setup	125.00		YES
		2101	Accts Payable-Module	Summ. Vendor Setup		125.00	YES
		D	Journal Difference	Summ. Products Setup		500.00	YES
		D	Journal Difference	Summ. Customer Setup		25.00	YES
				TOTAL TRANSACTION :	650.00	650.00	
				TOTAL TRANSACTION :	68350.00	68350.00	

OF ENTRIES PRINTED : 24

cial statements are prepared. You can post from a journal to a General Ledger periodically throughout a month. The number of transactions determines how often to post to a general ledger. A business with many transactions would normally post more often than a business with few transactions. Posting more often helps keep the workload evenly distributed throughout a month. Posting must be done at the end of a month.

Posting to the General Ledger

Note: Before you begin the posting procedure, it's important to back up your files to protect your data. A power or hardware failure during this operation would be detrimental to your entire accounting system.

To post transactions for a specific month, follow these steps:

1. Back up your account files (see Chapter 1 for instructions on how to make back-ups).
2. Highlight the Posting option from the Opening menu. Press Enter.
3. Press 1 to select the General Ledger Posting operation.
   The screen in Figure 3-6 will appear.
4. If your printer is off, turn it on at this time.
5. Press Enter to continue.
   Next, *DacEasy* will prompt you for the month to be posted.

Figure 3-6. The General Ledger Posting Screen

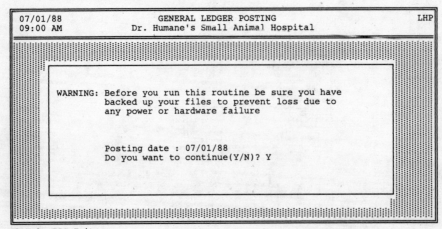

```
07/01/88                    GENERAL LEDGER POSTING                    LHP
09:00 AM               Dr. Humane's Small Animal Hospital


       WARNING: Before you run this routine be sure you have
                backed up your files to prevent loss due to
                any power or hardware failure


                Posting date : 07/01/88
                Do you want to continue(Y/N)? Y




F1-Help ESC-Exit
```

Figure 3-7. The Posting Printout

```
       Transactions with Journal Difference Account Movements :
       SU 0701
        SU 0701
        SU 0701
        SU 0101
        SU 0101
        SU 0101
        SU 0001
 Total Posted to G/L

Total Debits   :      67700.00

Total Credits  :      67700.00
```

6. Press Enter to accept 07, the date displayed on the screen.
7. Press Enter again to start the posting process.

Once posting is completed, the cursor will return to the Posting submenu. The posting process just printed should look like the one in Figure 3-7.

DacEasy's Purchase Order Transactions

Businesses purchase merchandise to sell and buy supplies/equipment for use in the business. A business from which merchandise is purchased or supplies are bought is called a *vendor*. When you need to purchase services, merchandise, or supplies, a *purchase order* must be created. A purchase order is a form describing the merchandise or supplies to be purchased, along with their quantity and price.

DacEasy's Purchase Order module lets you create purchase orders. Once created, this module also

- Lets you control back orders, price adjustments, and duplicate purchase orders.
- Lets you enter the actual amount of merchandise received or returned, and automatically updates the vendor file and product stock file.
- Automatically displays the product description and last purchase price once the product code is entered.
- Automatically updates your inventory system so you're aware of any items on order, thus preventing duplicate purchases.
- Handles purchase returns and adjusts your accounting system automatically.
- Updates vendor payables.

- Compiles a complete three-year history on vendor purchasing.
- Prints purchase orders, merchandise received, and merchandise returned transactions using plain or preprinted forms. *DacEasy* has a variety of preprinted forms available. For information on these forms and how to order them, see the back of *DacEasy Accounting*'s user's manual or contact Dac Software directly at 1-800-992-7779 or by mail at 17950 Preston Road, Suite 800, Dallas, TX 75252.
- Creates and updates a Purchases Journal that, when printed, summarizes the detail of each purchase order received or returned. Details on the Purchase Journal and printing the Purchase Journal Report are explained in Chapter 5.

To enter a purchase order, follow these steps:

1. Press 4 from the Transaction menu to select the Purchasing submenu.
2. Press 1 from the Purchasing submenu to select the Enter Purchase Order operation.
   The screen in Figure 3-8 will appear.

The cursor will be at the Purchase Order # field. This field uses a five-digit number to identify the purchase order. To enter a new purchase order, press Enter and *DacEasy* will automatically display the next available number. To review a purchase order

Figure 3-8. The Purchase Order Screen

```
                              Purchase Order #
    Vendor Code:               Remark:
                                             Via
                                             FOB
                                             Your Ref.
                                             Our Ref.
    Disc. Days      0 Disc. %  0.00 Due Days    0 Tax Code:   Rate:  0.000

     Item #      Desc. Ordered                    Price    Disc. Extended




     Sub Total    Sales Tax    Total
       0.00         0.00        0.00

F1-Help  F6-CANCEL  F10-Process  ALT D-Delete Line
```

that already exists, enter its number and press Enter. The details from that purchase order will appear.

3. Press Enter to display the next available number. The cursor will move to the Vendor Code field. Only a valid Vendor Code can be entered in this field (created in the Vendor File within the File menu). If you enter an incorrect code, *DacEasy* will alert you to the error and let you try again.

4. Type G015 and press Enter. The vendor's name, address, discount, and tax information will appear.

   Note: At this point you can change the vendor's name and address if, for example, the purchase order must be sent to another address. This change, however, is only temporary and only pertains to the specific purchase order being entered and printed. If you need to make any permanent changes regarding vendor information, it must be completed in the Vendor file within the File menu.

5. Press Enter until the cursor moves to the Remark field.

   The Remark field is used to enter any special information concerning the purchase order, such as a *Ship to* address, special instructions, and so on. A total of three lines is available, and you can enter up to 20 characters on each line.

6. Type *Please Deliver*. Press Enter. Type *Between 8–11 AM M–F*. Press Enter twice.

   The cursor will move to the VIA field. You can enter up to 15 alphanumeric characters to display the shipping method.

7. Type *Courier* and press Enter.

   The cursor will move to the FOB (Freight On Board) field. You can use up to 15 characters to enter the city where the freight (product) originates.

8. Type *San Diego* and press Enter.

   Your Ref. field. If the vendor has given you an invoice or reference number, enter it here; otherwise, press Enter to leave this field empty.

9. Type AX4119 and press Enter.

   Our Ref. field. If you have a reference number for this purchase order, enter it here; otherwise press Enter to leave this field empty.

10. Press Enter to leave this field empty.

    Discount Date, Discount %, and Due Days fields. These fields are automatically filled in by *DacEasy* using the information you entered and saved in the Vendor File. They may be modified if the terms of purchase change.

Note: If you do modify these fields, remember that the changes will only pertain to this purchase order. To permanently modify the discount terms for this vendor, you must make the changes in the Vendor File within the File menu.

11. Press Enter until the cursor moves to the Item # field.

The following four types of codes can be entered in the Item # field:

• The product/service code (Mandatory)
• Any applicable Purchasing codes
• Any message codes
• A special comment code

Only a valid product/service code can be entered in this field (created in the Product File or Service File within the File menu). If you enter a nonexistent code, *DacEasy* will alert you of the error and let you try again.

12. Type 4015 and press Enter. The description of the product will appear in the Description field.

The cursor is positioned at the Ordered field. The number of units or fractions ordered is entered here.

13. Type 25 and press Enter.

Price field. *DacEasy* automatically enters the last purchase price here. This amount can be modified.

14. Press Enter to move to the Discount field.

15. Type 3 and press Enter.

Extended, Subtotal, Tax, and Total fields. *DacEasy* automatically computes the total for each of these fields, taking into consideration any discounts entered.

16. Move the cursor to the next Item # field.

This field is also used to enter any special purchase order codes created in the Purchasing Codes operation within the File menu. For example, to enter packaging charges, follow these steps:

17. Type C and then press the space bar once. Next, type 3 and press Enter.

The purchase order code 3 corresponds to Packaging within the Purchasing Codes file. The word *Packaging* will appear in the Description field.

18. Press Enter. The cursor will move to the Extended field. Type 10 and press Enter.

    Special messages created in the Message Table within the Options menu can also be entered in the Item # field. To enter a message, follow these steps:

19. Type *M*, then press the space bar once. Next, type 1 and press Enter. The message that corresponds with the number 1 will appear in the Description field.

    DacEasy also lets you enter remarks within the purchase order. To enter any remarks, follow these steps:

20. Type *D* in the Item # field and press Enter. Next, enter the comments. You can use up to 40 characters per each line of comments.

21. Type *Our office will be closed on July 4th*. Press Enter. Type *D*, press Enter, and type in *Observance of Independence Day*. Press Enter.

    The following summarizes the special codes that can be used in the Item # field:

Code	Type
Purchasing Code	C, press space bar, enter a valid code (1–20).
Message Code	M, press space bar, enter the number of the message (1–40).
Comments	D, press Enter, enter comments in the body of the purchase order.

Review the data you entered. If you need to delete a line, move the cursor to it, then press Alt-D simultaneously. If you want to delete the entire transaction, press the F6 (Delete Transaction) function key.

The completed purchase order should look like the one in Figure 3-9.

Note: The entire body of the purchase order does not fit on the screen. You can review it, however, by pressing the up- and down-arrow keys.

Saving Your Work

To record the information entered in this purchase order, simply press the F10 (Process) function key. *DacEasy* automatically updates the amount owed to the vendor in the Vendor file.

Figure 3-9. The Completed Purchase Order

```
                              Purchase Order #    00101
  Vendor Code:    G015             Remark:
  Goodson's Drug Co.               Please Deliver        Via Courier
  Marjorie Miller                  Between 8-11 AM M-F    FOB San Diego
  1606 Pearl Street                                      Your Ref. AX4119
  San Diego      CA  92110-                              Our Ref.
  Disc. Days     15 Disc. % 3.00  Due Days     15  Tax Code: 0 Rate:  6.000

    Item #       Desc. Ordered                   Price    Disc. Extended

    4015         Amoxicillin
                   25.000                        5.000    3.00   121.25
    C 1          Freight
                                                                  10.00
    M 3          Check Discount with Manager

    D            Our office will be closed on July 4th


    Sub Total    Sales Tax    Total
      131.25        7.28      138.53
```

F1-Help F6-CANCEL F10-Process ALT D-Delete Line

22. Press F10 until a blank purchase order appears.

Printing a Purchase Order

To print the purchase order just entered, make sure you've set up the correct printer parameters, then follow these steps:

1. Press 4 to select the Print Purchase Orders operation within the Purchasing submenu.

    The screen in Figure 3-10 will appear.

Figure 3-10. The Print Purchase Orders Screen

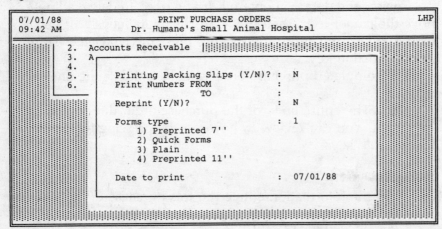

```
  07/01/88                    PRINT PURCHASE ORDERS                    LHP
  09:42 AM             Dr. Humane's Small Animal Hospital

      2. Accounts Receivable  |
      3. A
      4.
      5.        Printing Packing Slips (Y/N)? :  N
      6.        Print Numbers FROM             :
                              TO               :
                Reprint (Y/N)?                 :  N

                Forms type                     :  1
                   1) Preprinted 7''
                   2) Quick Forms
                   3) Plain
                   4) Preprinted 11''

                Date to print                  :  07/01/88
```

F1-Help F4-Change Date ESC-Exit

The cursor is at the Print Packing Slips field. To print packing slips, type *Y* and press Enter. *DacEasy* will print the packing slip; however, the Cost and Extended information will not appear.

2. Press Enter to select the *N* (No) option. The cursor will move to the Print Number FROM field.
3. Type 101 and press Enter.
4. At the Print Number TO field, type 101 and press Enter.

   The cursor will move to the Reprint field. If you press *Y* (Yes) in this field, the system will only print those purchase orders that have been printed before and have never been modified. If you press *N* (No) in this field, the system will only print those purchase orders that have never been printed or that have been modified since being printed.
5. Type *N* and press Enter.

   The cursor will move to the Forms type field. Choose the type of form you'll be using. If you select plain paper, *DacEasy* will print all column headings. If not, enter which preprinted forms you'll be using.
6. Select the plain paper option (3) and press Enter.

   The cursor will move to the Date to Print field. *DacEasy* automatically enters the current date; however, it can be changed.
7. Press Enter to select the default date.

   If you're using preprinted forms, the system helps you align the form by printing a test pattern of numbers just above the perforation on the left-hand side of the form. Once the test has been run, *DacEasy* will prompt you by asking if the form is aligned correctly. The test pattern will print again if you enter *N* (No). Realign the form before entering *N*. To skip the re-alignment option, press the F6 function key.
8. If you're using plain paper, press *Y* to start printing. Then press Enter.

   The printed purchase order should look like the one in Figure 3-11.

Entering Merchandise Received

A business needs to know all items ordered have been received and the prices are correct. The Merchandise Received operation lets you enter the product you received. You don't have to have a purchase order on file to receive merchandise.

Figure 3-11. The Printed Purchase Order

```
                    Dr. Humane's Small Animal Hospital
                           555 East Meadows Lane
                           San Diego, CA  92122
                             (619)555-3636
                         P u r c h a s e   O r d e r

   G015                                                  Ship to/Remarks
   Goodson's Drug Co.                                    Please Deliver
   Marjorie Miller                                       Between 8-11 AM M-F
   1606 Pearl Street
   San Diego CA 92110

                 Date 07/01/88    No. 00101 Page  1  Due Date  07/16/88
   --------------------------------------------------------------------------------
   Via Courier        FOB  San Diego   Disc.days 15 Disc.% 3.00 Net Days 15  Your #AX4119  Our #
   --------------------------------------------------------------------------------
   Inventory #   Description                  Ordered  Unit Price  Disc.%   Extended Price
   --------------------------------------------------------------------------------
   4015          Amoxicillin                  25.0C0     5.000      3.00         121.25
                 Packaging                                                        10.00
                 Check Credit Available
                 Our office will be closed on July 4th
                 in observance of Independence Day.




   --------------------------------------------------------------------------------
                                                 Sub-total      131.25
                                                 Tax              7.28
                                                 Total          138.53

                                                 Net to Pay     138.53
                                                 ------------
```

To enter Merchandise Received, follow these steps:

1. Press 2 to select the Enter Merchandise Received operation from within the Purchasing submenu.
   The screen in Figure 3-12 will appear.
2. Type 101 in the Purchase Order # field. The information contained in this purchase order will appear on the screen. If any

Figure 3-12. The Merchandise Received Screen

```
   ┌──────────────────────────────────────────────────────────────────────┐
   │    Merchandise Received from Purchase Order #                          │
   │ Vendor Code:                       Remark:                             │
   │                                                    Via                 │
   │                                                    FOB                 │
   │                                                    Your Ref.           │
   │                                                    Our Ref.            │
   │ Disc. Days      0 Disc. % 0.00  Due Days      0  Tax Code:  Rate: 0.000│
   │─────────────────────────────────────────────────────────────────────│
   │     Item #   Desc. Ordered   Received Back Ord.   Price   Disc. Extended│
   │                                                                        │
   │                                                                        │
   │                                                                        │
   │                                                                        │
   │                                                                        │
   │                                                                        │
   │─────────────────────────────────────────────────────────────────────│
   │   Sub Total   Sales Tax    Total                    Net to Pay         │
   │      0.00        0.00        0.00                       0.00           │
   └──────────────────────────────────────────────────────────────────────┘
```

F1-Help   F6-CANCEL   F10-Process   ALT D-Delete Line

information has changed (terms, discounts, prices), you can update it now.

Next, enter the quantity received. If the quantity is less than the original order, *DacEasy* displays the difference as a Back Order and recalculates the total price. If additional merchandise is received (not on the original order), it can be added.

Note: If you didn't use a purchase order to order merchandise, you may still use this operation to enter merchandise received as a new purchase order number.

3. Press Enter until the cursor moves to the Received field. Type 20 and press Enter.

DacEasy automatically refigures the totals as shown in Figure 3-13.

Once all the merchandise received has been entered and saved, *DacEasy* automatically updates the Vendor's File as to the amount due and the on-hand inventory. The Product File lets you know of any backordered merchandise.

Printing Merchandise Received

To print merchandise received, follow these steps:

1. Press 5 to choose the Print Merchandise Received operation from the Purchasing submenu.

Follow the same instructions used to print your purchase order.

Figure 3-13. Recalculated Figures on Merchandise Received Screen

```
    Merchandise Received from Purchase Order #      0010
Vendor Code:   G015                Remark:
Goodson's Drug Co.                 Please Deliver       Via Courier
Marjorie Miller                    Between 8-11 AM M-F  FOB San Diego
1606 Pearl Street                                       Your Ref. AX4119
San Diego      CA  92110-                               Our Ref.
Disc. Days     15 Disc. %  3.00  Due Days     15  Tax Code: 0 Rate:  6.000
─────────────────────────────────────────────────────────────────────────
    Item #     Desc. Ordered   Received Back Ord.   Price   Disc. Extended

    4015       Amoxicillin
               25.000         20.000     5.000      5.000  3.00       97.00
    C 3        Packaging
                                                                      10.00
    M 1        Check Credit Available

               Our office will be closed on July 4th


─────────────────────────────────────────────────────────────────────────
    Sub Total  Sales Tax    Total                     Net to Pay
    107.00        5.82      112.82                       112.82

F1-Help  F6-CANCEL  F10-Process  ALT D-Delete Line
```

Figure 3-14. The Merchandise Received Printout

```
                    Dr. Humane's Small Animal Hospital
                          555 East Meadows Lane
                          San Diego, CA  92122
                            (619)555-3636
                    M e r c h a n d i s e   R e c e i v e d

   G015                                                  Ship to/Remarks
   Goodson's Drug Co.                                    Please Deliver
   Marjorie Miller                                       Between 8-11 AM M-F
   1606 Pearl Street
   San Diego CA 92110

            Date 07/01/88      No. 00102 Page  1  Due Date   07/16/88
-----------------------------------------------------------------------------
Via Courier        FOB   San Diego   Disc.days 15 Disc.% 3.00 Net Days 15  Your #AX4119  Our #
-----------------------------------------------------------------------------
Inventory #   Description          Ordered   Received Backorder Unit Price Disc.%   Extended Price
-----------------------------------------------------------------------------
4015          Amoxicillin          25.000    20.000    5.000    5.000    3.00          97.00
              Packaging                                                                10.00
              Check Credit Available
              Our office will be closed on July 4th
              in observance of Independence Day.




                                                  Sub-total      107.00
                                                  Tax              5.82
                                                  Total          112.82

                                                  Net to Pay     112.82
                                                  ------------
```

Once printed, the Merchandise Received form should look like the example in Figure 3-14.

Entering Purchase Returns

A business may not want to keep a product that's inferior in quality or is damaged when received. You, the buyer, may be allowed to return part or all of the product purchased. A product returned by a buyer for credit is called a purchase return.

DacEasy's Purchase Order module lets you enter purchase returns (using the Enter Returns operation) and automatically reverses entries made to the product and general ledger files.

To enter a purchase return, follow these steps:

1. Press 3 from the Purchasing submenu to select the Enter Returns operation.

   The screen in Figure 3-15 will appear.

   The cursor is positioned at the Purchase Return # field.

2. Press Enter to assign the next available Purchase Return #.
   Next, enter the Vendor Code.

3. Type G015 and press Enter. The name, address, discount, and tax information for this vendor will appear. Press Enter until the cursor moves to the Item # field.

Figure 3-15. The Purchase Return Screen

```
                              Purchase Return #
    Vendor Code:                   Ship To:
                                                Via
                                                FOB
                                                Your Ref.
                                                Our Ref.
    Disc. Days      0 Disc. %  0.00  Due Days      0  Tax Code:   Rate:  0.000

      Item #       Desc.            Shipped          Price    Disc. Extended




    Sub Total     Sales Tax     Total
       0.00          0.00        0.00
```

F1-Help F6-CANCEL F10-Process ALT D-Delete Line

4. Type 4015 and press Enter.

    The description of this number will appear in the Description field.

5. In the Shipped field, type 1. Move the cursor to the Discount field.

6. Type 3. Move the cursor to the next Item # field.

    To enter a message:

7. Type *D,* then press Enter.

8. Type *Returned due to out-dated expiration.* Press Enter. *DacEasy* automatically refigures the totals as shown in Figure 3-16.

Figure 3-16. Completed Purchase Return Screen

```
                              Purchase Return #    00016
    Vendor Code:    G015           Ship To:
    Goodson's Drug Co.                              Via
    Marjorie Miller                                FOB
    1606 Pearl Street                              Your Ref.
    San Diego      CA  92110-                      Our Ref.
    Disc. Days     15 Disc. %  3.00  Due Days     15  Tax Code: 0 Rate:  6.000

      Item #       Desc.            Shipped          Price    Disc. Extended

      4015         Amoxicillin
                                     1.000           5.000    3.00       4.85
                   Returned due to out-dated expiration.




    Sub Total     Sales Tax     Total
       4.85          0.29        5.14
```

F1-Help F6-CANCEL F10-Process ALT D-Delete Line

Saving Your Work

To record this transaction, simply press the F10 (Process) function key. *DacEasy* will save it and a blank record will appear. Press Esc to go back to the Purchasing submenu.

9. Press F10 until a blank record appears. Then press Esc.

Printing Purchase Returns

To print purchase returns, follow these steps:

1. Press 6 to select the Print Returns option from the Purchasing submenu.

    The screen in Figure 3-17 will appear.

    Follow the same instructions used to print a purchase order, entering the appropriate numbers.

    When you've printed the purchases return form, it should look like Figure 3-18.

Accounts Payable Transactions

DacEasy's Accounts Payable Module lets you keep track of the money you owe to your vendors. When vendor files are created and purchase orders are processed, accounts payable are automatically updated by the Accounts Payable Module. However, items not purchased through the purchase order system (telephone bills, utilities, rent, credit cards, bank loans, and so on)

Figure 3-17. The Print Returns Screen

```
 07/01/88                    PRINT PURCHASE RETURNS                      LHP
 10:24 AM              Dr. Humane's Small Animal Hospital

         2.  Accounts Receivable  |
         3.  A
         4.
         5.       Printing Packing Slips (Y/N)? :  N
         6.       Print Numbers FROM             :
                              TO                 :
                  Reprint (Y/N)?                 :  N

                  Forms type                     :  1
                     1) Preprinted 7''
                     2) Quick Forms
                     3) Plain
                     4) Preprinted 11''

                  Date to print                  :  07/01/88




 F1-Help F4-Change Date   ESC-Exit
```

Figure 3-18. The Purchases Return Printout

```
                         Dr. Humane's Small Animal Hospital
                                555 East Meadows Lane
                                San Diego, CA  92122
                                   (619)555-3636
                         P u r c h a s e   O r d e r   R e t u r n

    G015                                                          Ship to/Remarks
  Goodson's Drug Co.
  Marjorie Miller
  1606 Pearl Street
  San Diego CA 92110

                      Date 07/01/88      No. 00016 Page  1
  ------------------------------------------------------------------------------------

  ------------------------------------------------------------------------------------
  Inventory #    Description                        Returned  Unit Price  Disc.%   Extended Price
  ------------------------------------------------------------------------------------
  4015           Amoxicillin                          1.000     5.000      3.00            4.85
                 Returned due to out-dated expiration.




  ------------------------------------------------------------------------------------
                                                              Sub-total              4.85
                                                              Tax                    0.29
                                                              Total                  5.14

                                                                 ------------
```

must be entered using the Accounts Payable Transaction Entry operation.

When the vendor invoices for these items are entered, *DacEasy* completes the following:

- Automatically computes due dates for your payments and informs you of any discounts available for early payment.
- Lets you issue payments many ways. You can
  - Withhold payments.
  - Make partial payments.
  - Record manual checks.
  - Generate computer-printed checks.
  - Take discounts.
- Tracks both manual and computer-printed checks.
- Allows you to reprint computer checks, and automatically voids the original checks.
- Automatically updates your accounting system.
- Prints payable reports, such as cash flow, aging reports, statistical reports on vendors, and payment reports.
- Prints vendor directories, mailing labels, and statements.

To enter Accounts Payable transactions, follow these steps:

1. Press 3 from the Transactions menu to select the Accounts Payable submenu.
2. Press 1 to select the Transaction Entry operation.
   The screen in Figure 3-19 will appear.

The cursor is positioned at the Transaction # field. This field is used to identify the transaction being entered. To assign a four-digit number, press Enter. *DacEasy* automatically assigns the next available number. To view a transaction that already exists, enter the number for that transaction and press Enter; the details from that transaction will appear.

3. Press Enter to assign the next available number.
   The cursor will move to the Vendor Code field. Enter the code assigned to the appropriate vendor. If you enter a code that doesn't exist, *DacEasy* will display an error message and let you try again.
4. Type U008 and press Enter.
   DacEasy automatically displays the vendor's name in the Vendor Name field.
   The cursor will move to the Transaction Code field and a status box displaying three options for this field will appear on the screen. To enter invoices not generated through the Purchase Order system, type *I* (Invoice) and press Enter. To enter

Figure 3-19. Accounts Payable Transaction Screen

```
                    ACCOUNTS PAYABLE TRANSACTION ENTRY
  Trans. #   :                       Reference/Check #  :
  Vendor Code:                       Transaction Date   :   /  /
  Vendor Name:                       Due Date           :   /  /
  Trans. Code:                       Discount Date      :   /  /
  Invoice #  :                       Discount Available :        0.00
 ┌──────────────────────────────────────────────────────────────────┐
 │ Acct.#   Account Name          Description          Debit    Credit│
 ├──────────────────────────────────────────────────────────────────┤
 │                                                                    │
 │                                                                    │
 │                                                                    │
 │                                                                    │
 │                                                                    │
 │                                                                    │
 │                                                                    │
 │                                                                    │
 ├───────────────────────────────┬────────────────────────────────────┤
 │ Total Debits :                 │ Total Credits :                    │
 └───────────────────────────────┴────────────────────────────────────┘
 F1-Help F6-Delete F9-Auto Entry F10-Process ALT D-Delete line
```

miscellaneous debits or payments to this account that aren't
generated by the check printing operations, type *D* (Miscellaneous Debit) and press Enter. To enter miscellaneous credits
that aren't generated by the Purchase Order system to this
account, type *C* (Miscellaneous Credit) and press Enter.
5. Type *I* and press Enter.

   The cursor will move to the Invoice # field. You can use
up to eight alphanumeric characters to identify the vendor's
invoice #.
6. Type 6053853 and press Enter.

   The cursor will move to the Reference/Check # field. You
can use up to six alphanumeric characters to designate a check
number or other reference that relates to this transaction. This
field does not effect your accounting information; it's used for
memo purposes only.
7. Type *Bill* and press Enter.

   The cursor will move to the Transaction Date field. The
date entered during logon procedures will automatically appear in this field. To accept the date, press Enter; to change it,
simply type the new date, then press Enter.
8. Type 0630 and press Enter.

   The cursor is now at the Due Date field. The due date is
automatically computed by *DacEasy* by adding the number of
days entered in the Due Days field in the Vendor File to the
date entered in the Transaction Date field. This date can be
changed.
9. Press Enter to accept the due date displayed.

   Discount Date, and Discount Available fields. *DacEasy*
automatically computes these discounts and enters them in the
appropriate fields. *DacEasy* computes the discount date by taking the date from the Transaction Date field and adding it to
the number of days in the Discount Days field from the Vendor File. *DacEasy* computes the discount available for early
payment of an invoice by multiplying the invoice total by the
Discount % field from the Vendor file.

   The cursor should be positioned at the Acct. # field. The
account # on the first line will always be the Accounts Payable
account from the G/L Interface Table. *DacEasy* automatically
enters this account on the first line. Subsequent Account #
fields can only have valid detail accounts entered in them.
10. Move the cursor to the Description field. You can use up to 24
characters to enter a description of the debit or credit entered.

Once entered, this description will default to the subsequent lines (thus saving you keystrokes); however, this field may be edited.

11. Type *June 1988 Payment* and press Enter.

The Debit field. Any application of funds is entered in the debit field. When a debit is entered, the Total Debits field located at the bottom of the screen will be updated. The cursor will then move to the Acct. # field on the next line.

The Credit field. Any source of funds is entered in the credit field. When a credit is entered, the Total Credits field located at the bottom of the screen will be updated. The cursor will then move to the Acct. # field on the next line.

12. Move the cursor to the Credit field and type 253. Press Enter.
13. At the next Acct. # field type 5214 and press Enter. The word *Utilities*, taken from the Chart of Accounts, will appear in the Account Name field.

The cursor will move to the Description field and automatically enter *June 1988 Payment*.

14. Press the F9 (Auto Entry) function key. The amount 253.00 automatically appears in the Debit field.

Review the information entered. To delete a line, move the cursor to it, then press Alt-D simultaneously. *DacEasy* automatically adjusts the Total Debits and Total Credits fields. To delete this transaction, press the F6 (Delete Transaction) function key.

Saving Your Work

To record this transaction, simply press the F10 (Process) Function Key. *DacEasy* not only saves this transaction, it also automatically updates both the Vendor File and General Ledger. Figure 3-20 displays this completed transaction.

15. Press F10.

Entering Payments and Adjustments

As you learned earlier in this section, you can issue payments several ways. The Enter Payments operation lets you choose whether an outstanding balance will be paid partially or totally.

To enter the payment for the transaction just completed, follow these steps:

Figure 3-20. The Completed Accounts Payable Transaction Screen

```
                    ACCOUNTS PAYABLE TRANSACTION ENTRY
Trans. #   : 0001                    Reference/Check #   : Bill
Vendor Code: U008                    Transaction Date    : 06/30/88
Vendor Name: Utilities Co. of San Diego   Due Date       : 07/07/88
Trans. Code: I                       Discount Date       : 06/30/88
Invoice #  : 6053853                 Discount Available  :        0.00

Acct.#    Account Name          Description          Debit        Credit

2101    Accts Payable-ModuleJune 1988 Payment                     253.00
5214    Utilities            June 1988 Payment       253.00




Total Debits :       253.00     │  Total Credits :       253.00
```
F1-Help F6-Delete F9-Auto Entry F10-Process ALT D-Delete line

1. Press 2 from the Accounts Payable submenu to select the Enter Payments operation.

    The screen in Figure 3-21 will appear.

The cursor is positioned at the Transaction # field. This field is used to identify the transaction being entered. To assign a four-digit number, press Enter. *DacEasy* automatically assigns the next available number. To view a transaction that already exists, enter

Figure 3-21. The Payments and Adjustments Screen

```
                    PAYMENTS AND ADJUSTMENTS
Transaction # :                      Date     : 07/01/88
Vendor    Code :                     Check #  :
          Name :                     Amount   :        0.00
Transac. Type :                      Applied  :        0.00
Account #     :                      To Apply :        0.00

Inv. #   Date      Due      Amount   Disc.Avail  Amt.Applied  Disc.taken





```
F1-Help F2-Advance F5-Balance F6-Delete F8-Sort F9-Auto apply F10-Process

the number for that transaction and press Enter. The details from that transaction will appear.

2. Press Enter to assign the next available number.

   The cursor will move to the Vendor Code field. Enter the code assigned to the appropriate vendor. *DacEasy* will display an error message if you enter a nonexistent code.
3. Type U008 and press Enter. The vendor's name is automatically displayed in the Name field.

   The bottom of the screen will flash and display the phrase *Loading Open Invoice.* Then the first two lines of the body will automatically be completed.

   The cursor will move to the Transaction Type field and a status box displaying three options for this field will appear. To enter a check payment, type *K* and press Enter. To enter a manual payment (a check not printed through the computer system), type *P.* To enter an adjustment, type *A.*
4. Type *K* and press Enter.

   The cursor will move to the Date field. The date you entered during logon procedures will appear in this field. To accept it, press Enter. To change it, type the new date, then press enter.
5. Press Enter to accept the default date.

   The cursor is positioned at the Amt. Applied field.
6. Press the F9 (Auto Apply) function key. The entire amount due appears in the field.
7. Move the cursor to the next Amt. Applied field. Type 100 and press Enter.

   The screen should look like the one in Figure 3-22.

Saving Your Work

To record this transaction, simply press the F10 (Process) function key.

8. Press F10.

Printing Checks

DacEasy's Print Checks operation is used to make payments for selected invoices. Consecutive numbers are usually printed on the checks. Consecutive numbers help a business keep track of all checks to assure that no blank checks are lost or misplaced. To

Figure 3-22. The Completed Payments and Adjustments Screen

```
                        PAYMENTS AND ADJUSTMENTS
   Transaction # :0002                        Date    : 07/01/88
   Vendor   Code :U008                         Check # :
            Name :Utilities Co. of San Diego   Amount  :       353.00
   Transac. Type :K                            Applied :       353.00
   Account #     :                             To Apply:         0.00

   Inv. #    Date      Due        Amount    Disc.Avail  Amt.Applied  Disc.taken

   6053853  06/30/88  07/07/88      253.00      0.00       253.00       0.00
   23478    07/01/88  07/08/88      225.00      0.00       100.00       0.00
```

F1-Help F2-Advance F5-Balance F6-Delete F8-Sort F9-Auto apply F10-Process

properly align the checks with your printer, *DacEasy* always voids
the first check as shown in Figure 3-24.

To print a check, follow these steps:

1. Press 3 to select the Accounts Payable submenu within the
   Transaction menu. Next, press 4 to select the Print Checks operation.

   The screen in Figure 3-23 will appear.

Figure 3-23. The Print Checks Screen

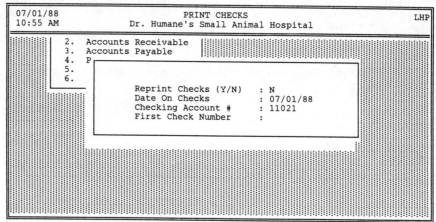

```
 07/01/88                    PRINT CHECKS                          LHP
 10:55 AM           Dr. Humane's Small Animal Hospital

         2.  Accounts Receivable
         3.  Accounts Payable
         4.  P
         5.
         6.
                        Reprint Checks (Y/N)   : N
                        Date On Checks         : 07/01/88
                        Checking Account #     : 11021
                        First Check Number     :
```

F1-Help F4-Change Date   ESC-Exit

Figure 3-24. The Printed Check

1111111111111111111111111111

```
          ***** VOID — VOID *****
          ***** VOID — VOID *****
       ***** CHECK NUMBER : 000001 *****
```

Dr. Humane's Small Animal Hospital

Invoice No.		Amount	Discount	Net Amt.
23478		100.00	0.00	100.00
6053853		253.00	0.00	253.00

Date   07/01/88

Check No.   000002

Dr. Humane's Small Animal Hospital   First Bank of San Diego   **15-4**
   555 East Meadows Lane   San Diego, CA   **1660**
   San Diego, CA 92122

                                                         CHECK NO: 000002

** THREE HUNDRED FIFTY THREE DOLLARS AND 00/CENTS **

                                    DATE   AMOUNT
                                    07/01/88   ******353.00

PAY TO THE   Utilities Co. of San Diego
ORDER OF   6222 Lakeshore Drive   _____
             San Diego, CA 92102   Dr. I. M. Humane

The cursor is positioned at Reprint Checks. To reprint checks, enter *Y* (Yes). *DacEasy* will ask for the beginning and ending check numbers. Once entered and printed, *DacEasy* also voids the checks from the first printing. Enter *N* (No) if you want to print checks for all selected invoices.

2. Type *N* and press Enter.

   The cursor will move to the Date on Checks field. The date you want printed on all the checks is entered in this field.

   DacEasy automatically displays the current date. However, it can be edited.

3. Press Enter to accept the default.

   The Bank Checking account number, taken from the G/L Interface Table will automatically appear in the Checking Account # field. If needed, this field can be edited to reflect another valid detail account.

4. Move the cursor to the First Check Number field. The number of your first check is entered here. Note: Remember that this check will be voided.

5. Type 00001 and press Enter.

   The check in Figure 3-24 will print.

Chapter 4

A Detailed Look at Billing, Accounts Receivable, and Inventory Transactions

As stated in Chapter 3, transactions change assets, liabilities, or an owner's equity, and each transaction makes at least two changes in the accounting equation.

The following tutorials in this chapter (Billing, Accounts Receivable, and Inventory) will show you, hands on, how transactions change your accounting equation.

DacEasy's Billing Transactions

DacEasy created a special Billing Submenu (located within the Transaction Menu) where customer invoices and sales returns operations are performed. The Billing module serves many valuable purposes:

- It notifies your customer of monies owed.
- It provides proof of payment if your customer pays in cash.
- It controls any sales tax due.
- It expedites packing and shipping products.
- It updates inventory levels.
- It handles nonrecurring items like the disposal of assets that are neither product or service (freight, packaging, insurance, and so on).
- It notifies you when you're in an out-of-stock situation, as well as the amount of product available and the amount on order.
- It automatically updates your general ledger, customer file, and the product file whenever transactions are entered.
- It allows you to perform credit transactions when you have to refund money, and automatically updates the general ledger, customer file, product file, and sales activity report accordingly.
- It automatically creates and updates a Sales Journal that, when printed, summarizes the detail of each invoice or sales return.

Note: For more details about the Sales Journal and printing the Sales Journal Report, see Chapter 5.

The *DacEasy* Billing operation also takes care of the repetitive and time-consuming job of entering information that remains the same (customer name, address, payment and discount terms, and so on). This problem is annoying in manual accounting systems, but *DacEasy* automatically enters this information when invoices are entered.

Customer information entered when you set up the customer's file is used during the billing operation, thus ensuring accuracy and saving time. When in the Enter Invoice operation, simply enter the customer's code and the code of the product or service purchased; the billing module takes care of everything else.

Entering a Service Invoice

To enter an invoice involving the sale of services, follow these steps:

1. Press 5 from the Transaction Menu to select the Billing submenu.
2. Press 1 to select the Enter Invoices operation.
   The screen in Figure 4-1 will appear.

The cursor will move to the Invoice # field.

Figure 4-1. Invoice Screen

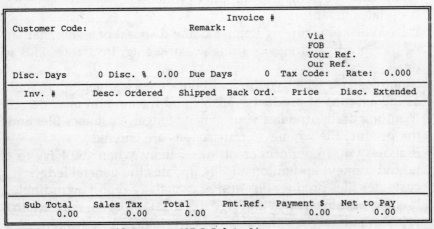

```
                                  Invoice #
   Customer Code:            Remark:
                                             Via
                                             FOB
                                             Your Ref.
                                             Our Ref.
   Disc. Days      0 Disc. % 0.00 Due Days      0 Tax Code:  Rate:  0.000

    Inv. #      Desc. Ordered   Shipped  Back Ord.   Price    Disc. Extended




     Sub Total   Sales Tax    Total   Pmt.Ref.  Payment $   Net to Pay
        0.00        0.00       0.00                 0.00        0.00
```

F1-Help F6-CANCEL F10-Process ALT D-Delete Line

3. Press Enter to create a new invoice number.
4. Type B016 in the Customer Code field and press Enter. Review the screen, then press any key to continue.

   Move the cursor to the Remark field.
5. Type *Services Rendered*. Press Enter. Type *July 1, 1988*. Press Enter.
6. Next, press Enter five times to skip the following fields: VIA, FOB, Your Ref., Our Ref.

   DacEasy will automatically complete the discount fields if necessary.
7. At the Inventory # field, type E001 and press Enter. The word *Emergency* will appear in the Description field. Press Enter.
8. Type 1 in the Ordered field. (This number describes the unit price per emergency.) Press Enter.

   DacEasy automatically fills in the Shipped and Extended fields.

   Move the cursor to the next Inventory # field.
9. Type S001 and press Enter. The word *Surgery* will appear in the Description field and the Price field will automatically display the unit price (100.00).

   Move the cursor to the Ordered field.
10. Press 4 (This number denotes the actual hours in surgery; the Extended price reflects this.)

    Move the cursor to the next Inventory # field.
11. Type *D* and press Enter. Next type *Emergency Surgery to Repair Broken*. Press Enter. Type *D* and Press Enter. Type *Front Leg and Broken Pelvis*. Press Enter.

    DacEasy automatically computes the Extended, Subtotal, Tax, Total, and Net to Pay fields.
12. Press the F10 function key. The cursor will move to the Pmt. Ref. field.
13. Your customer paid the emergency fee, so at the Pmt. Ref. field type 0322 to identify the check number of the deposit. Press Enter.
14. Next, enter the amount of the payment in the Payment $ field. Type 50 and press Enter.

    DacEasy automatically computes the Net to Pay field by subtracting the Payment $ field from the Total field. It also automatically debits this amount to the customer account.

    Before saving your work, look the invoice over to ensure accuracy. If you need to correct an error or change any part

123

of the invoice, use the arrow keys to move to the specific field and then type the necessary changes. Press Alt-D if you want to delete any line. (You must be on the line you want to delete.) Any adjustments will automatically be made. Press the F6 function key if you want to delete the entire transaction.

Saving Your Work

To record this invoice, simply press the F10 (Process) function key.

15. Press F10. To see the invoice you just entered, type its Invoice # at the Invoice # field on a blank record. Press Enter. The invoice will appear.

    The invoice should look like the one in Figure 4-2.

Printing Invoices

To print the invoice just entered, make sure you've set up printer parameters; then follow these steps:

1. Press 5 to select the Billing Submenu from within the Transaction Menu. Press 3 to select the Print Invoice operation. The screen in Figure 4-3 will appear.

    The cursor is at the Print Packing Slips field. To print packing slips, type *Y* and press Enter. *DacEasy* will print the packing slip;

Figure 4-2. The Completed Invoice

```
                              Invoice #  00354
  Customer Code: B016         Remark:
  Champ                       Services Rendered    Via
  Bud Boswell                 July 1, 1988.        FOB
  868 River Drive                                  Your Ref.
  San Diego      CA  92117-                        Our Ref.
  Disc. Days      0 Disc. %  0.00  Due Days       0  Tax Code: 0 Rate:  6.000

    Inv. #       Desc. Ordered    Shipped  Back Ord.   Price    Disc. Extended

    E001         Emergency
                   1.000          1.000      0.000     50.000  0.00       50.00
    S001         Surgery
                   4.000          4.000      0.000    100.000  0.00      400.00
                 Emergency Surgery to Repair Broken

                 Front Leg and Broken Pelvis.


    Sub Total   Sales Tax    Total    Pmt.Ref.   Payment $   Net to Pay
      450.00        3.00     453.00     0322          50.00      403.00

  F1-Help  F6-CANCEL  F10-Process  ALT D-Delete Line
```

124

Figure 4-3. The Print Invoices Screen

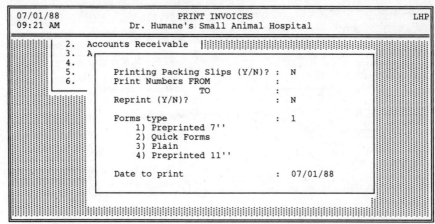

```
07/01/88                      PRINT INVOICES                          LHP
09:21 AM               Dr. Humane's Small Animal Hospital

           2.   Accounts Receivable  |
           3.   A
           4.
           5.        Printing Packing Slips (Y/N)? :   N
           6.        Print Numbers FROM             :
                                   TO              :
                     Reprint (Y/N)?                 :   N

                     Forms type                     :   1
                        1) Preprinted 7''
                        2) Quick Forms
                        3) Plain
                        4) Preprinted 11''

                     Date to print                  :   07/01/88
```

F1-Help F4-Change Date   ESC-Exit

however, the cost and extended information will not appear.

2. Press Enter to select the *N* (No) option. The cursor will move to the Print Numbers FROM field.
3. Type 354 and press Enter.
4. At the Print Numbers TO field, type 354 and press Enter.

   The cursor will move to the Reprint field. If you press *Y* (Yes) in this field, the system will only print those invoices that have been printed before and have not been modified. If you press *N* (No) in this field, the system will only print those invoices that have not been printed or have been modified since the last printing.

5. Press Enter to accept the *N* default.

   The cursor will move to the Forms type field. This field lets you choose the type of forms you'll be using. If you select plain paper, *DacEasy* will print all column headings. If not, enter which preprinted forms you'll be using.

6. Select the Plain Paper option (3) and press Enter.

   The cursor will move to the Date to Print field. *DacEasy* automatically enters the current date; however, it can be modified.

7. Press Enter to select the default date.

   If you're using preprinted forms, the system helps you align the form by printing a test pattern of numbers just above the perforation of the left-hand side of the form. Once the test has been run, *DacEasy* will prompt you by asking if the form is

Figure 4-4. The Printed Invoice

```
                      Dr. Humane's Small Animal Hospital
                            555 East Meadows Lane
                            San Diego, CA  92122
                              (619)555-3636
                              I n v o i c e

     B016                                               Ship to/Remarks
     Champ                                              Services Rendered
     Bud Boswell                                        July 1, 1988.
     868 River Drive
     San Diego CA 92117

              Date 07/01/88      No. 00354 Page   1  Due Date   07/01/88
     --------------------------------------------------------------------------------

     --------------------------------------------------------------------------------
     Inventory #   Description        Ordered   Shipped   Backorder Unit Price  Disc.%   Extended Price
     --------------------------------------------------------------------------------
     E001          Emergency                     1.000 @   50.000                              50.00
     S001          Surgery                       4.000 @  100.000                             400.00
                   Emergency Surgery to Repair Broken
                   Front Leg and Broken Pelvis.



     --------------------------------------------------------------------------------
                                                           Sub-total      450.00
                                                           Tax              3.00
                                                           Total          453.00
                                                           Payment    (    50.00)
                                                           Net to Pay     403.00
                                                           ------------
```

aligned correctly. The test pattern will print again if you enter
N (No).

   Realign the form before entering *N* (No).

   Press the F6 function key to skip the alignment option.

8. Press Enter to start printing.

   DacEasy will print the invoice shown in Figure 4-4.

Entering a Product Invoice

The same type of invoice is used for entering the sale of a product (flea spray, dog/cat food, and so on). To enter an invoice involving the sale of a product, follow these steps:

1. Highlight the Transaction option from the Opening Menu. Press Enter.
2. Press 5 to select the Billing submenu.
3. Press 1 to select the Enter Invoices operation. The screen in Figure 4-5 will appear.

   The cursor is positioned at the Invoice # field. This field uses a five-digit number to identify the invoice.

Figure 4-5. Invoice Screen

```
                                    Invoice #
   Customer Code:               Remark:
                                             Via
                                             FOB
                                             Your Ref.
                                             Our Ref.
   Disc. Days      0 Disc. % 0.00 Due Days      0 Tax Code:  Rate: 0.000

    Inv. #        Desc. Ordered   Shipped Back Ord.   Price   Disc. Extended




   Sub Total    Sales Tax    Total      Pmt.Ref.  Payment $   Net to Pay
      0.00         0.00       0.00                    0.00        0.00
```

F1-Help F6-CANCEL F10-Process ALT D-Delete Line

To enter a new invoice number, press Enter. The next available number will appear. To review an invoice that already exists, enter its number and the details from that invoice will appear.

4. Press Enter to display the next available number.

   The cursor will move to the Customer Code field. Only a valid customer code can be entered in this field (created in the customer file within the File Menu). If you enter an incorrect code, *DacEasy* will alert you of the error and let you try again.

5. Type A001 and press Enter. A message from the message code and the customer's credit and balance information appears on the screen for your review. Press any key and the customer's name and address will appear.

   Note: At this point, you can change the customer's name and address if, for example, the invoice and product is to be shipped to a different address. This change, however, is only temporary and only pertains to the specific invoice being entered and printed. If you need to make any permanent changes regarding customer information, it must be done in the Customer file within the File menu.

6. Press Enter until the cursor is at the Remark field.

   This field is used to enter any special remarks concerning the invoice such as a "ship to" address, special handling instructions, service rendered information, and so on. A total of three lines is available, and you can enter up to 20 characters on each line.

7. Type *c/o Jody Sommers*. Press Enter. Type *45 West Way*. Press Enter. Type *San Diego, CA 92123*. Press Enter.

    The cursor will move to the VIA field. You can enter up to 15 alphanumeric characters to display the shipping method.

8. Type *UPS* and press Enter.

    The cursor will move the to FOB (Freight On Board) field. You can use to up 15 characters to enter the city where the freight originates.

9. Type *San Diego* and press Enter.

    The cursor will move to the Your Ref. field. If your customer has given you a reference number, you can enter it here. Otherwise press Enter to leave it empty.

10. Press Enter to leave this field empty.

    The cursor will move to the Our Ref. field. If you have a reference number for this invoice, enter it here; otherwise, press enter to leave it empty.

11. Press Enter to leave this field empty.

    The Discount Days, Discount %, Due Days, and Sales Tax Rate fields are all automatically filled in by *DacEasy*. (It uses the information you entered and saved in the Customer File.) These fields may be modified if the terms of this particular sale are different. If you do modify these fields, remember that the changes will only be temporary and will only pertain to this particular invoice. To permanently modify the data for this customer, you must make the changes in the Customer File within the File menu.

    At this point your screen should look like the one in Figure 4-6.

12. Press Enter until the cursor moves to the Inventory # field.

    Four codes can be entered in this field:

- The product or service code (mandatory)
- Any special invoice (billing) codes
- Any applicable message codes
- A special comments code

    Only a valid product or service code can be entered in this field (created in the Product File or Service File within the File

Figure 4-6. The Partially Filled Invoice Screen

```
                                Invoice #  00355
  Customer Code: A001            Remark:
  Buffy Adams                    c/o Jody Sommers       Via UPS
  Mr. & Mrs. John Adams          45 West Way            FOB San Diego
  66 Flamingo Street             San Diego, CA 92123    Your Ref.
  San Diego       CA  92101-                            Our Ref.
  Disc. Days      30 Disc. % 15.00  Due Days      30 Tax Code: 0 Rate:  6.000

    Inv. #      Desc. Ordered    Shipped  Back Ord.   Price    Disc. Extended




    Sub Total    Sales Tax    Total      Pmt.Ref.   Payment $   Net to Pay
       0.00         0.00       0.00                     0.00        0.00
```

F1-Help F6-CANCEL F10-Process ALT D-Delete Line

Menu). If you enter an incorrect code, *DacEasy* will alert you of the error and let you try again.

13. Type: 2601 and press Enter. The description of the product will appear.

    With the cursor positioned at the Ordered field,

14. Type 24 and press Enter. (The purchase is 24 cans of dog food.)

    The Shipped, Price, and Extended fields are all automatically entered by the system. If there's enough product on hand, the Shipped and Ordered fields will equal. If there's not enough product, the quantity available will appear in the Shipped field. The Back Ordered field is then automatically used to show the difference between the Ordered and the Shipped fields.

    Move your cursor to the Discount field.

15. Type 15 and press Enter. At this point, *DacEasy* will compute prices, taking into consideration this discount.

    Now move your cursor to the next Inventory # line. This field is also used to enter any special invoice codes created in the Billing Codes operation within the File Menu. For example, to enter freight charges, follow these steps:

16. Type *C*, then press the space bar once. Next, type 1 and press Enter. (The invoice code 1 corresponds to *Freight* within the Billing Codes file.) The word *Freight* will appear in the Description field.

17. Press Enter. The cursor will move to the Extended field.
18. Type 3.50 and press Enter.

    Move the cursor to the next Inventory # line. You can use this field to enter any special messages created in the Message Table within the Options Menu. To enter a message, follow these steps:

19. Type *M*, then press the space bar once. Next, type 5 and press Enter. The message *15% Sr. Citizen Discount.* will appear in the Description field.

    DacEasy also lets you enter special remarks within the invoice. To enter any remarks, follow these steps:

20. Type *D* in the Inventory # field and press Enter. Next, type in the comments. You can use up to 40 characters per line of comments.
21. Type *August is "Vaccinate Your Pet Month."* Press Enter. Type *D.* Press Enter. Type *All vaccines are 1/2 price.* Press Enter.
22. Press the F10 (Process) function key.

    The cursor will move to the Pmt. Ref. field. This field is used to enter a check number or reference number if you receive an advance payment with an order. You can enter up six alphanumeric characters.

23. Press Enter to leave this field empty.

    The Payment $ field is used to enter the amount received from an advance payment. Once entered, *DacEasy* automatically debits this amount to the Bank Checking account of the G/L Interface Table. The Net to Pay field is also automatically computed by *DacEasy*. The amount for this field is computed by subtracting the Payment $ field from the Total field. *DacEasy* also debits this amount to the customer account.

    Review the data you entered. To make any changes, use the arrow keys to move the cursor to the appropriate field, then type the change. If you want to delete a line, press Alt-D. If you want to delete the entire transaction press the F6 (Delete Transaction) function key.

Saving Your Work

To save the information entered in this invoice, simply press the F10 (Process) function key. *DacEasy* will not only record the information for this particular invoice, it will also update the General Ledger, sales statistics, and inventory adjustments, as well as post your customer's balance due, and store a profitability analysis by customer and product.

24. Press F10.

The completed invoice should look like the one in Figure 4-7.

Entering a Sales Return

Businesses that sell products expect to have some merchandise returned because a customer decides not to keep it. A customer may have received the wrong style, the wrong size, or damaged goods. A customer may return merchandise and ask for a credit on account or a cash refund. Product returned by a customer for a credit on account or a cash refund is called a *sales return*. With *DacEasy*, entering sales returns is handled the same way as entering invoices; however, the Customer, Product, and General Ledger files are all affected in the opposite manner.

To enter a sales return, follow these steps:

1. Press 5 from the Transaction Menu to select the Billing Submenu.
2. Press 2 from within the Billing Submenu to select the Enter Sales Returns operation.

The screen in Figure 4-8 will appear.

Figure 4-7. The Completed Invoice Screen

```
                                   Invoice #   00355
Customer Code: A001            Remark:
Buffy Adams                    c/o Jody Sommers        Via UPS
Mr. & Mrs. John Adams          45 West Way             FOB San Diego
66 Flamingo Street             San Diego, CA 92123     Your Ref.
San Diego        CA  92101-                            Our Ref.
Disc. Days       30 Disc. % 15.00  Due Days      30  Tax Code: 0 Rate:  6.000

   Inv. #        Desc. Ordered   Shipped  Back Ord.   Price    Disc. Extended

   2601          Dog Food
                     24.000      24.000     0.000    1.000 15.00      20.40
     C 1         Freight
                                                                      3.50

                 15% Sr. Citizen Discount.

                 August is "Vaccinate Your Pet Month."


   Sub Total    Sales Tax    Total    Pmt.Ref.  Payment $   Net to Pay
     23.90         1.22      25.12                  0.00        25.12

F1-Help  F6-CANCEL  F10-Process  ALT D-Delete Line
```

Figure 4-8. The Sales Return Screen

```
                                Sales Return #
   Customer Code:               Remark:
                                              Via
                                              FOB
                                              Your Ref.
                                              Our Ref.
   Disc. Days      0 Disc. %  0.00  Due Days    0  Tax Code:   Rate:  0.000

     Item #      Desc.            Received           Price    Disc. Extended




      Sub Total    Sales Tax    Total
        0.00         0.00       0.00
```

F1-Help F6-CANCEL F10-Process ALT D-Delete Line

The cursor is positioned at the Sales Return # field. To select the next available number, press Enter. To select a transaction that already exists, enter that number, then press Enter. The details from that transaction will appear.

3. Press Enter. The next available number will appear in this field.
4. The cursor will move to the Customer Code field. Type S135 and press Enter.
   The screen will display any messages and credit information. Review this information, then press any key to continue.
5. Move the cursor to the Item # field.
6. Type 2602 and press Enter.
   Cat Food will appear in the Description field and the unit price will appear in the price field.
   The cursor is positioned at the Received field.
7. Type 6 and press Enter. Next, press Enter until the cursor moves to the discount field. Type 15 and press Enter.
8. At the next Item # field type *D* and press Enter (to enter a message).
9. Type *Six cans returned due to damaged cans.* Press Enter.
10. Type *D*, press Enter, then type *Sorry for any inconvenience.* Press Enter.

Review this transaction. If you need to make any corrections or changes, use the arrow keys to move to the specific field, then enter the necessary change. To delete a line, move the cursor to it; then press Alt-D simultaneously. To delete this transaction, press the F6 function key.

The completed Sales Return should look like the one in Figure 4-9.

Saving Your Work

To record this transaction, simply press the F10 (Process) function key.

11. Press F10.

Printing a Sales Return

To print this return, press the F7 (Print Sales Return) function key. Follow the steps that appear on the screen.

Once completed, the Sales Return should look like the one in Figure 4-10.

Accounts Receivable Transactions

DacEasy's Accounts Receivable Module lets you control the monies owed to you. Without additional work, this module provides you with the following information:

Figure 4-9. The Completed Sales Return Screen

```
                                    Sales Return #    00069
        Customer Code: S135         Remark:
        Lady                                          Via
        Betsy Shaw                                    FOB
        166 State Street                              Your Ref.
        San Diego      CA  92103-                     Our Ref.
        Disc. Days     30 Disc. % 15.00  Due Days    30 Tax Code: 0 Rate:  6.000
        ┌──────────────────────────────────────────────────────────────────┐
        │  Item #      Desc.          Received         Price   Disc. Extended │
        ├──────────────────────────────────────────────────────────────────┤
        │  2602        Cat Food                                               │
        │                             6.000            1.000 15.00      5.10  │
        │  D           Six cans returned due to damaged cans.                 │
        │                                                                     │
        │  D           Sorry for any inconvenience.                           │
        │                                                                     │
        │                                                                     │
        ├──────────────────────────────────────────────────────────────────┤
        │  Sub Total   Sales Tax    Total                                     │
        │     5.10        0.31       5.41                                     │
        └──────────────────────────────────────────────────────────────────┘
        F1-Help  F6-CANCEL  F10-Process  ALT D-Delete Line
```

Figure 4-10. The Printed Sales Return Form.

```
                    Dr. Humane's Small Animal Hospital
                         555 East Meadows Lane
                         San Diego, CA  92122
                            (619)555-3636
                         S a l e s   R e t u r n

      S135                                                    Ship to/Remarks
      Lady
      Betsy Shaw
      166 State Street
      San Diego CA 92103

                Date 07/01/88      No. 00069 Page  1
    -------------------------------------------------------------------------

    -------------------------------------------------------------------------
    Inventory #   Description                Returned  Unit Price  Disc.%   Extended Price
    -------------------------------------------------------------------------
    2602          Cat Food                     6.000     1.000    15.00             5.10
                  Six cans returned due to damaged cans.
                  Sorry for any inconvenience.




    -------------------------------------------------------------------------
                                                     Sub-total          5.10
                                                     Tax                0.31
                                                     Total              5.41
```

- Sales quotas by salesperson or customer
- Buying trends
- Mailing labels
- Cash flow forecasting
- Three years of online history for every customer
- Reports such as customer statements, aging reports, cash flow, customer directories, and sales reports by customer

Because *DacEasy* provides a Billing module, entering invoices through the Accounts Receivable submenu is not necessary. However, miscellaneous transactions, such as special discounts or late charges should be entered through the Accounts Receivable Transaction Entry operation. To assign a number, press Enter. *DacEasy* automatically assigns the next available number. To view a transaction that already exists, enter that number and press Enter. The details from that transaction will appear. To enter an Accounts Receivable Transaction, follow these steps:

1. Press 2 from the Transaction Menu to select the Accounts Receivable Submenu.
2. Press 1 from the Accounts Receivable Submenu to select the Transaction Entry operation.
   The screen in Figure 4-11 will appear.

Figure 4-11. The Accounts Receivable Transaction Entry Screen

```
                ACCOUNTS RECEIVABLE TRANSACTION ENTRY
   Trans. #   :                        Reference/Check #  :
   Customer # :                        Transaction Date   :   /  /
   Cust. Name :                        Due Date           :   /  /
   Trans. Code:                        Discount Date      :   /  /
   Invoice #  :                        Discount Available :        0.00

   Acct.#  Account Name           Description         Debit      Credit




   Total Debits :                    Total Credits :
```
F1-Help F6-Delete F9-Auto Entry F10-Process ALT D-Delete line

The cursor is positioned at the Transaction # field. A four-digit number in this field identifies the transaction being entered.

3. Press Enter to assign the next available number.
   The cursor will move to the Customer # field. The customer's code is entered in this field. If you enter a nonexistent code, *DacEasy* will display an error message and let you try again.
4. Type R050 and press Enter.
   The customer's name will automatically appear in the Customer Name field. Any messages, credit information, and balance information will appear on the screen (Figure 4-12). Review this information, then press any key to continue.

The cursor will move to the Transaction Code field and three options are displayed in a status box that appears on the screen (Figure 4-13). To enter an invoice not generated through the Billing operation, type *I* and press Enter. To enter a miscellaneous debit (miscellaneous charges, such as a returned-check charge) not generated through the billing operation, type *D* and press Enter. To enter a miscellaneous credit (such as an overcharge), type *C* and press Enter.

135

Figure 4-12. Message, Credit, Balance Information

```
                   ACCOUNTS RECEIVABLE TRANSACTION ENTRY
    Trans. #  : 0001                  Reference/Check #  :
    Customer # : R050                 Transaction Date   : 07/01/88
    Cust. Name : Mittens              Due Date           : 07/01/88
    Trans. Code:                      Discount Date      : 07/01/88
    Invoice # :                       Discount Available :      0.00
   ┌─────────────────────────────────────────────────────────────┐
    Acct.#   Accoun┌────────────────────────────────────┐   Credit
                   │ 15% Sr. Citizen Discount.          │
                   │ Credit Limit...............$   500.00 │
                   │ Current Balance............    0.00 │
                   │ Credit Available...........  500.00 │
                   │                                    │
                   │ Press <ANYKEY> to continue...      │
                   │                                    │
                   └────────────────────────────────────┘

    Total Debits :              │  Total Credits :
```
F1-Help F6-Delete F9-Auto Entry F10-Process ALT D-Delete line

5. Type *D* and press Enter.

    The cursor will move to the Invoice # field. You can use up to eight alphanumeric characters to identify the invoice number.

6. Type 99 and press Enter.

    The cursor will move to the Reference/Check # field. You can use up to six alphanumeric characters to specify a check number or reference connected with this transaction. This

Figure 4-13. Transaction Codes

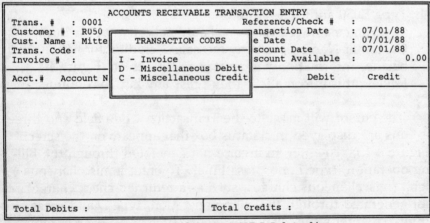

```
                   ACCOUNTS RECEIVABLE TRANSACTION ENTRY
    Trans. #  : 0001                  Reference/Check #  :
    Customer # : R050        ┌────────────────────┐ansaction Date : 07/01/88
    Cust. Name : Mitte       │  TRANSACTION CODES │e Date         : 07/01/88
    Trans. Code:             │                    │scount Date    : 07/01/88
    Invoice # :              │ I - Invoice        │scount Available :  0.00
                             │ D - Miscellaneous Debit │
    Acct.#   Account N       │ C - Miscellaneous Credit │  Debit    Credit
                             └────────────────────┘




    Total Debits :              │  Total Credits :
```
F1-Help F6-Delete F9-Auto Entry F10-Process ALT D-Delete line

field in no way affects your accounting system. It's used for memo purposes only.

7. Type *Debit* and press Enter.

    The cursor will move to the transaction Date field. *DacEasy* automatically enters the date you used during logon procedures. Press Enter to accept this date or type the new date and then press Enter.

8. Press Enter to accept the default date.

    Due Date, Discount Date, and Discount Available fields. *DacEasy* automatically enters the appropriate information in these fields. However, they may be modified for this particular transaction. Remember, if you want to edit any customer information permanently, it must be edited in the Customer File within the File menu.

9. Press Enter until the cursor moves to the Acct. # field.

    A General Ledger detail account number is entered in this field. *DacEasy* automatically enters (on the first line) the Accounts Receivable account number taken from the G/L Interface Table.

    The cursor will then move to the Description field. You can use up to 24 characters to describe the debit or credit entered. To save keystrokes, the description you enter will default to the subsequent Description fields. However, it may be changed.

10. Type *Returned Check Charge* and press Enter.

    Debit field. An application of funds is entered in the debit field. When a debit is entered, the Total Debits field, located at the bottom of the screen, is updated. The cursor will then move to the Account # field on the next line.

    Credit field. Any source of funds is entered in the credit field. When a credit is entered, the Total Credits field, located at the bottom of the screen, is updated. The cursor will then move to the Account # field on the next line.

11. Move the cursor to the debit field and type 10. Press Enter.

12. At the next Account # field, type 5403 and press Enter. *DacEasy* automatically displays the account name that corresponds with this number (in the Account Name field). The Description field is also automatically filled in.

13. Press the F9 (Auto Apply) function key. *DacEasy* automatically enters the amount of $10.00 in the appropriate credit field.

Review the information entered. To make any changes, use the arrow keys to move the cursor to the specific field, then make your change. To delete a line, move the cursor to it, then press Alt-D. *DacEasy* automatically adjusts the Total Debits and Total Credits fields. To delete this transaction, press the F6 (Delete Transaction) function key.

If you make any changes prior to saving your work, remember that before pressing the F10 (Process) function key, the Total Debits and Total Credits fields must be equal. *DacEasy* will not let you leave the operation until these fields are equal.

Saving Your Work

To record this transaction, simply press the F10 (Process) function key. *DacEasy* not only saves this transaction, it also automatically updates both the Customer File and General Ledger.

Figure 4-14 displays this completed transaction.

14. Press F10. Press Esc until the cursor returns to the Accounts Receivable submenu.

Entering Cash Receipts

Sometimes transactions involve the receipt of cash. Most cash receipts are for (1) cash and credit card sales, and (2) cash received from customers on account. *DacEasy* automatically records

Figure 4-14. The Completed, Updated Transaction Screen

```
                 ACCOUNTS RECEIVABLE TRANSACTION ENTRY
 Trans. #   : 0001                 Reference/Check #  : Debit
 Customer # : R050                 Transaction Date   : 07/01/88
 Cust. Name : Mittens              Due Date           : 07/01/88
 Trans. Code: D                    Discount Date      : 07/01/88
 Invoice #  : 99                   Discount Available :       0.00

 Acct.#  Account Name         Description      Debit     Credit

 11051   Accts Rec'ble ModuleReturned Check Charge      10.00
 5403    Miscellaneous LossesReturned Check Charge                10.00




 Total Debits :     10.00   | Total Credits :     10.00
```

F1-Help F6-Delete F9-Auto Entry F10-Process ALT D-Delete line

cash receipts transactions in the Accounts Receivable Payments Journal (also known as the Cash Receipts Journal).

Note: Details on the Cash Receipts Journal are discussed in Chapter 5.

To enter a cash payment, follow these steps:

1. Press 2 from the Transaction menu to select the Accounts Receivable submenu.
2. Press 2 from the Accounts Receivable submenu to select the A/R Cash Receipts operation.

    The screen in Figure 4-15 will appear.

The cursor is positioned at the Transaction # field. A four-digit number in this field identifies the transaction being entered. To assign a number, press Enter. *DacEasy* automatically assigns the next available number. To view a transaction that already exists, enter that number and press Enter. The details from that transaction will appear.

3. Press Enter to assign the next available number.

    The cursor will move to the Customer Code field. The customer's code is entered in this field. If you enter a nonexistent code, *DacEasy* will display an error message and let you try again.
4. Type B016 and press Enter. The customer's name will automatically appear in the Customer Name field.

Figure 4-15. The Cash Receipts and Adjustments Screen

```
                     CASH RECEIPTS AND ADJUSTMENTS
   Transaction # :                          Date     : 07/01/88
   Customer Code :                          Check #  :
           Name :                           Amount   :        0.00
   Transac. Type :                          Applied  :        0.00
   Account #     :                          To Apply :        0.00
  ─────────────────────────────────────────────────────────────────
   Inv. #   Date      Due      Amount    Disc.Avail  Amt.Applied  Disc.taken




  F1-Help F2-Advance F5-Balance F6-Delete F8-Sort F9-Auto apply F10-Process
```

The cursor will move to the Transaction Type field. Two options are displayed in a status box that appears on the screen (Figure 4-16). To enter a payment to an existing invoice, type *P* (Check Payment). To enter an advance or credit to the account, type *A* (Adjustment).

5. Type *P* and press Enter.

The Account # field will automatically display the Bank Check account number taken from the G/L Interface Table. You may change this account to another detail account if necessary.

6. Press Enter.

Note: If you entered *A* (Adjustments) in the Transaction Type field, this field is disregarded because the transaction does not affect cash.

Date field. *DacEasy* automatically enters the date used during logon procedures; however, it can be changed.

7. Press Enter to accept the default date.

The cursor will move to the Check # field. You can use up to six alphanumeric characters to record the check number or reference connected with this transaction. This field in no way affects your accounting system. It's used for memo purposes only.

8. Type *Cash* and Press Enter.

The cursor will move to the Amount field. The payment or advance is entered here. This field is disregarded if this transaction is an adjustment.

Figure 4-16. Transaction Types

```
                        CASH RECEIPTS AND ADJUSTMENTS
   Transaction # :0002                              Date     : 07/01/88
   Customer Code :B016                              Check #  :
          Name :Champ    ┌─── TRANSACTION TYPES ───┐ Amount   :        0.00
   Transac. Type :9      │                         │ Applied  :        0.00
   Account #    :        │ P - Payment             │ To Apply :        0.00
                         │ A - Adjustment          │
   Inv. #   Date    D    │                         │ il Amt.Applied  Disc.taken

   202      06/02/88 06  └─────────────────────────┘ 0.00         0.00        0.00
   00354    07/01/88 07/01/88        403.00          0.00         0.00        0.00
```

F1-Help F2-Advance F5-Balance F6-Delete F8-Sort F9-Auto apply F10-Process

9. Type 20 and press Enter.

    Applied field. *DacEasy* continuously updates this field whenever a portion of a payment is applied.

    To Apply field. *DacEasy* also automatically updates this field by displaying the difference between the Amount and Applied fields.

    Invoice # field. The outstanding balance per invoice appears in due date order here.

    Note: The F8 (Sort) function key lets you sort the invoices by discount date.

    Date field. *DacEasy* automatically displays the invoice date here.

    Due/Discount fields. These fields toggle back and forth. To sort invoices by discount date, press the F8 (Sort) function key.

    Amount field. *DacEasy* automatically displays the invoice balance in this field.

    Discount Available field. *DacEasy* automatically displays any discounts available due to early payment of an invoice.

10. Move the cursor to the Amt. Applied field. The amount applied to this invoice is entered here.

11. Type 20 and press Enter.

    If any discounts are to be taken, *DacEasy* automatically enters the dollar amount in the Discount Taken field. *DacEasy* also adjusts this amount each time an amount is applied to each invoice, thus ensuring that the discounts taken do not exceed the invoice balance.

    Review the information entered. To change any information, use the arrow keys to move the cursor to the specific field, then type the necessary changes. To delete a line, move the cursor to it, then press Alt-D. To delete this transaction, press the F6 (Delete Transaction) function key.

    The completed transaction should look like the one in Figure 4-17.

Saving Your Work

To record this transaction, simply press the F10 (Process) function key.

12. Press F10.

Figure 4-17. The Completed Cash Receipts and Adjustments Screen

```
                      CASH RECEIPTS AND ADJUSTMENTS
     Transaction # :0002                    Date      : 07/01/88
     Customer Code :B016                     Check #   : Cash
            Name :Champ                      Amount    :       20.00
     Transac. Type :P                        Applied   :       20.00
     Account #     :11021  Checking Account  To Apply  :        0.00

     Inv. #   Date      Due        Amount   Disc.Avail  Amt.Applied  Disc.taken

     202      06/02/88 06/02/88      60.00      0.00        20.00         0.00
     00354    07/01/88 07/01/88     403.00      0.00          .           0.00
```

F1-Help F2-Advance F5-Balance F6-Delete F8-Sort F9-Auto apply F10-Process

Managing Your Inventory

Knowing the size of inventory to maintain requires frequent analysis of purchases, sales, and inventory records. Your business may fail because too much or too little merchandise inventory is kept on hand. Sometimes the wrong merchandise is kept on hand. If the merchandise is not sold, less revenue is received. In addition, greater costs result from storing merchandise that sells slowly.

Merchandise inventory larger than needed may decrease the net income of your business for several reasons.

1. Excess inventory requires expensive store and warehouse space.
2. Excess inventory requires capital that could be invested to better advantage in other assets.
3. Excess inventory increases taxes and insurance premiums paid on merchandise inventory on hand.
4. Excess inventory may become obsolete and unsalable.

Merchandise inventory smaller than necessary may decrease the net income of your business for several reasons.

1. Sales will be lost to competitors if items wanted by customers are not on hand.

2. Sales will be lost if there is an insufficient variety of merchandise that customers want.
3. Merchandise reordered often and in small quantities costs more than that ordered in larger quantities.

In order to figure the cost of merchandise sold, you must know what inventory is on hand at the end of a fiscal period. Two types of inventory systems are used by businesses to determine the quantity of each type of merchandise on hand:

• Physical inventory
• Perpetual inventory

The *physical inventory* system determines merchandise inventory by counting, weighing, or measuring items of merchandise on hand. A physical inventory is normally taken at the end of a fiscal year because it's usually a large task.

The *perpetual inventory* system determines merchandise inventory by keeping a continuous record of increases, decreases, and balance on hand. This system provides day-to-day information about the quantity of merchandise on hand.

DacEasy's Inventory module lets you take full advantage of all product- and/or service-related functions.

Most of the work required to operate this program was accomplished when you set up your purchase order system and when you used the billing process. Once you enter physical inventory levels, information such as which products sell best, which products generate greater profits, which products have the best turnover rate, and so on, will be at your fingertips. Various reports, including activity reports, sales reports, alert reports, and comparative reports are accessed through this module. Catalogs, count sheets, and price listings can also be printed.

Before you can enter inventory, count sheets should be printed. Count sheets are forms used to record all inventory on hand. When you or your employees perform periodic inventories, the actual count of the number of units on hand is written on these count sheets. *DacEasy* lets you choose several ways to sort and rank the information printed on them.

To print count sheets, follow these steps:

1. Highlight the Reports option from the Opening menu. Press Enter.
2. Press 3 to select the Inventory submenu.

Figure 4-18. The Count Sheets Screen

```
07/01/88                        Count Sheets                          LHP
05:34 PM                Dr. Humane's Small Animal Hospital

        Sort By :                           Rank By :

        1  Inventory #                      1  Inventory #
        2  Description                      2  Description
        3  Department                       3  Sales Units
        4  Bin                              4  Sales Dollars
        5  Vendor                           5  Last Sales Date
                                            6  Purchase Units
        Enter Your Selection :              7  Purchase Dollars
                                            8  Last Purchase Date
                                            9  On Hand Units
                                            10 On Hand Dollars
                                            11 Profit
                                            12 Turns
                                            13 Gross Profit

                                            Enter Your Selection :
```

3. Press 6 to select the Print Count Sheets operation.
   The screen in Figure 4-18 will appear.

   You can choose 5 different ways to sort and 13 different ways
to rank your count sheets.
   To sort your count sheets by Inventory #:

4. Type 1 and press Enter.
   The screen in Figure 4-19 will appear.
5. Press Enter at the From field. The words *First Record* will appear.

Figure 4-19. The Count Sheets Screen After Choosing Inventory

```
07/01/88                        Count Sheets                          LHP
09:26 AM                Dr. Humane's Small Animal Hospital

                                            Rank By :

        Sorted by : Inventory #
                                            1  Inventory #
        From :                              2  Description
        To   :                             3  Sales Units
                                            4  Sales Dollars
                                            5  Last Sales Date
                                            6  Purchase Units
                                            7  Purchase Dollars
                                            8  Last Purchase Date
                                            9  On Hand Units
                                            10 On Hand Dollars
                                            11 Profit
                                            12 Turns
                                            13 Gross Profit

                                            Enter Your Selection :
```

Figure 4-20. The Count Sheets Printout

```
Date : 07/01/88                    Dr. Humane's Small Animal Hospital                    Page no. 1
Time : 09:31 AM                         555 East Meadows Lane
                                         San Diego, CA  92122
                                          (619)555-3636

Sorted by: Inventory #                          Count Sheets                        Ranked by: Description

   Inventory #   Description      Unit  Frac  Dept  Bin   Vendor   Units   Fractions   Remarks
   -----------   -----------      ----  ----  ----  ----  ------   -----   ---------   -------
   4015          Amoxicillin      Each   1     01   0005  G015     _____  ._____   _____
   2602          Cat Food         Case   24    01   0011  A001     _____  ._____   _____
   2601          Dog Food         Case   24    01   0010  A001     _____  ._____   _____
   0038188       Flea Powder      Case   36    01   0001  A001     _____  ._____   _____

               Total Products : 4 records
```

6. Press Enter at the To field. The words *Last Record* will appear.
   To rank your count sheets by Description:
7. Type 2 and press Enter.
8. Press Enter at the From field. The words *First Record* will appear.
9. Press Enter at the To field. The words *Last Record* will appear.
   Your count sheet will automatically begin printing. Note: To stop printing, press Esc. Once printed, your count sheet should look like the one in Figure 4-20.

Entering Physical Inventory

DacEasy's Enter Physical Inventory operation lets you enter the products that were recorded by hand on the count sheets during physical inventory. This operation allows you to enter the product number (Inventory number) and the actual number of units and/or fractions counted.

To enter physical inventory, follow these steps:

1. Highlight the Transaction menu from the Opening menu. Press Enter.
2. Press 6 to select the Inventory submenu.
3. Press 2 to select the Enter Physical Inventory operation. The screen in Figure 4-21 will appear.

The cursor should be positioned at the Product # field.

4. Type 4015 and press Enter.
   DacEasy automatically enters both the Description and the Previous Count fields. If the Previous Count field displays a quantity (entered during a past physical inventory entry operation), it's added to the quantity you enter in the Counted field. This feature comes in handy if your business has more

145

Figure 4-21. The Physical Inventory Screen

```
07/01/88                    PHYSICAL INVENTORY                      LHP
09:33 AM              Dr. Humane's Small Animal Hospital


                                        Previous
          Product #     Description       Count      Counted     Total
          -------------  ------------------  ----------  -----------  ----------
```

F1-Help F6-Delete   ESC-Exit

than one warehouse because you can enter the quantities
counted as you receive each count sheet. That is, you don't
have to wait to receive all the count sheets before entering
the information.

   The cursor should be positioned at the Counted field.

5. Type 30 and press Enter.

   DacEasy then automatically enters the Total.

   At the next Product # field:

6. Type 2602 and press Enter.

Figure 4-22. The Completed Physical Inventory Screen

```
07/01/88                    PHYSICAL INVENTORY                      LHP
09:33 AM              Dr. Humane's Small Animal Hospital


                                        Previous
          Product #     Description       Count      Counted     Total
          -------------  ------------------  ----------  -----------  ----------
          4015          Amoxicillin         0.000       30.000      30.000
          2602          Cat Food            0.000       72.000      72.000
          2601          Dog Food            0.000       53.000      53.000
          0038188       Flea Powder         0.000       38.000      38.000
```

F1-Help F6-Delete   ESC-Exit

146

7. Type 72 at the Counted field. Press Enter.
8. Type 2601 at the next Product # field. Press Enter.
9. Type 53 at the Counted field and press Enter.
10. Type 0038188 at the Product # field and press Enter.
11. Type 38 at the Counted field and press Enter.

Your screen should look like the one in Figure 4-22.

12. Press Esc to record this operation. You'll return to the Inventory submenu.

As mentioned earlier in this section, you can print various inventory reports that allow you to analyze the inventory activity of your business accurately.

To learn more about the inventory report options, see Chapter 6.

Chapter 5
Using *DacEasy's* Accounting Journals and Posting Operations

Transactions could be recorded directly in general ledger accounts. However, the first permanent record in which transaction information is recorded is a *journal*. The reasons for recording transactions first in a journal and not directly in general ledger accounts are as follows:

Accuracy

A journal entry includes the debit and credit parts of each transaction in one place. The equality of debits and credits for a transaction can be checked easily by looking at a journal entry. If transactions were recorded directly in general ledger accounts, each account would show only a part of a transaction. Omissions could be easily overlooked. Errors in recording a transaction can be corrected in a journal before transferring the information to accounts. Thus, information in accounts is more likely to be accurate.

Chronological Order

Transactions are recorded in a journal by date. Day-to-day activities of a business are listed in the order they occur. When, weeks or months later, all the facts are needed about a specific transaction, a journal is an easy source to check. The debit and credit parts of transactions are recorded in different general ledger accounts. If transactions were recorded directly in general ledger accounts, information about any single transaction would be difficult to find in one place.

Double-Entry Accounting

The recording of debit and credit parts of a transaction is called double-entry accounting. Double-entry accounts provide a complete record of each transaction. Complete accounting is double-entry accounting. Most well-managed businesses use double-entry accounting.

DacEasy provides several special journals where specific information is automatically entered. *DacEasy's* Print Journal Reports options let you print the various journals so they can be reviewed.

The Purchase Journal

A special journal used to record only purchases on account transactions is called a *purchase journal*. *DacEasy's* Purchase Journal is located within the Journals menu. Every time you record and print a transaction in the Enter Merchandise Received or Enter Returns operations, *DacEasy* automatically updates this journal. To review the Purchase Journal, use the Print Purchase Journal operation.

Printing the Purchase Journal

When the Purchase Journal Report is printed, it's broken down into detail and summary sections.

The first section, entitled *Purchase Journal Report*, contains details of each purchase order received or returned on a given day, as well as vendor information and totals. This section lets you review your vendor's performance:

• Have you returned a large quantity of merchandise to them?
• Have vendors delivered or sent your merchandise in a timely manner?

It also lets you keep track of daily totals that reflect growth in your liabilities.

The second section, entitled *Purchase Journal Report Summary by Inventory and Code,* contains a summary of each miscellaneous code (that is, codes used for freight, packaging, and so on) and the amount of product received. The last price paid and the new price with a percent (%) variance for each product is also included. This section is extremely beneficial for accounting and auditing purposes because it proves that the accounting transactions entered in the purchase order posting operation are accurate. A single error in posting to a ledger account causes several problems in your business' accounting system:

- The trial balance can be out of balance
- The income statement can be understated or overstated
- Vendors can be overpaid or underpaid

To print the Purchase Journal, follow these steps:

1. Highlight the Journals menu from the Opening menu. Press Enter.
2. Press 7 from the Journals menu to select the Purchase Journals operation.
   The screen in Figure 5-1 will appear.

Note: Before you can print the Purchase Journal, all Merchandise Receipts and Purchase Returns must be printed. *DacEasy* will

Figure 5-1. The Purchase Journal Report Screen

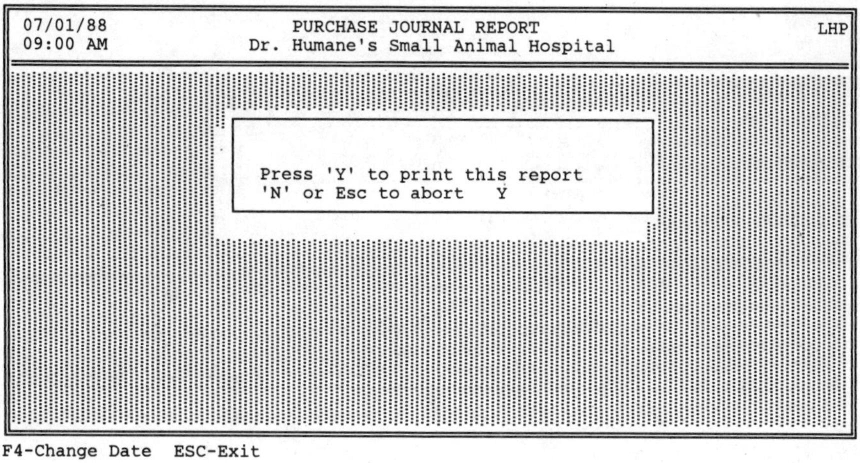

```
07/01/88                    PURCHASE JOURNAL REPORT                      LHP
09:00 AM              Dr. Humane's Small Animal Hospital



                     ┌─────────────────────────────────┐
                     │                                 │
                     │  Press 'Y' to print this report │
                     │  'N' or Esc to abort    Y       │
                     │                                 │
                     └─────────────────────────────────┘




F4-Change Date   ESC-Exit
```

display a message on the screen if you still need to print these operations.

3. Press Esc to begin printing.

When printed, the Purchase Journal should look like the one in Figure 5-2. The cursor will return to the Journals menu.

Use the Purchase Journal to verify that all Purchase Order transactions are accurate before you post them to the general ledger.

PO (Purchase Order) Status Report

DacEasy's PO Status Report lists all purchase orders still pending and all products ordered. Any purchase order listed on this report can be deleted using the Enter Purchase Order operation within the Transaction menu.

Printing the PO Status Report

To print the PO Status Report, follow these steps:

1. Highlight the Journals menu from the Opening menu. Press Enter.
2. Press 8 from the Journals menu to select the PO Status Report operation.

The screen in Figure 5-3 will appear.

Figure 5-2. The Purchase Journal Printout

```
Date : 07/01/88                        Dr. Humane's Small Animal Hospital                 Page no. 1
Time : 09:19 AM                              555 East Meadows Lane
                                            San Diego, CA  92122
                                              (619)555-3636

                                          PURCHASE JOURNAL REPORT

          Vend.  PO.    Vendor
   Type   Dept.  Number Code              Name         Date      Gross       Tax       Total
   ------- ----- ------ ------  --------------------- -------- ---------- -------- ------------
PURCHASE   02    00102  G015    Goodson's Drug Co.    07/01/88    107.00     5.82      112.82
                                Purchase Total :                 107.00     5.82      112.82
RETURN     02    00016  G015    Goodson's Drug Co.    07/01/88     -4.85    -0.29       -5.14
                                Purch.Returns Total  :            -4.85    -0.29       -5.14
                                Department Total :               102.15     5.53      107.68

                                Grand Totals :                   102.15     5.53      107.68
```

```
        07/01/88                        Dr. Humane's Small Animal Hospital                 Page no. 2
Time : 09:19 AM                              555 East Meadows Lane
                                            San Diego, CA  92122
                                              (619)555-3636

                                          PURCHASE JOURNAL REPORT
                                       SUMMARY BY INVENTORY AND CODE
Dept.  Type   Item/Acct #  Description                       Units     Amount    Avg./Unit  Last P.Price % Variance
-----  ------ -----------  --------------------------------  --------- ---------- ---------- ------------- ----------
       CODE   52083        Packaging                                     10.00
                           Code total :                                  10.00
                           Department Total :                            10.00

                           Grand Totals :                                10.00
```

152

Figure 5-3. The PO Status Report Screen

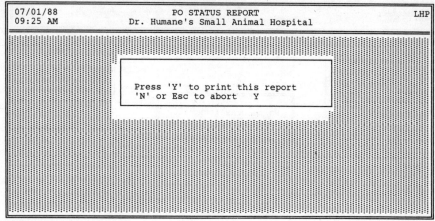

```
07/01/88                      PO STATUS REPORT                          LHP
09:25 AM              Dr. Humane's Small Animal Hospital




                  ┌─────────────────────────────────────┐
                  │                                     │
                  │    Press 'Y' to print this report   │
                  │    'N' or Esc to abort    Y         │
                  │                                     │
                  └─────────────────────────────────────┘



F4-Change Date   ESC-Exit
```

3. Press Enter. The PO Status Report will begin printing.
   When printed, the report should look like the one in Figure 5-4.

   If there are no transactions to be printed on this report, *DacEasy* will display the message in Figure 5-5.

4. Press any key to return to the Journals menu.

Sales Journal

A special journal used to record only sales on account is called a *Sales Journal. DacEasy*'s Sales Journal is located within the Journals menu. Every time you record and print a transaction in the Enter Invoices or Enter Sales Returns operations, *DacEasy* automatically updates this journal. To review the Sales Journal, use the Print Sales Journal operation.

Figure 5-4. The PO Status Report Printout

```
Date : 07/01/88                      Dr. Humane's Small Animal Hospital                    Page no. 1
Time : 09:27 AM                             555 East Meadows Lane
                                            San Diego, CA  92122
                                              (619)555-3636

                                             PO STATUS REPORT


        Vend.   PO.    Vendor
        Type   Number   Code        Name          Date      Gross       Tax       Total     Status    Printed
        -----  ------  ------  ----------------  --------  ----------  --------  ---------  --------  ----------
         02    00103    G015   Goodson's Drug Co.  07/01/88   131.25     7.28     138.53   On Order    YES
                               Department Total :           131.25      7.28     138.53

                               Grand Totals :               131.25      7.28     138.53
```

153

Figure 5-5. Message Displayed When No Transactions Are Available

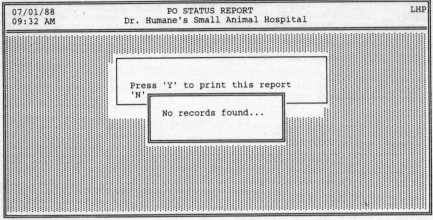

```
07/01/88                    PO STATUS REPORT                      LHP
09:32 AM              Dr. Humane's Small Animal Hospital
```

```
            Press 'Y' to print this report
            'N'
                    No records found...
```

```
SORTING . . .
```

Printing the Sales Journal

When the Sales Journal is printed, it's broken down into detail
and summary sections. The first section, entitled *Sales Journal Report*, contains details of each invoice sent or returned, as well as
customer information, totals of invoices and returns, and whether
they've been paid or are still outstanding (need to be paid). Keeping an eye on the amount of returned merchandise is important,
and this journal can keep you on top of any problem that might
arise (unhappy customers, decrease in sales, lost commissions,
cost of restocking, and so on). This section also lets you see who
is buying your products and in what quantity, and tells you your
receivables (money still owed to you) and the amount of money
received each day.

The second section, entitled *Sales Journal Report Summary by
Inventory and Code*, contains the amounts of miscellaneous codes,
and the sales price and average dollars per sale. This way, you'll
know which products are selling the best, and what their average
selling price is. This section is also excellent for auditing purposes:

- It gives you the amount of money to be deposited in the bank
  by providing details of totals collected each day (including cash
  receipts).
- The Tax field total also reflects the credit to the Sales Tax
  account.

154

- The Net to Pay field gives you the debit to the Accounts Receivable account.
- The Amount Paid field gives you the debit to the bank (the deposit slip also backs this up).

It's suggested that you keep a copy of all invoices and sales returns with the Sales Journal so they can easily be reviewed.

To print the Sales Journal Report, follow these steps:

1. Highlight the Journals menu from the Opening menu. Press Enter.
2. Press 9 to select the Sales Journal option.
   The screen in Figure 5-6 will appear.
3. Press Enter. The report will begin printing.
   Note: You must print all Invoices and Sales Returns before running this operation. If any still need to be printed, the message in Figure 5-7 will appear on the screen. Go to the Transaction menu to complete the printing operations.

The completed Sales Journal Report should look like the one in Figure 5-8.

Use the Sales Journal to verify that all Sales transactions are accurate before you post them to the general ledger.

Figure 5-6. The Last Opportunity to Abort Printout

```
07/01/88                    SALES JOURNAL REPORT                        LHP
09:00 AM               Dr. Humane's Small Animal Hospital


                      Press 'Y' to print this report
                      'N' or Esc to abort     Y




F4-Change Date  ESC-Exit
```

Figure 5-7. Warning to Print All Invoices and Sales Returns Before Printing the Sales Journal Report

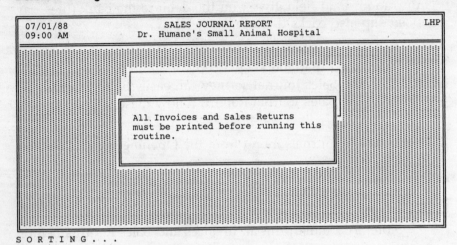

```
07/01/88                    SALES JOURNAL REPORT                        LHP
09:00 AM              Dr. Humane's Small Animal Hospital




              ┌─────────────────────────────────┐
              │                                 │
              │                                 │
              │    All Invoices and Sales Returns│
              │    must be printed before running this│
              │    routine.                     │
              │                                 │
              │                                 │
              └─────────────────────────────────┘



```

S O R T I N G . . .

Figure 5-8. The Sales Journal Report Printout

```
Date : 07/01/88                    Dr. Humane's Small Animal Hospital              Page no. 1
Time : 09:12 AM                         555 East Meadows Lane
                                         San Diego, CA  92122
                                          (619)555-3636

                                        SALES JOURNAL REPORT
```

Type	Cust. Dept.	Inv/Ret Number	Customer Code	Name	Date	Gross	Tax	Total	Amount Pd	Net To Pay
RETURN	CAT	00069	S135	Lady	07/01/88	-5.10	-0.31	-5.41		
				Invoice Return Total :		-5.10	-0.31	-5.41	0.00	-5.41
				Department Total :		-5.10	-0.31	-5.41	0.00	-5.41
INVOICE	DOG	00354	B016	Champ	07/01/88	450.00	3.00	453.00	50.00	403.00
INVOICE	DOG	00355	A001	Buffy Adams	07/01/88	23.90	1.22	25.12	0.00	25.12
				Invoice Total :		473.90	4.22	478.12	50.00	428.12
				Department Total :		473.90	4.22	478.12	50.00	428.12
				Grand Totals :		468.80	3.91	472.71	50.00	422.71

```
Date : 07/01/88                    Dr. Humane's Small Animal Hospital              Page no. 2
Time : 09:12 AM                         555 East Meadows Lane
                                         San Diego, CA  92122
                                          (619)555-3636

                                        SALES JOURNAL REPORT
                                  SUMMARY BY INVENTORY AND CODE
```

Dept.	Type	Item/Acct #	Description	Units	Amount	Avg./Unit	Sale Price	% Variance
	CODE	4301	Freight		3.50			
			Code total :		3.50			
			Department Total :		3.50			
01	PRODUCT	2601	Dog Food	24.000	20.40	0.85	1.00	-15.00
01	PRODUCT	2602	Cat Food	-6.000	-5.10	0.85	1.00	-15.00
			Product total :		15.30			
01	SERVICE	E001	Emergency	1.000	50.00	50.00	50.00	0.00
01	SERVICE	S001	Surgery	4.000	400.00	100.00	100.00	0.00
			Service Total :		450.00			
			Department Total :		465.30			
			Grand Totals :		468.80			

156

Accounts Receivable Journal

A special journal used to record accounts receivable transactions not recorded in *DacEasy's* Billing system is called an *Accounts Receivable Journal.*

DacEasy has provided an Accounts Receivable Journal where miscellaneous transactions (that is, adjustments) are entered. This journal will probably not be used often if all of your selling is done through the Billing process. However, if you're not using *DacEasy's* Billing system, the report printed from the Accounts Receivable Journal will be as beneficial as the Sales Journal because all accounts receivable and sales transactions need to be entered in the A/R Transaction Entry operation within the Transaction menu.

Printing the Accounts Receivable Journal

To print the Accounts Receivable Journal, follow these steps:

1. Highlight the Journals menu from the Opening menu. Press Enter.
2. Press 3 to select the A/R Transactions option.
   The screen in Figure 5-9 will appear.
3. Press Enter twice to print all transactions.
   The completed Accounts Receivable Journal should look like the one in Figure 5-10.

Figure 5-9. The Accounts Receivable Transaction Screen

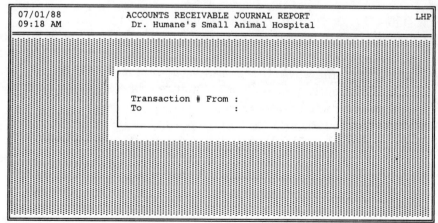

```
07/01/88              ACCOUNTS RECEIVABLE JOURNAL REPORT              LHP
09:18 AM                Dr. Humane's Small Animal Hospital




                    Transaction # From :
                    To                 :




F1-Help F4-Change Date   ESC-Exit
```

Figure 5-10. The Accounts Receivable Journal Printout

```
Date : 07/01/88                      Dr. Humane's Small Animal Hospital                    Page no. 1
Time : 09:24 AM                            555 East Meadows Lane
                                          San Diego, CA  92122
                                            (619)555-3636

                                        Accounts Receivable Journal

 Tran Custom.                              Ref. #  Due   Discount  Discount   Trans.
 No.  Code     Customer name   Invoice#  Date Chk. #  Date   Date     Available   Type      Debit      Credit
 ---- ------   -------------   -------- -------- -----  -----  --------  ---------  ------- --------- ---------
 0001 R050     Mittens           99     07/01/88 Debit  07/01/88 07/01/88          DEBIT
      11051    Accts Rec'ble Module              Returned Check Charge                                  10.00
      5403     Miscellaneous Losses             Returned Check Charge                                            10.00
                                                                      Totals:    TRANSACTION   2       10.00    10.00

                                                     Grand Total :    TRANSACTIONS   2       10.00    10.00


                                     Dr. Humane's Small Animal Hospital                    Page no. 2
 Time : 09:24 AM                           555 East Meadows Lane
                                          San Diego, CA  92122
                                            (619)555-3636

                     GENERAL LEDGER TRANSFER SUMMARY
 Acct #       Acct. name         Description              Debit        Credit
 ------  ------------------- ------------------------  ------------  ------------
 11051  Accts Rec'ble Module Summary From AR Post        10.00
 5403   Miscellaneous Losses Summary From AR Post                      10.00
                             Summary Total :             10.00        10.00
```

Use the Accounts Receivable Journal to verify that all Accounts Receivable transactions are accurate before you post them to the general ledger.

Cash Receipts Journal

A special journal used to record only transactions involving the receipt of cash is called a Cash Receipts Journal. *DacEasy's* Accounts Receivable Cash Receipts Journal is located within the Journals menu. Every time you record and print a transaction in the Enter Cash Receipts operation, *DacEasy* automatically updates this journal. The benefits of this journal are:

- It states the amount of money received each day.
- It lets you know if your customers are taking advantage of any discounts you're offering.
- It lets you examine whether it's more advantageous to offer discounts for early payment or to finance a line of credit established by your receivables.
- It provides an audit trail so cash deposits can be validated.
- It states any adjustments made or advances paid.

The Accounts Receivable Cash Receipts Journal is usually printed by account (for instance, bank account) so you'll be able to validate the amount of money deposited in each bank account.

Printing the Accounts Receivable Cash Receipts Journal

To print the Accounts Receivable Cash Receipts Journal, follow these steps:

1. Highlight the Journals menu from the Opening menu. Press Enter.
2. Press 4 to select the Accounts Receivable Cash Receipts Journal operation.

    The screen in Figure 5-11 will appear.
3. Press Enter twice to print all Accounts Receivable Cash Receipts transactions.

    The report will begin printing. The completed report should look like the one in Figure 5-12.

    Use the Accounts Receivable Cash Receipts Journal to verify all bank deposit slips and receipts of cash.

Accounts Payable Journals

Three separate Accounts Payable Journals are provided with *DacEasy's* Accounting program:

1. Transactions
2. Payments
3. Checks to Print

Figure 5-11. The Accounts Receivable Cash Receipts Journal Screen

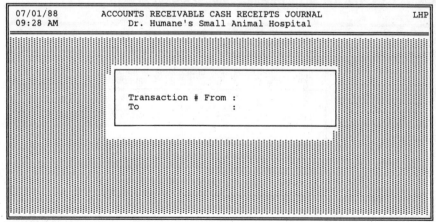

```
07/01/88          ACCOUNTS RECEIVABLE CASH RECEIPTS JOURNAL              LHP
09:28 AM                Dr. Humane's Small Animal Hospital




                        Transaction # From :
                        To          :




F1-Help F4-Change Date   ESC-Exit
```

Figure 5-12. The Accounts Receivable Cash Receipts Journal Printout

```
Date : 07/01/88                    Dr. Humane's Small Animal Hospital                      Page no. 1
Time : 09:32 AM                         555 East Meadows Lane
                                        San Diego, CA  92122
                                          (619)555-3636

                           ACCOUNTS RECEIVABLE CASH RECEIPTS JOURNAL

 Tran.
 No.   Acct #  Cust.        Customer Name      Invoice#   Date    Chk #  Type  Inv. Amount  Disc. Taken  Chk. Amount
 ----  ------  ------  ---------------------   --------  --------  -----  ----  -----------  -----------  -----------
 0002  11021   B016    Champ                     202    07/01/88  Cash   PMT.     20.00         0.00         20.00
                       Acct. Total:                                               20.00         0.00         20.00


                       Grand Total:  # of Transactions    1                       20.00         0.00         20.00
```

Two of the journals (Transactions and Payments) are accessed through the Journals menu. The Checks to Print Journal is accessed through the Accounts Payable submenu within the Transaction menu. All three journals are updated when transactions relating to them occur.

The Accounts Payable Transactions Journal keeps track of all transactions involving vendors who aren't controlled through the Purchase Order system (such as telephone, utilities, rent, temporary services, and so on). The detailed information printed for this journal (due dates, amounts owed, available discounts, and so on) helps you keep track of these transactions. This information is useful because you can see at a glance if you can take any early payment discount options.

This journal also prints petty cash transactions. Thus, it provides complete audit information.

Figure 5-13. The Accounts Payable Journal Report Screen

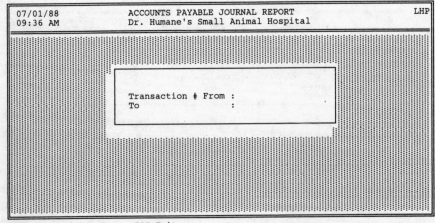

```
07/01/88          ACCOUNTS PAYABLE JOURNAL REPORT            LHP
09:36 AM          Dr. Humane's Small Animal Hospital




                  Transaction # From :
                  To               :




F1-Help F4-Change Date   ESC-Exit
```

Figure 5-14. The Accounts Payable Journal Report Printout

```
Date : 07/01/88                    Dr. Humane's Small Animal Hospital                              Page no. 1
Time : 09:36 AM                          555 East Meadows Lane
                                          San Diego, CA  92122
                                            (619)555-3636

                                        Accounts Payable Journal

Tran Vendor                             Ref. #  Due    Discount  Discount  Trans.
No.  Code    Vendor Name    Invoice#  Date  Chk. #  Date   Date      Available Type      Debit        Credit
---- ------  -------------- --------  ----  ------  ----   --------  --------- ------    ------------ ------------
0001 U008    Utilities Co. of San D 6053853  06/30/88 Bill  07/07/88 06/30/88   0.00 INVOICE
     2101    Accts Payable-Module              June 1988 Payment                                          253.00
     5214    Utilities                         June 1988 Payment                          253.00
                                                             Totals:  TRANSACTION   2     253.00          253.00

                                                          Grand Total :  TRANSACTIONS   2    253.00       253.00



Date : 07/01/88                    Dr. Humane's Small Animal Hospital                              Page no. 2
Time : 09:36 AM                          555 East Meadows Lane
                                          San Diego, CA  92122
                                            (619)555-3636

                  GENERAL LEDGER TRANSFER SUMMARY
       Acct #     Acct. name      Description          Debit         Credit
       ------  ---------------- -------------------  ------------  ------------

       2101    Accts Payable-Module Summary From AP Post                253.00
       5214    Utilities            Summary From AP Post   253.00
                                    Summary Total :        253.00       253.00
```

To print the Accounts Payable Transactions Journal, follow these steps:

1. Highlight the Journals menu from the Opening menu. Press Enter.
2. Press 5 to select the Accounts Payable Transactions option.
   The screen in Figure 5-13 will appear.
3. Press Enter twice to print all Accounts Payable transactions.
   The report will begin printing.
   When completed, the Accounts Payable Journal should look like the one in Figure 5-14.

Use this report to verify that all Accounts Payable transactions are accurate before you post them to the general ledger.

Accounts Payable Payments Journal

It's important that you account for all checks, even voided ones. The Accounts Payable Payments Journal gives you a list of checks printed, whether they're printed by the computer, handwritten, or voided, or even if they're electronic transfers, or automatic charges to your bank.

To print the Accounts Payable Payment Journal, follow these steps:

1. Highlight the Journals menu from the Opening menu. Press Enter.

161

Figure 5-15. The Accounts Payable Payments Journal Screen

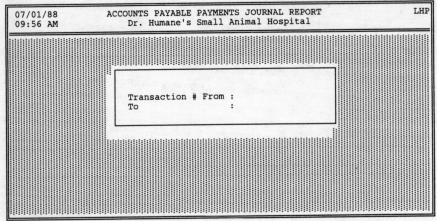

```
07/01/88          ACCOUNTS PAYABLE PAYMENTS JOURNAL REPORT              LHP
09:56 AM                 Dr. Humane's Small Animal Hospital
```

```
            Transaction # From :
            To               :
```

F1-Help F4-Change Date   ESC-Exit

2. Press 6 to select the A/P Payments option.
    The screen in Figure 5-15 will appear.
3. Press Enter twice to print all Accounts Payable Payments transactions.
    When printed, the completed Payments Journal should look like the one in Figure 5-16.

    Use this report to verify that specific checks have been printed.

Checks to Print Journal

The Checks to Print Journal lets you review and edit any checks to print before the figures are transferred to a preprinted check.

Figure 5-16. The Accounts Payable Payments Journal Printout

```
Date : 07/01/88                    Dr. Humane's Small Animal Hospital              Page no. 1
Time : 09:54 AM                          555 East Meadows Lane
                                         San Diego, CA  92122
                                           (619)555-3636

                                  ACCOUNTS PAYABLE PAYMENTS JOURNAL

Tran.
No.   Acct # Vendor      Vendor Name         Invoice#   Date    Chk #  Type Inv. Amount Disc. Taken Chk. Amount
----  ------ ------  ---------------------   --------  -------- -----  ---- ----------- ----------- -----------
0003                 ****** V O I D ******   VOID      07/01/88 000001 VOID        0.00        0.00        0.00
                     Check Total: # of Transactions     1                          0.00        0.00        0.00

                     Acct. Total:                                                  0.00        0.00        0.00

0002  11021  U008    Utilities Co. of San Diego 6053853 07/01/88 000002 CHECK    253.00        0.00      253.00
0002  11021  U008    Utilities Co. of San Diego 23478   07/01/88 000002 CHECK    100.00        0.00      100.00
                     Check Total: # of Transactions     2                        353.00        0.00      353.00

                     Acct. Total:                                                353.00        0.00      353.00


                     Grand Total: # of Transactions     3                        353.00        0:00      353.00
```

162

Figure 5-17. The Checks to Print Journal Screen

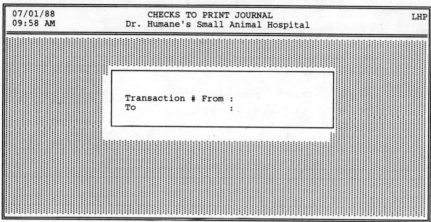

```
07/01/88                      CHECKS TO PRINT JOURNAL                    LHP
09:58 AM                  Dr. Humane's Small Animal Hospital



                    ┌──────────────────────────────────────┐
                    │                                      │
                    │                                      │
                    │     Transaction # From :             │
                    │     To               :               │
                    │                                      │
                    │                                      │
                    └──────────────────────────────────────┘




F1-Help F4-Change Date   ESC-Exit
```

This journal is advantageous because it allows you to

- Decrease a payment or payments due to your current bank balance.
- Reprint checks if needed.

To print the Checks to Print Journal, follow these steps:

1. Highlight the Transactions menu from the Opening menu. Press Enter.
2. Press 3 to select the Accounts Payable submenu.
3. Press 3 to select the Checks to Print Journal option. The screen in Figure 5-17 will appear.
4. Press Enter twice to print all checks that need to be printed. When completed, the Checks to Print Journal will resemble the one in Figure 5-18.

Figure 5-18. The Checks to Print Journal Printout

```
Date : 07/01/88                    Dr. Humane's Small Animal Hospital                    Page no. 1
Time : 10:23 AM                          555 East Meadows Lane
                                         San Diego, CA  92122
                                           (619)555-3636

                                 ACCOUNTS PAYABLE CHECKS TO PRINT JOURNAL

       Tran.
       No.  Vendor        Vendor Name           Invoice# Inv. Amount Disc. Taken Amt. to Pay
       ---- ------ ------------------------------ -------- ----------- ----------- -----------
       0004 A001   Ace Veterinary Supplies        H053669      125.00        2.50      122.50
                   Check Total: # of Transactions       1      125.00        2.50      122.50

                   Grand Total: # of Transactions       1      125.00        2.50      122.50
```

Figure 5-19. The Screen Notifying You that No Checks Are Awaiting Printing

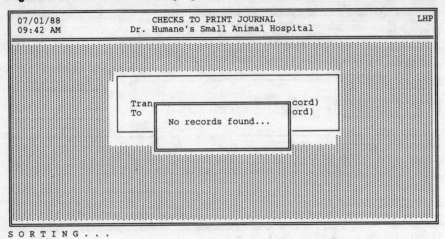

```
07/01/88              CHECKS TO PRINT JOURNAL                      LHP
09:42 AM           Dr. Humane's Small Animal Hospital




              Tran┌─────────────────────────┐cord)
              To   │                         │ord)
                   │   No records found...   │
                   │                         │
                   └─────────────────────────┘




SORTING . . .
```

If there are no checks waiting to be printed, the screen will display the message shown in Figure 5-19.

General Ledger Journal

DacEasy's General Ledger Journal option lets you print any of the journals created in the general ledger. You can also print any of the summary journals created such as:

- Accounts Receivable (AR)
- Accounts Payable (AP)
- Billing (BI)
- Inventory (IN)
- Purchase Order (PO)
- Set Up (SU)

This journal sorts information transaction by transaction for a given period.

One journal or a range of journals can be printed by entering the two-character journal codes in the Journal Code From and To fields. If you want to print all journals, press Enter at each of these fields.

Figure 5-20. The General Ledger Journal Report Screen

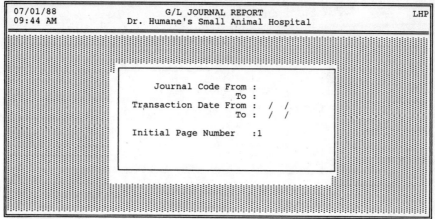

```
07/01/88                     G/L JOURNAL REPORT                        LHP
09:44 AM              Dr. Humane's Small Animal Hospital
```

```
                    Journal Code From :
                              To :
              Transaction Date From :   /  /
                              To :   /  /

              Initial Page Number    :1
```

```
F1-Help ESC-Exit
```

Printing the General Ledger Journal

To print the General Ledger Journal, follow these steps:

1. Highlight the Journals menu from the Opening menu. Press
   Enter.
2. Press 1 to select the General Ledger Journal operation.
   The screen in Figure 5-20 will appear.

   The cursor should be positioned at the Journal Code From
   field. To print only the Journal used to set up balances, type *SU*
   at the To field.

3. Type *SU* and press Enter.
   The cursor will move to the Transaction Date From field.
4. Press Enter. *DacEasy* will enter the words *First Date* and the
   cursor will move to the To field.
5. Press Enter again. *DacEasy* will enter the words *Last Date* and
   the cursor will move to the Initial Page Number field.
   The screen should look like the one in Figure 5-21.
6. Press Enter to accept the default.
   The report will begin printing.
   The first page of the completed report will resemble the
   one in Figure 5-22.

Figure 5-21. The General Ledger Journal Screen Prepared to Print Set Up

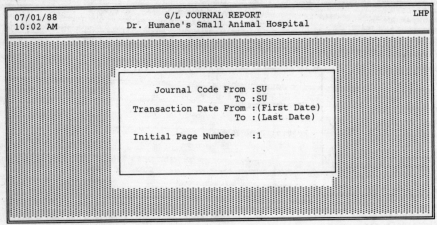

```
07/01/88              G/L JOURNAL REPORT                    LHP
10:02 AM        Dr. Humane's Small Animal Hospital



          ┌──────────────────────────────────────────┐
          │                                          │
          │      Journal Code From :SU               │
          │                   To :SU                 │
          │   Transaction Date From :(First Date)     │
          │                   To :(Last Date)        │
          │                                          │
          │      Initial Page Number    :1           │
          │                                          │
          │                                          │
          └──────────────────────────────────────────┘



```

F1-Help ESC-Exit

Account Activity Detail Report

DacEasy's Account Activity Detail Report provides the same information as the General Ledger Journal. However, it will be sorted by account. You'll probably find that this report will be one of the most valuable management tools in your accounting system because of the many details this report provides. This report can be printed summarizing a range of accounts, one account, or all ac-

Figure 5-22. The General Ledger Journal Report Printout

```
Date : 07/01/88                    Dr. Humane's Small Animal Hospital              Page no. 1
Time : 09:56 AM                           555 East Meadows Lane
                                          San Diego, CA  92122
                                            (619)555-3636

                                      General Ledger Journal Report

   Journal
   Trans.#    Date    Acct. #   Account Name        Description        Debits      Credits   Posted?
   -------  --------  -------   ------------------  ----------------  ----------  ----------  -------
   SU 0001  07/01/88  1101      Petty Cash          Set-Up Balance      1500.00                 YES
                      12021     Original Value      Set-Up Balance      5000.00                 YES
                      12031     Original Value      Set-Up Balance     60000.00                 YES
                      13031     Insurance           Set-Up Balance      1000.00                 YES
                      14013     Utilities           Set-Up Balance       200.00                 YES
                      2102      Notes Payable       Set-Up Balance                 10000.00     YES
                      210411    Federal Income W/H  Set-Up Balance                   250.00     YES
                      210416    State Income W/H    Set-Up Balance                   100.00     YES
                      21042     Sales Tax Payable   Set-Up Balance                  2000.00     YES
                      4101      Sales Dept. 01      Set-Up Balance                  5500.00     YES
                      4301      Freight             Set-Up Balance                  1500.00     YES
                      520111    Salaries            Set-Up Balance                 10000.00     YES
                      520112    Hourly              Set-Up Balance                  6000.00     YES
                      5211      Office Supplies     Set-Up Balance                   500.00     YES
                      5217      Licenses/Permits    Set-Up Balance                   250.00     YES
                      5218      Memships/Dues/Subscr Set-Up Balance                  125.00     YES
                      5401      Cash Short          Set-Up Balance                    80.00     YES
                      D         Journal Difference  Reconcile Trans. Differ.        31395.00    YES

                                                    TOTAL TRANSACTION :  67700.00   67700.00

   SU 0701  07/01/88  11051     Accts Rec'ble Module Summ. Customer Setup   85.00                 YES
                      11071     Inventory - Module  Summ. Products Setup    403.00                 YES
                      D         Journal Difference  Summ. Vendor Setup      725.00                 YES
                      2101      Accts Payable-Module Summ. Vendor Setup                 725.00     YES
                      D         Journal Difference  Summ. Products Setup                403.00     YES
                      D         Journal Difference  Summ. Customer Setup                 85.00     YES

                                                    TOTAL TRANSACTION :   1213.00    1213.00
```

166

counts, and shows beginning balances, debits/credits, and current balances for all designated account numbers.

This report can also be printed summarizing a range of dates, one day, or all days.

Printing the Account Activity Detail Report

To print the Account Activity Detail Report, follow these steps:

1. Highlight the Journals menu from the Opening menu. Press Enter.
2. Press 2 from the Journals menu to select the General Ledger Activity option.

    The screen in Figure 5-23 will appear.

    The cursor is positioned at the Print Account # From field.

3. Type 1101 and press Enter.

    The cursor will move to the To field.
4. Type 14013 and press Enter.

    The cursor will move to the Transaction Date From field.
5. Press Enter. *DacEasy* will enter the words *First Date* and the cursor will move to the To field.
6. Press Enter again. *DacEasy* will enter the words *Last Date* and the cursor will move to the Initial Page Number field.

Figure 5-23. The Account Activity Report Screen

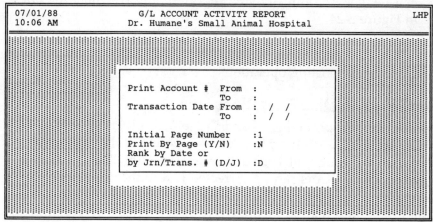

```
07/01/88              G/L ACCOUNT ACTIVITY REPORT              LHP
10:06 AM           Dr. Humane's Small Animal Hospital



              Print Account #  From  :
                                 To   :
              Transaction Date From  :  /  /
                                 To   :  /  /

              Initial Page Number    :1
              Print By Page (Y/N)    :N
              Rank by Date or
              by Jrn/Trans. # (D/J)  :D




F1-Help ESC-Exit
```

Figure 5-24. The General Ledger Account Activity Detail Report Printout

```
Date : 07/01/88                        Dr. Humane's Small Animal Hospital              Page no. 1
Time : 10:12 AM                               555 East Meadows Lane
                                              San Diego, CA  92122
                                                 (619)555-3636

                                        G/L Account Activity Detail Report
                                           Complete Monthly Activity

        Journal
        Trans.#   Date    Acct. #   Account Name        Description          Debits      Credits   Posted?
        -------  -------- -------   -----------------   -----------------   ----------   --------   -------
                          1101      Petty Cash          BEGINNING BALANCE        0.00
        SU 0001  07/01/88                               Set-Up Balance        1500.00                 YES
                                                        CURRENT BALANCE       1500.00

                          11051     Accts Rec'ble Module BEGINNING BALANCE       0.00
        SU 0701  07/01/88                               Summ. Customer Setup    85.00                 YES
        SU 0701  07/01/88                               Summ. Customer Setup    25.00                 YES
                                                        CURRENT BALANCE        110.00

                          11071     Inventory - Module  BEGINNING BALANCE        0.00
        SU 0701  07/01/88                               Summ. Products Setup   403.00                 YES
        SU 0701  07/01/88                               Summ. Products Setup   500.00                 YES
                                                        CURRENT BALANCE        903.00

                          12021     Original Value      BEGINNING BALANCE        0.00
        SU 0001  07/01/88                               Set-Up Balance        5000.00                 YES
                                                        CURRENT BALANCE       5000.00

                          12031     Original Value      BEGINNING BALANCE        0.00
        SU 0001  07/01/88                               Set-Up Balance       60000.00                 YES
                                                        CURRENT BALANCE      60000.00

                          13031     Insurance           BEGINNING BALANCE        0.00
        SU 0001  07/01/88                               Set-Up Balance        1000.00                 YES
                                                        CURRENT BALANCE       1000.00

                          14013     Utilities           BEGINNING BALANCE        0.00
        SU 0001  07/01/88                               Set-Up Balance         200.00                 YES
                                                        CURRENT BALANCE        200.00
```

7. Press Enter to accept the default.

     The cursor will move to the Print By Page field.

8. Press Enter to accept the default.

     Note: Type Y and press Enter if you want each account to start on a new page.

     The cursor will move to the Rank by Date or by Jrn/Trans # field.

9. Press Enter to accept the default.

     Your report will start printing. When completed, the General Ledger Account Activity Report should resemble the one in Figure 5-24.

     Now that you've printed and reviewed each journal, you're ready to begin posting operations.

DacEasy's Posting Operations

Most computer programs work using either a *batch* system or an *online* system. A batch system lets you verify all data before it's distributed throughout your accounting system. This is advantageous because errors can be corrected before they're spread throughout the system. The disadvantage of a batch system is that timely information regarding your customers, vendors, or inventory is not updated immediately. This causes problems like losing sales or overextending credit.

An online system lets you update information immediately. This is advantageous because your accounting system is always up-to-date. The disadvantage of an online system is that inaccuracies are immediately spread throughout your entire accounting system.

DacEasy Version 3.0 has taken the advantages of both systems and combined them into one. For example, operations that should be updated immediately, such as Invoicing, Merchandise Received, Merchandise Returned, Payments, and Purchase Orders operate using the online system. These operations are immediately processed throughout your accounting system.

DacEasy also uses the batch system for operations that require daily or monthly postings. For example, the general ledger is an area where the batch system is used. It's not completely updated until postings have occurred. However, if you need complete up-to-date balance information, the General Ledger Account Activity Detail Report provides this data.

After you've printed and reviewed the various accounting journals, you can post the journal entries. Transferring information from journal entries to ledger accounts is called *posting*. It's important that you complete the print journal operations before proceeding to the posting operations. When you print the various journals, you can review them for accuracy. If you need to make a correction, go to the appropriate transaction and make the change. Then print the journal again. If you find an error after the posting operation, you must enter an adjustment in the general ledger transaction entry operation. Posting sorts journal entry information so all changes affecting each account are brought together in one place. For example, all information about changes in cash are brought together in the cash account.

DacEasy's Posting menu lets you post transactions for a selected month. This feature is beneficial because you can enter the daily activities of the next month while the previous month is still open.

With *DacEasy* you can prepare invoices, make payments, collect money, and purchase supplies for the next month before you close the previous month, and the information you enter won't get mixed in with other months. The only operation you shouldn't perform in a current month while a previous month is still open is the posting operation. If you post a new month before the previous month is posted, your accounting system will be inaccurate.

After you've entered all the previous month's general ledger transactions, and after you've reviewed, corrected, posted, and printed financial statements for the previous month, you can close the month, then post to the general ledger for the next month.

Before running the general ledger posting operations, it's important that you make a backup of your *DacEasy* data files. That way, if there's a power or hardware failure during this operation, valuable information won't be lost.

When you complete the posting operation, *DacEasy* automatically sends a summary transaction to the general ledger transaction file, and updates your customer, vendor, inventory, and general ledger files.

To post your journals, highlight the Posting menu from the Opening menu. Press Enter.

The screen in Figure 5-25 will appear.

As you can see, six posting options are available. These options are described below.

General Ledger. The General Ledger posting option is used to update general ledger account balances with entries recorded in the transaction file. It's important to back up your *DacEasy* date files before running this operation.

Figure 5-25. The Posting Menu

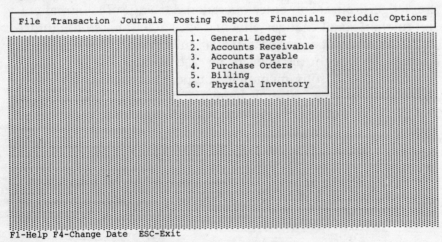

```
 File  Transaction  Journals  Posting  Reports  Financials  Periodic  Options

                              1.  General Ledger
                              2.  Accounts Receivable
                              3.  Accounts Payable
                              4.  Purchase Orders
                              5.  Billing
                              6.  Physical Inventory
```

```
F1-Help F4-Change Date   ESC-Exit
```

Accounts Receivable. The Accounts Receivable posting option is used to update customer balances. This operation also provides summary transactions for the general ledger. Back up your data files before running this operation.

Accounts Payable. The Accounts Payable posting option is used to update vendor balances. This operation also prepares the check register for your checking accounts and provides summary transactions for the general ledger. Back up your data files before running this operation.

Purchase Orders. The Purchase Order posting option is used to update the statistical history in your product and vendor files. This operation also updates the general ledger.

Billing. The Billing posting option is used to update the statistical history in your product and customer files. The general ledger is also updated.

Physical Inventory. The Physical Inventory option is used to post the differences (adjustments). Make sure you've entered the physical inventory count accurately before running this operation. After you've run this posting operation, the Inventory and Cost of Goods Sold accounts (indicated in the G/L Interface table) will receive the adjustments.

Posting Accounts Payable Transactions

To select the Accounts Payable posting operation, follow these steps:

1. Highlight the Posting menu from the Opening menu. Press Enter.
2. Press 3 from the Posting menu to select the Accounts Payable posting operation.

    The screen in Figure 5-26 will appear.

    If you need to back up your data files, do so at this time. Note: The Accounts Receivable and Physical Inventory posting operations will also display this screen.

    The cursor should be positioned at the field that reads *Do you want to continue.* Type *N* and press Enter to exit this operation and back up your files or press Enter to continue.

3. Press Enter.

    DacEasy will post all Accounts Payable transactions to the general ledger, and the amount will be printed as shown on following page:

171

Figure 5-26. DacEasy Awaiting Confirmation Before Posting

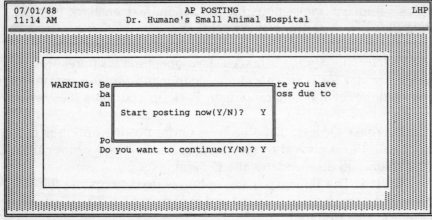

```
07/01/88                          AP POSTING                              LHP
11:14 AM                Dr. Humane's Small Animal Hospital


        WARNING: Be ┌─────────────────────────────────┐ re you have
                 ba │                                 │ oss due to
                 an │                                 │
                    │    Start posting now(Y/N)?   Y  │
                    │                                 │
                    │                                 │
                 Po └─────────────────────────────────┘
                    Do you want to continue(Y/N)? Y

```

F1-Help ESC-Exit

Posted to G/L
Total Debits: 731.00
Total Credits: 731.00

Posting Purchase Order Transactions

Purchase Orders should be posted next. If you attempt to post
Billing transactions before Purchase Orders, the message in Figure 5-27 will appear.

Figure 5-27. Warning to Post Purchase Orders Before Billing Transactions

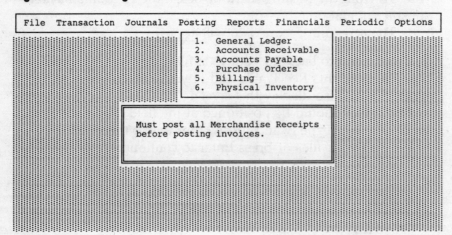

```
File   Transaction  Journals  Posting  Reports  Financials  Periodic  Options

                              1.   General Ledger
                              2.   Accounts Receivable
                              3.   Accounts Payable
                              4.   Purchase Orders
                              5.   Billing
                              6.   Physical Inventory

                   ┌──────────────────────────────────┐
                   │  Must post all Merchandise Receipts│
                   │  before posting invoices.          │
                   └──────────────────────────────────┘
```

To select the Purchase Order posting operation, follow these steps:

1. Highlight the Posting menu from the Opening menu. Press Enter.
2. Press 4 from the Posting menu to select the Purchase Orders posting operation.

    The screen in Figure 5-28 will appear.

    Note: The Billing posting operation will also display this screen.

    The cursor should be positioned at the field that reads *Do you want to continue*. Type *N* and press Enter to exit this operation (for instance, if you need to run any of the operations that appear on the screen). Otherwise, press Enter to accept the default.

3. Press Enter.

    The screen in Figure 5-29 will appear.
4. Press Enter again to start the posting process.

    When the purchase order transactions are posted, the screen will display the Posting menu.

Posting to the General Ledger

The General Ledger posting operation updates the general ledger account balances with all entries processed in the transaction file.

Figure 5-28. Confirm Intention to Continue Posting

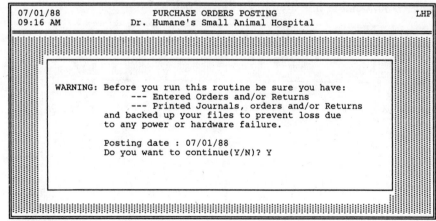

```
07/01/88                    PURCHASE ORDERS POSTING                         LHP
09:16 AM              Dr. Humane's Small Animal Hospital




          WARNING: Before you run this routine be sure you have:
                      --- Entered Orders and/or Returns
                      --- Printed Journals, orders and/or Returns
                   and backed up your files to prevent loss due
                   to any power or hardware failure.

                   Posting date : 07/01/88
                   Do you want to continue(Y/N)? Y




F1-Help ESC-Exit
```

Figure 5-29. DacEasy Awaits Confirmation Before Posting Purchase Orders

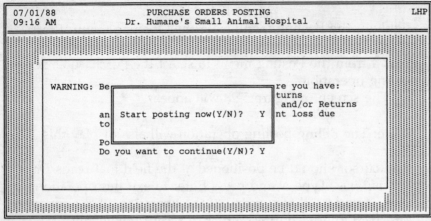

To select the General Ledger posting operation, follow these steps:

1. Highlight the Posting menu from the Opening menu. Press Enter.
2. Press 1 from the Posting menu to select the General Ledger posting operation.

   The screen in Figure 5-30 will appear.

The cursor should be located at the field that reads *Do you want to continue*. Type *N* and press Enter to exit this operation (for

Figure 5-30. Confirm Intention to Continue Posting

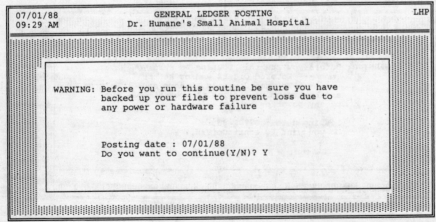

Figure 5-31. Enter Month to Be Posted

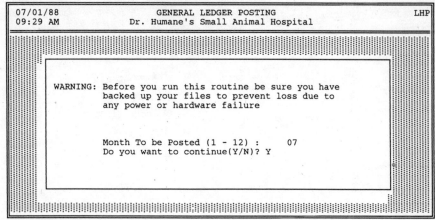

```
07/01/88                GENERAL LEDGER POSTING                    LHP
09:29 AM           Dr. Humane's Small Animal Hospital


         WARNING: Before you run this routine be sure you have
                  backed up your files to prevent loss due to
                  any power or hardware failure



         Month To be Posted (1 - 12) :      07
         Do you want to continue(Y/N)? Y
```

F1-Help ESC-Exit

instance, if you need to back up your files) or press Enter to continue.

3. Press Enter.

The screen will change as shown in Figure 5-31.

DacEasy gives you the option to post to a selected month. This feature is beneficial because you can enter the daily activities of the next month while the previous month is still open. When you post to a previous month, any transactions entered for the current month will not be included. Press Enter to accept *DacEasy*'s default, or type the month you want to post, then press Enter.

4. Press Enter.
5. Press Enter again to start the posting process.

DacEasy will post all applicable transactions to the general ledger, and information will be printed as shown below.

Transactions with Journal Difference Account Movements:
SU 0701
SU 0701
SU 0701
SU 0701
SU 0001

Total Posted to G/L
Total Debits: 1861.19
Total Credits: 1861.19

175

Chapter 6
DacEasy's Report Operations

DacEasy's Reports

DacEasy lets you print comprehensive reports for three of its modules:

- Accounts Receivable
- Accounts Payable
- Inventory

These reports are extremely beneficial for evaluating several aspects of your business including providing a balance between purchases and disbursement management, providing a balance between sales and collection management, and providing necessary information regarding product quotas, promotion planning, purchase negotiations, marketing, and price assignments.

Note: To ensure accuracy of all reports, print them after all your accounting transactions have been posted to the general ledger.

The following describes all of the Report menu's options.

Accounts Receivable Reports

DacEasy's Accounts Receivable reports include:

- Statements
- Aging
- Directory
- Labels

The Accounts Receivable Statements Report

The Statements option provides five sorts and ten rankings you can select when printing statements. Reminding customers of any invoices that may still be open is just one useful way this statement operation benefits your business.

Printing the Accounts Receivable Statements Report. To print the Accounts Receivable Statements Report, follow these steps:

1. Highlight the Reports menu from the Opening menu. Press Enter.
2. Press 1 to select the Accounts Receivable Reports submenu.
3. Press 1 to select the Statements option.
    The screen in Figure 6-1 will appear.

The cursor should be positioned at the first Enter Your Selection field. To sort the Statements Report by Code:

4. Type 1 and press Enter.
    The screen in Figure 6-2 will appear.

To print all records by Code:

5. Press Enter twice.
    DacEasy will automatically enter the words *First Record* at the From field and *Last Record* at the To field. The cursor will then move to the second Enter Your Selection field.
    To rank the Statements Report by Code:
6. Type 1 and press Enter.
    To print all records ranked by Code:
7. Press Enter twice.

Figure 6-1. The Accounts Receivable Statements Screen

```
 07/01/88           Accounts Receivable Statements           LHP
 09:33 AM          Dr. Humane's Small Animal Hospital


    Sort By :                          Rank By :

    1  Code                           1  Code
    2  Name                           2  Name
    3  Department                     3  Credit Limit
    4  Sales Person                   4  Credit Available
    5  Zip Code                       5  Balance
                                      6  Last Sales Date
    Enter Your Selection :            7  Last Payment Date
                                      8  Sales Units
                                      9  Sales Dollars
                                     10  Profit

                                      Enter Your Selection :
```

Figure 6-2. The Sorting Screen

```
07/01/88                 Accounts Receivable Statements                    LHP
09:33 AM                 Dr. Humane's Small Animal Hospital


                                               Rank By :
         Sorted by : Code
                                               1  Code
         From :                                2  Name
         To   :                                3  Credit Limit
                                               4  Credit Available
                                               5  Balance
                                               6  Last Sales Date
                                               7  Last Payment Date
                                               8  Sales Units
                                               9  Sales Dollars
                                              10  Profit

                                               Enter Your Selection :




F1-Help F4-Change Date  ESC-Exit
```

DacEasy will automatically enter the words *First Record* at
the From field and *Last Record* at the To field. Then the closing date will appear on the screen. Press Enter to accept the
date that's displayed or type the new date, then press Enter.
8. Press Enter.

The screen in Figure 6-3 will appear.

If you're using preprinted forms, type *Y* and press Enter. If
you're using plain paper, press Enter to accept the default. This
will indicate to *DacEasy* that column headings should be printed
in the report.

Figure 6-3. Setup to Rank by Code

```
07/01/88                 Accounts Receivable Statements                    LHP
09:58 AM                 Dr. Humane's Small Animal Hospital


         Sorted by : Code                      Ranked by : Code

         From : (First Record)                 From : (First Record)
         To   : (Last Record)                  To   : (Last Record)

                        Closing Date: 07/01/88
                        Preprinted forms(Y/N)? N
```

Figure 6-4. Screen to Confirm Whether to Print Only Those Customers with Outstanding Balances

```
07/01/88              Accounts Receivable Statements            LHP
09:33 AM              Dr. Humane's Small Animal Hospital


   Sorted by : Code                  Ranked by : Code

   From : (First Record)             From : (First Record)
   To   : (Last Re┌──────────────────────────────────┐cord)
                   │ Do you want to include Customers │
                   │ with zero balance (Y/N) ?    Y   │
                   │                                  │
                   │                                  │
                   └──────────────────────────────────┘




```

F1-Help F4-Change Date   ESC-Exit

9. Press Enter.

    The screen in Figure 6-4 will appear.

If you want to include all customers, press Enter. If you only want to include customers with outstanding balances, type *N*, then press Enter.

10. Press Enter.

    DacEasy will display a message asking if you want to print the Code in the statement. If you do, type *Y* and press Enter. If you don't, press Enter to accept the default.

11. Press Enter.

    The Statements Report will start printing.

The Accounts Receivable Aging Report

The Accounts Receivable Aging Report option provides five sorts and ten rankings you can select when printing this report. You also have the option to print this report in detail (by each invoice entry) or in summary (by invoice totals). If you want to analyze your business' cash flow, you can also print an Accounts Payable Aging Report (explained later in this chapter). Use the same sort and ranking when defining both reports. Then, when you place both reports next to each other, you'll easily be able to analyze and compare cash flow.

Printing the Accounts Receivable Aging Report. To print the Accounts Receivable Aging Report, follow these steps:

1. Highlight the Reports menu from the Opening menu. Press Enter.
2. Press 1 to select the Accounts Receivable Reports submenu.
3. Press 2 to select the Aging Report option.
     The screen in Figure 6-5 will appear.

     The cursor should be positioned at the first Enter Your Selection field.
     To sort the Aging Report by Name:

4. Type 2 and press Enter.
     To print all records sorted by Name:
5. Press Enter twice.
     DacEasy will automatically enter the words *First Record* at the From field and *Last Record* at the To field.
     The screen in Figure 6-6 will appear.

     The cursor will move to the second Enter Your Selection field.
     To rank the Aging Report by Balance:

6. Type 5 and press Enter.
     The screen in Figure 6-7 will appear.

     At this point you can enter the minimum to maximum balances you want *DacEasy* to print.

Figure 6-5. The Accounts Receivable Aging Report Screen

```
07/01/88              Accounts Receivable Aging Report              LHP
09:58 AM              Dr. Humane's Small Animal Hospital


      Sort By :                          Rank By :

      1  Code                            1  Code
      2  Name                            2  Name
      3  Department                      3  Credit Limit
      4  Sales Person                    4  Credit Available
      5  Zip Code                        5  Balance
                                         6  Last Sales Date
      Enter Your Selection :             7  Last Payment Date
                                         8  Sales Units
                                         9  Sales Dollars
                                        10  Profit

                                         Enter Your Selection :

```

Figure 6-6. Screen Prepared to Sort by Name

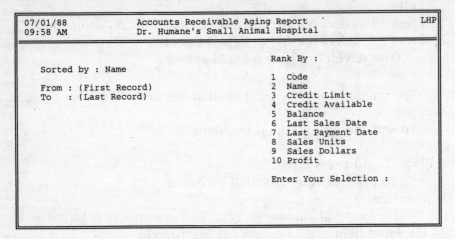

```
07/01/88            Accounts Receivable Aging Report           LHP
09:58 AM            Dr. Humane's Small Animal Hospital

                                     Rank By :

   Sorted by : Name                  1   Code
                                     2   Name
   From : (First Record)             3   Credit Limit
   To   : (Last Record)             4   Credit Available
                                     5   Balance
                                     6   Last Sales Date
                                     7   Last Payment Date
                                     8   Sales Units
                                     9   Sales Dollars
                                     10  Profit

                                     Enter Your Selection :
```

7. Type 50 at the From field. Press Enter.
8. Type 2000 at the To field. Press Enter.

    The closing date will appear on the screen. Press Enter to accept the date that's displayed or type the new date, then press Enter.

9. Press Enter.

    The screen in Figure 6-8 will appear.

    To print the Aging Report by Detail (by each invoice entry), press Enter. To print the report by Summary (by invoice totals), type *S*, then press Enter.

Figure 6-7. Screen Prepared to Rank by Balance

```
07/01/88            Accounts Receivable Aging Report           LHP
09:58 AM            Dr. Humane's Small Animal Hospital


   Sorted by : Name                  Ranked by : Balance

   From : (First Record)             From :
   To   : (Last Record)             To   :
```

Figure 6-8. Minimum and Maximum Balances Entered

```
07/01/88                Accounts Receivable Aging Report              LHP
10:08 AM                Dr. Humane's Small Animal Hospital


    Sorted by : Name                    Ranked by : Balance

    From : (First Record)               From :        50.000
    To   : (Last Record)                To   :      2000.000

            Closing Date: 07/01/88
            (D)etail or (S)ummary Report? D

                          From      To
            Column    1:  9999 -     61
                      2:    60 -     31
                      3:    30 -      1
                      4:     0 -    -30
                      5:   -31 -    -60
                      6:   -61 -    -90
                      7:   -91 - -9999
```

10. Press Enter.

    DacEasy will display a message asking if you want to edit the aging schedule. Type *Y* and press Enter to edit the schedule; press Enter to leave it as is.

11. Press Enter.

    The Aging Report will start printing.

The Accounts Receivable Customer Directory

The Accounts Receivable Directory option provides five sorts and ten rankings so you can print customer directories.

Printing the Accounts Receivable Directory. To print the Accounts Receivable Directory, follow these steps:

1. Highlight the Reports menu from the Opening menu. Press Enter.
2. Press 1 to select the Accounts Receivable Reports submenu.
3. Press 3 to select the Directory option.

    The screen in Figure 6-9 will appear.

    The cursor should be positioned at the first Enter Your Selection field.

    To sort the Directory by Name:

4. Type 2 and press Enter.

    To print all records sorted by Name:

5. Press Enter twice.

Figure 6-9. The Customer Directory Screen

```
07/01/88                    Customer Directory                    LHP
10:19 AM              Dr. Humane's Small Animal Hospital

       Sort By :                        Rank By :

       1  Code                          1  Code
       2  Name                          2  Name
       3  Department                    3  Credit Limit
       4  Sales Person                  4  Credit Available
       5  Zip Code                      5  Balance
                                        6  Last Sales Date
       Enter Your Selection :           7  Last Payment Date
                                        8  Sales Units
                                        9  Sales Dollars
                                        10 Profit

                                        Enter Your Selection :
```

DacEasy will automatically enter the words *First Record* at
the From field and *Last Record* at the To field.

The screen will look like the one in Figure 6-10.

The cursor will move to the second Enter Your Selection
field.

To rank the Directory by Code:

6. Type 1 and press Enter.

To print all records ranked by Code:

Figure 6-10. The Screen Prepared to Sort the Entire Customer Directory

```
07/01/88                    Customer Directory                    LHP
10:26 AM              Dr. Humane's Small Animal Hospital

                                        Rank By :

       Sorted by : Name                 1  Code
                                        2  Name
       From : (First Record)            3  Credit Limit
       To   : (Last Record)             4  Credit Available
                                        5  Balance
                                        6  Last Sales Date
                                        7  Last Payment Date
                                        8  Sales Units
                                        9  Sales Dollars
                                        10 Profit

                                        Enter Your Selection :
```

7. Press Enter twice.

    DacEasy will automatically enter the words *First Record* at the From field and *Last Record* at the To field.

    The Directory will start printing.

The Accounts Receivable Labels Operation

The Labels option provides five sorts and ten rankings so you can print labels for mailings, phone/address cards, and so on. Each label has a default height of six lines. However, this default can be changed to suit the size of your labels.

    Printing Accounts Receivable Labels. To print customer labels, follow these steps:

1. Highlight the Reports menu from the Opening menu. Press Enter.
2. Press 1 to select the Accounts Receivable Reports submenu.
3. Press 4 to select the Labels option.

    The screen in Figure 6-11 will appear.

    The cursor should be positioned at the first Enter Your Selection field.

    To sort labels by zip code (if you're sending a bulk mailing, sorting by zip code is the most efficient option):

4. Type 5 and press Enter.

    To print all records sorted by zip code:

Figure 6-11. The Customer Labels Screen

```
07/01/88                      Customer Labels                        LHP
10:30 AM             Dr. Humane's Small Animal Hospital


     Sort By :                            Rank By :

     1  Code                              1  Code
     2  Name                              2  Name
     3  Department                        3  Credit Limit
     4  Sales Person                      4  Credit Available
     5  Zip Code                          5  Balance
                                          6  Last Sales Date
     Enter Your Selection :               7  Last Payment Date
                                          8  Sales Units
                                          9  Sales Dollars
                                          10 Profit

                                          Enter Your Selection :
```

Figure 6-12. The Screen Prepared to Sort by Zip Code

```
┌─────────────────────────────────────────────────────────────────┐
│ 07/01/88                    Customer Labels                  LHP  │
│ 10:30 AM          Dr. Humane's Small Animal Hospital             │
├─────────────────────────────────────────────────────────────────┤
│                                      Rank By :                   │
│      Sorted by : Zip Code                                        │
│                                      1  Code                     │
│      From : (First Record)           2  Name                     │
│      To   : (Last Record)            3  Credit Limit            │
│                                      4  Credit Available         │
│                                      5  Balance                  │
│                                      6  Last Sales Date          │
│                                      7  Last Payment Date        │
│                                      8  Sales Units              │
│                                      9  Sales Dollars            │
│                                      10 Profit                   │
│                                                                  │
│                                      Enter Your Selection :      │
│                                                                  │
│                                                                  │
└─────────────────────────────────────────────────────────────────┘
```

5. Press Enter twice.

   DacEasy will automatically enter the words *First Record* at the From field and *Last Record* at the To field.

   The screen will look like the one in Figure 6-12.

   The cursor will move to the second Enter Your Selection field.

   To rank the labels by Name:

6. Type 2 and press Enter.

   To print all records ranked by Name:

7. Press Enter twice.

   DacEasy will automatically enter the words *First Record* at the From field and *Last Record* at the To field.

   The screen in Figure 6-13 will appear.

   If you want the customer code included on the label, press Enter to accept the default. If you don't, type *N*, then press Enter.

8. Type *N*, then press Enter.

   DacEasy will display a message asking if you want the customer's phone number included on the label. Press Enter to include the phone number; type *N*, then press Enter if you don't want the phone number to appear.

Figure 6-13. The Screen Prepared to Sort Customer Labels by Zip Code and Name

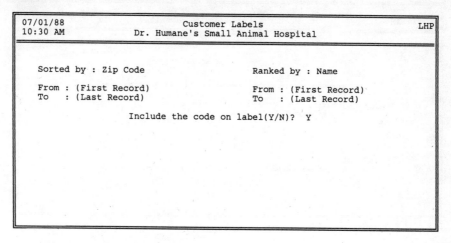

```
07/01/88                      Customer Labels                         LHP
10:30 AM              Dr. Humane's Small Animal Hospital


     Sorted by : Zip Code                Ranked by : Name

     From : (First Record)               From : (First Record)
     To   : (Last Record)                To   : (Last Record)

                 Include the code on label(Y/N)?  Y
```

9. Type *N* and press Enter.

   The screen in Figure 6-14 will appear.

DacEasy lets you choose the maximum number of lines you want printed on each label. Make sure the number you choose corresponds with the size of the label you're using.

10. Press Enter to accept the default.

    The screen in Figure 6-15 will appear.
11. Position your labels in the printer; then press any key to check the alignment.

Figure 6-14. The Current Customer Labels Screen

```
07/01/88                      Customer Labels                         LHP
10:30 AM              Dr. Humane's Small Animal Hospital


     Sorted by : Zip Code                Ranked by : Name

     From : (First Record)               From : (First Record)
     To   : (Last Record)               To   : (Last Record)

                 Include the code on label(Y/N)?  N
                 Include the phone on label(Y/N)?  N
                 Lines per label...:   6
```

Figure 6-15. Initial Label-Alignment Screen

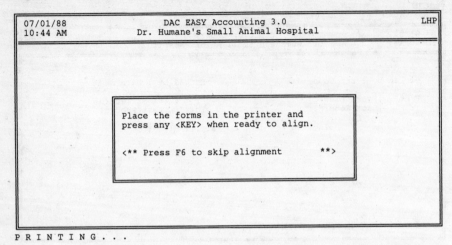

A row of 1s (11111111111) will print at the top of your form. *DacEasy* will then display a message asking you if the forms are aligned. Press Enter if they are. If they're not aligned, realign them, then type *N* and press Enter. The alignment test will repeat.

12. Press Enter.

The labels will start printing.

Accounts Payable Reports

DacEasy's Accounts Payable Reports include

- Statements
- Aging
- Directory
- Labels
- Payment Report
- Print 1099s

The Accounts Payable Statements Report

The Accounts Payable Statements option provides five sorts and nine rankings so you can print statements reminding vendors of invoices that are still open.

Printing the Accounts Payable Statements Report. To print the Accounts Payable Statements Report, follow these steps:

1. Highlight the Reports menu from the Opening menu. Press Enter.
2. Press 2 to select the Accounts Payable Reports submenu.
3. Press 1 to select the Statements option.
   The screen in Figure 6-16 will appear.

The cursor should be positioned at the Enter Your Selection field.
   To sort the Statements Report by Code:

4. Type 1 and press Enter.
   The screen in Figure 6-17 will appear.
5. Press Enter twice.
   DacEasy will automatically enter the word *First Record* at the From field and *Last Record* at the To field. The cursor will then move to the second Enter Your Selection field.
   To rank the Statements Report by Code:
6. Type 1 and press Enter.
   The screen in Figure 6-18 will appear.

To print all records ranked by Code:

7. Press Enter twice.
   DacEasy will automatically enter the words *First Record* at the From field and *Last Record* at the To field. Then the closing date will appear on the screen. Press Enter to accept the date displayed or type the new date, then press Enter.

Figure 6-16. The Accounts Payable Statements Screen

```
07/01/88                 Acccounts Payable Statements                    LHP
10:35 AM             Dr. Humane's Small Animal Hospital
═══════════════════════════════════════════════════════════════════════════

      Sort By :                          Rank By :

      1  Code                            1  Code
      2  Name                            2  Name
      3  Type                            3  Credit Limit
      4  Territory                       4  Credit Available
      5  Zip Code                        5  Balance
                                         6  Last Purchase Date
      Enter Your Selection :             7  Last Payment Date
                                         8  Purchase Units
                                         9  Purchase Dollars

                                         Enter Your Selection :
```

Figure 6-17. The Screen Prepared to Sort by Code

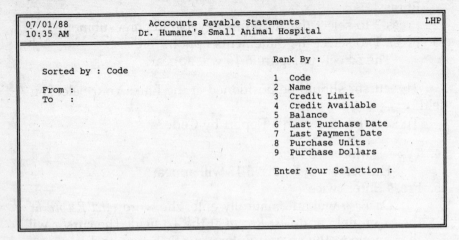

```
07/01/88                Acccounts Payable Statements              LHP
10:35 AM              Dr. Humane's Small Animal Hospital

                                    Rank By :

    Sorted by : Code
                                    1  Code
    From :                          2  Name
    To  :                           3  Credit Limit
                                    4  Credit Available
                                    5  Balance
                                    6  Last Purchase Date
                                    7  Last Payment Date
                                    8  Purchase Units
                                    9  Purchase Dollars

                                    Enter Your Selection :
```

To print all records by Code:

8. Press Enter.
     The screen in Figure 6-19 will appear.

If you're using preprinted forms, type *Y* and press Enter. If you're using plain paper, press Enter to accept the default. This will indicate to *DacEasy* that column headings should be printed in the report.

9. Press Enter.
     The screen in Figure 6-20 will appear.

Figure 6-18. The Screen Prepared to Sort and Rank by Code

```
07/01/88                Acccounts Payable Statements              LHP
10:40 AM              Dr. Humane's Small Animal Hospital


    Sorted by : Code                 Ranked by : Code

    From : (First Record)            From :
    To   : (Last Record)            To   :
```

Figure 6-19. The Screen Inquires Whether Preprinted Forms Are Being Used

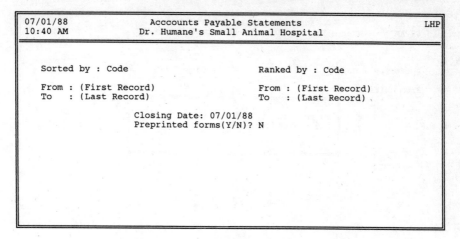

```
07/01/88                 Acccounts Payable Statements            LHP
10:40 AM              Dr. Humane's Small Animal Hospital


   Sorted by : Code                   Ranked by : Code

   From : (First Record)              From : (First Record)
   To   : (Last Record)              To   : (Last Record)

                     Closing Date: 07/01/88
                     Preprinted forms(Y/N)? N
```

If you want to include all vendors, press Enter. If you only want to include vendors who you owe money to, type *N*, then press Enter.

10. Press Enter.

The screen in Figure 6-21 will appear.

If you want to print the code in the statement, type *Y* and press Enter. If you don't want to print the code in the statement, press Enter to accept the default.

Figure 6-20. The Option of Printing Vendors with Zero Balances

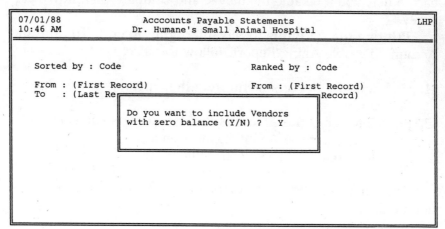

```
07/01/88                 Acccounts Payable Statements            LHP
10:46 AM              Dr. Humane's Small Animal Hospital


   Sorted by : Code                   Ranked by : Code

   From : (First Record)              From : (First Record)
   To   : (Last Re┌──────────────────────────────┐Record)
                  │  Do you want to include Vendors │
                  │  with zero balance (Y/N) ?   Y  │
                  │                                 │
                  └──────────────────────────────┘
```

Figure 6-21. The Screen Inquires Whether to Print the Code

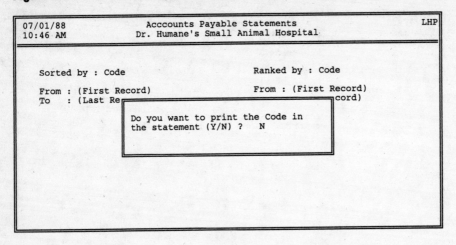

```
07/01/88              Acccounts Payable Statements              LHP
10:46 AM           Dr. Humane's Small Animal Hospital


  Sorted by : Code                    Ranked by : Code

  From : (First Record)               From : (First Record)
  To   : (Last Re┌────────────────────────────────┐cord)
                 │ Do you want to print the Code in│
                 │ the statement (Y/N) ?   N       │
                 │                                 │
                 └────────────────────────────────┘



```

11. Press Enter.

    The Statements Report will start printing.

The Accounts Payable Aging Report

The Aging Report option provides five sorts and nine rankings
you can select when printing this report. You have the option to
print this report in detail (by each invoice entry) or in summary
(by invoice totals). If you want to analyze the cash flow of your
business, you can also print an Accounts Receivable Aging Report
(discussed earlier in this chapter). Use the same sort and ranking
when defining both reports; then if you place both reports next to
each other, you'll be able to analyze and compare cash flow
easily.

Printing the Accounts Receivable Aging Report. To print the
Accounts Payable Aging Report, follow these steps:

1. Highlight the Reports menu from the Opening menu. Press
   Enter.
2. Press 2 to select the Accounts Payable Reports submenu.
3. Press 2 to select the Aging Report option.

   The screen in Figure 6-22 will appear.

The cursor should be positioned at the first Enter Your Selection field.

Figure 6-22. The Accounts Payable Aging Report Screen

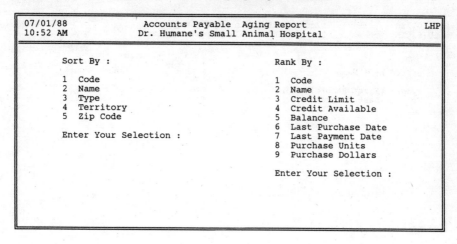

```
07/01/88                Accounts Payable  Aging Report             LHP
10:52 AM                Dr. Humane's Small Animal Hospital

        Sort By :                              Rank By :

        1   Code                              1   Code
        2   Name                              2   Name
        3   Type                              3   Credit Limit
        4   Territory                         4   Credit Available
        5   Zip Code                          5   Balance
                                              6   Last Purchase Date
        Enter Your Selection :                7   Last Payment Date
                                              8   Purchase Units
                                              9   Purchase Dollars

                                              Enter Your Selection :
```

To sort the Aging Report by Name:

4. Type 2 and press Enter.

   To print all records sorted by Name:
5. Press Enter twice.

   DacEasy will automatically enter the words *First Record* at the From field and *Last Record* at the To field.

   The screen in Figure 6-23 will appear.

Figure 6-23. Screen Prepared to Sort by Name

```
07/01/88                Accounts Payable  Aging Report             LHP
10:52 AM                Dr. Humane's Small Animal Hospital

                                             Rank By :
        Sorted by : Name
                                             1   Code
        From : (First Record)                2   Name
        To   : (Last Record)                 3   Credit Limit
                                             4   Credit Available
                                             5   Balance
                                             6   Last Purchase Date
                                             7   Last Payment Date
                                             8   Purchase Units
                                             9   Purchase Dollars

                                             Enter Your Selection :
```

193

Figure 6-24. Screen to Sort by Name and Rank by Balance

```
07/01/88              Accounts Payable  Aging Report              LHP
10:52 AM              Dr. Humane's Small Animal Hospital


  Sorted by : Name                    Ranked by : Balance

  From : (First Record)               From :       .
  To   : (Last Record)                To   :
```

The cursor will move to the second Enter Your Selection field.

To rank the Aging Report by Balance:

6. Type 5 and press Enter.
   The screen in Figure 6-24 will appear.

At this point you can enter the minimum to maximum balances you want *DacEasy* to print.

7. Type 25 at the From field. Press Enter.
8. Type 5000 at the To field. Press Enter.
   The closing date will appear on the screen. Press Enter to accept the date displayed, or type the new date, then press Enter.
9. Press Enter.
   The screen in Figure 6-25 will appear.

To print the Aging Report by Detail (by each invoice entry), press Enter. To print the report by Summary (by invoice totals), type *S*, then press Enter.

10. Press Enter.
    DacEasy will display a message asking if you want to edit the aging schedule. Type *Y* and press Enter to edit the schedule; press Enter to leave it as is.

Figure 6-25. The Accounts Payable Aging Report Screen with Closing Date Entered

```
07/01/88              Accounts Payable  Aging Report            LHP
10:52 AM             Dr. Humane's Small Animal Hospital


   Sorted by : Name                    Ranked by : Balance

   From : (First Record)               From :        25.000
   To   : (Last Record)                To   :      5000.000

               Closing Date: 07/01/88
               (D)etail or (S)ummary Report? D

                           From     To
               Column  1:  9999 -     61
                       2:    60 -     31
                       3:    30 -      1
                       4:     0 -    -30
                       5:   -31 -    -60
                       6:   -61 -    -90
                       7:   -91 - -9999
```

11. Press Enter.

    The Aging Report will start printing.

The Accounts Payable Vendor Directory

The Accounts Payable Directory option provides five sorts and nine rankings so you can print vendor directories.

Printing the Accounts Payable Directory. To print the Accounts Payable Directory, follow these steps:

1. Highlight the Reports menu from the Opening menu. Press Enter.
2. Press 2 to select the Accounts Payable Reports submenu.
3. Press 3 to select the Directory option.

    The screen in Figure 6-26 will appear.

    The cursor should be positioned at the first Enter Your Selection field.

    To sort the Directory by Name:

4. Type 2 and press Enter.

    To print all records sorted by Name:

5. Press Enter twice.

    DacEasy will automatically enter the words *First Record* at the From field and *Last Record* at the To field.

Figure 6-26. The Vendor Directory Screen

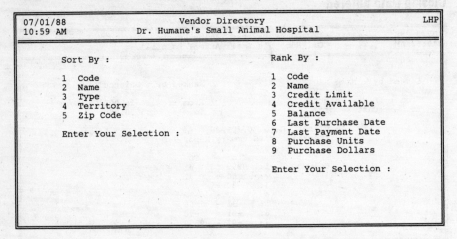

```
07/01/88                    Vendor Directory                      LHP
10:59 AM            Dr. Humane's Small Animal Hospital


    Sort By :                           Rank By :

    1  Code                             1  Code
    2  Name                             2  Name
    3  Type                             3  Credit Limit
    4  Territory                        4  Credit Available
    5  Zip Code                         5  Balance
                                        6  Last Purchase Date
    Enter Your Selection :              7  Last Payment Date
                                        8  Purchase Units
                                        9  Purchase Dollars

                                        Enter Your Selection :
```

The cursor will move to the second Enter Your Selection field.

To rank the Directory by Code:

6. Type 1 and press Enter.

The screen in Figure 6-27 will appear.

To print all records ranked by Code:

7. Press Enter twice.

DacEasy will automatically enter the words *First Record* at the From field and *Last Record* at the To field.

The Directory will start printing.

Figure 6-27. Sorting the Vendor Directory by Name and Ranking by Code

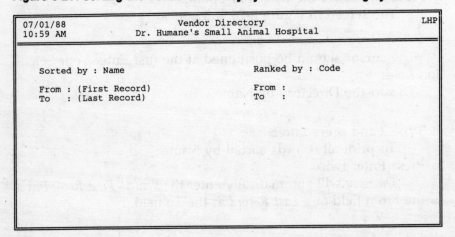

```
07/01/88                    Vendor Directory                      LHP
10:59 AM            Dr. Humane's Small Animal Hospital


    Sorted by : Name                    Ranked by : Code

    From : (First Record)               From :
    To   : (Last Record)                To   :
```

The Accounts Payable Labels Operation

The Accounts Payable Labels option provides five sorts and nine rankings so you can print labels for mailings, phone/address cards, and so on. Each label has a default height of six lines; however, this default can be changed to suit the size of your labels.

Printing Accounts Payable Labels. To print vendor labels, follow these steps:

1. Highlight the Reports menu from the Opening menu. Press Enter.
2. Press 2 to select the Accounts Payable Reports submenu.
3. Press 4 to select the Labels option.
   The screen in Figure 6-28 will appear.

The cursor should be positioned at the first Enter Your Selection field.

To sort labels by zip code (if you're sending a bulk mailing, sorting by zip code is the most efficient option):

4. Type 5 and press Enter.
   To print all records sorted by zip code:
5. Press Enter twice.
   DacEasy will automatically enter the words *First Record* at the From field and *Last Record* at the To field.
   The screen will look like the one in Figure 6-29.

Figure 6-28. The Vendor Labels Screen

```
07/01/88                     Vendor Labels                      LHP
11:04 AM          Dr. Humane's Small Animal Hospital

       Sort By :                          Rank By :

       1  Code                            1  Code
       2  Name                            2  Name
       3  Type                            3  Credit Limit
       4  Territory                       4  Credit Available
       5  Zip Code                        5  Balance
                                          6  Last Purchase Date
       Enter Your Selection :            7  Last Payment Date
                                          8  Purchase Units
                                          9  Purchase Dollars

                                          Enter Your Selection :
```

Figure 6-29. The Screen Prepared to Sort by Zip Code

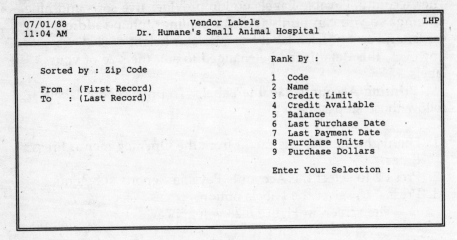

```
07/01/88                    Vendor Labels                       LHP
11:04 AM            Dr. Humane's Small Animal Hospital

                                     Rank By :

     Sorted by : Zip Code            1   Code
                                     2   Name
     From : (First Record)           3   Credit Limit
     To   : (Last Record)            4   Credit Available
                                     5   Balance
                                     6   Last Purchase Date
                                     7   Last Payment Date
                                     8   Purchase Units
                                     9   Purchase Dollars

                                     Enter Your Selection :
```

The cursor will move to the second Enter Your Selection field.

To rank the labels by Name:

6. Type 2 and press Enter.

   To print all records ranked by Name:

7. Press Enter twice.

   DacEasy will automatically enter the words *First Record* at the From field and *Last Record* at the To field.

   The screen in Figure 6-30 will appear.

Figure 6-30. The Screen Prepared to Sort by Zip Code and Rank by Name

```
07/01/88                    Vendor Labels                       LHP
11:04 AM            Dr. Humane's Small Animal Hospital


     Sorted by : Zip Code            Ranked by : Name

     From : (First Record)           From : (First Record)
     To   : (Last Record)            To   : (Last Record)

              Include the code on label(Y/N)?   Y
```

If you want the vendor's code included on the label, press Enter to accept the default. If you don't want the vendor's code included on the label, type *N*, then press Enter.

8. Type *N*, then press Enter.

    DacEasy will display a message asking if you want the vendor's phone number included on the label. Press Enter to include the phone number; type *N*, then press Enter if you don't want the phone number to appear.
9. Type *N* and press Enter.

    The screen in Figure 6-31 will appear.

DacEasy lets you choose the maximum number of lines you want printed on each label. Make sure the number you choose corresponds with the size of the label you're using.

10. Press Enter to accept the default.

    The screen in Figure 6-32 will appear.
11. Position your labels in the printer; then press any key to check the alignment.

    A row of 1s (111111111111) will print at the top of your form.

    DacEasy will display a message asking you if the forms are aligned. Press Enter if they are; if they're not, realign them, then type *N* and press Enter. The alignment test will repeat.

Figure 6-31. The Current Vendor Label Screen

```
07/01/88                       Vendor Labels                            LHP
11:04 AM           Dr. Humane's Small Animal Hospital


   Sorted by : Zip Code                  Ranked by : Name

   From : (First Record)                 From : (First Record)
   To   : (Last Record)                  To   : (Last Record)

                   Include the code on label(Y/N)?  N
                   Include the phone on label(Y/N)? N
                   Lines per label...:   6




```

Figure 6-32. The Alignment Screen

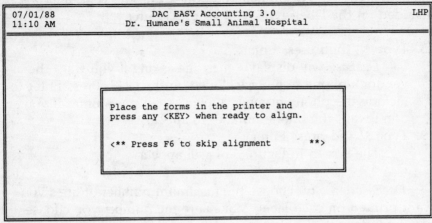

```
07/01/88                    DAC EASY Accounting 3.0                      LHP
11:10 AM                Dr. Humane's Small Animal Hospital




              ┌──────────────────────────────────────────┐
              │                                            │
              │   Place the forms in the printer and       │
              │   press any <KEY> when ready to align.     │
              │                                            │
              │   <** Press F6 to skip alignment      **>  │
              │                                            │
              └──────────────────────────────────────────┘




PRINTING . . .
```

12. Press Enter.
    The labels will begin printing.

The Accounts Payable Payments Report

The Accounts Payable Payments Report lets you generate a report
listing all invoices, when they're due, and any applicable discounts. Two sorting options are available when you print this
report. It can be subtotaled by:

• Date
• Vendor

Printing the Accounts Payable Payments Report. To print the
Accounts Payable Payment Report, follow these steps:

1. Highlight the Reports menu from the Opening menu. Press
   Enter.
2. Press 2 to select the Accounts Payable Reports submenu.
3. Press 5 to select the Payments Report option.
       The screen in Figure 6-33 will appear.

   To print the report subtotaled by vendor,

4. Type 2 and press Enter.
       The screen in Figure 6-34 will appear.

200

Figure 6-33. The Accounts Payable Payment Report Screen

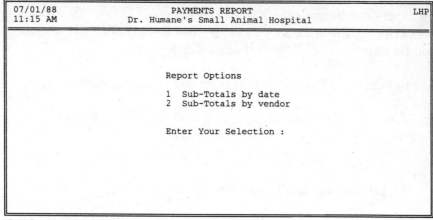

```
07/01/88                    PAYMENTS REPORT                        LHP
11:15 AM             Dr. Humane's Small Animal Hospital
═══════════════════════════════════════════════════════════════════════



                         Report Options

                         1   Sub-Totals by date
                         2   Sub-Totals by vendor


                         Enter Your Selection :




```
F1-Help F4-Change Date   ESC-Exit

To print all applicable records subtotaled by vendor:

5. Press Enter twice.

DacEasy will automatically enter the words *First Date* at the From field and *Last Date* at the To field.

The Payments Report will start printing.

The Accounts Payable 1099 Report

The Print 1099s option is a new feature *DacEasy* added to Version 3.0. It prints a listing of all vendors who must receive federal

Figure 6-34. The Screen Prompts You to Enter Beginning and Ending Dates

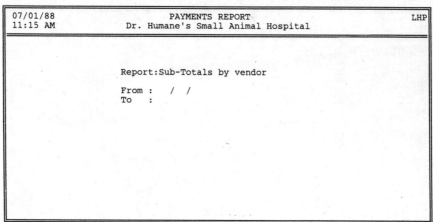

```
07/01/88                    PAYMENTS REPORT                        LHP
11:15 AM             Dr. Humane's Small Animal Hospital
═══════════════════════════════════════════════════════════════════════


                  Report:Sub-Totals by vendor

                  From :   /  /
                  To   :





```
F1-Help F4-Change Date   ESC-Exit

form 1099 from you at the end of the calendar year. You must enter both the vendor's Tax Id. Number and the minimum payment amount before printing this report.

Printing the Accounts Payable 1099 Report. To print the Accounts Payable 1099 Report, follow these steps:

1. Highlight the Reports menu from the Opening menu. Press Enter.
2. Press 2 to select the Accounts Payable Reports submenu.
3. Press 6 to select the Print 1099s option.
   The screen in Figure 6-35 will appear.

   To print all applicable vendors:

4. Enter the vendor's Tax Id. Number at the first field. Press Enter.
   The screen in Figure 6-36 will appear.
5. Press Enter to start printing the report.

Inventory Reports

DacEasy's Inventory Reports include:

• Product Listing
• Product Price List

Figure 6-35. The Initial Print 1099s Screen

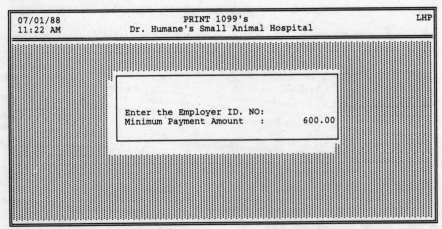

```
07/01/88                    PRINT 1099's                        LHP
11:22 AM          Dr. Humane's Small Animal Hospital




               Enter the Employer ID. NO:
               Minimum Payment Amount    :        600.00



F1-Help F4-Change Date   ESC-Exit
```

- Product Activity Report
- Product Alert Report
- Service Report
- Print Count Sheets
- Physical Perpetual Comparison Report

The Product Listing Report

The Product Listing option provides 5 sorts and 13 rankings so you can print a product catalog.

Printing the Product Listing Report. To print the Product Listing Report, follow these steps:

1. Highlight the Reports menu from the Opening menu. Press Enter.
2. Press 3 to select the Inventory Reports submenu.
3. Press 1 to select the Product Listing option.
    The screen in Figure 6-37 will appear.

    The cursor should be positioned at the first Enter Your Selection field.
    To sort the Product Listing Report by Description:

4. Type 2 and press Enter.
    To print all products sorted by Description:

Figure 6-36. Screen Awaiting Confirmation

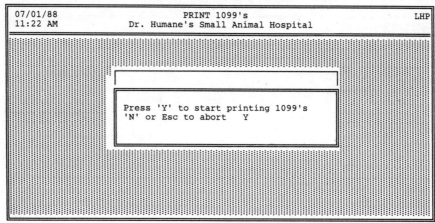

```
07/01/88                    PRINT 1099's                              LHP
11:22 AM             Dr. Humane's Small Animal Hospital
```

```
              Press 'Y' to start printing 1099's
              'N' or Esc to abort     Y
```

F1-Help F4-Change Date   ESC-Exit

Figure 6-37. The Product Listing Screen

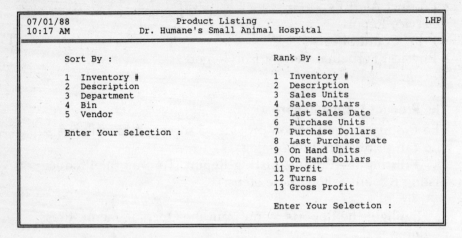

```
07/01/88                      Product Listing                        LHP
10:17 AM              Dr. Humane's Small Animal Hospital

       Sort By :                         Rank By :

       1  Inventory #                    1  Inventory #
       2  Description                    2  Description
       3  Department                     3  Sales Units
       4  Bin                            4  Sales Dollars
       5  Vendor                         5  Last Sales Date
                                         6  Purchase Units
       Enter Your Selection :            7  Purchase Dollars
                                         8  Last Purchase Date
                                         9  On Hand Units
                                         10 On Hand Dollars
                                         11 Profit
                                         12 Turns
                                         13 Gross Profit

                                         Enter Your Selection :
```

5. Press Enter twice.

    DacEasy automatically enters the words *First Record* at the From field and *Last Record* at the To field.

    The screen will look like the one in Figure 6-38.

    The cursor will then move to the second Enter Your Selection field.

    To rank the Products Listing Report by Inventory #:

6. Type 1 and press Enter.

    To print all products ranked by Inventory #:

Figure 6-38. The Screen Prepared to Sort by Description

```
07/01/88                      Product Listing                        LHP
10:17 AM              Dr. Humane's Small Animal Hospital

                                         Rank By :
    Sorted by : Description
                                         1  Inventory #
    From : (First Record)                2  Description
    To   : (Last Record)                 3  Sales Units
                                         4  Sales Dollars
                                         5  Last Sales Date
                                         6  Purchase Units
                                         7  Purchase Dollars
                                         8  Last Purchase Date
                                         9  On Hand Units
                                         10 On Hand Dollars
                                         11 Profit
                                         12 Turns
                                         13 Gross Profit

                                         Enter Your Selection :
```

7. Press Enter twice.

DacEasy automatically enters the words *First Record* at the From field and *Last Record* at the To field.

The Products Listing Report will start printing.

The Product Price List Report

The Product Price List provides 5 sorts and 13 rankings so you can print a comprehensive report displaying the product name, unit of measure and fractions per unit, department, location (bin), vendor code, and tax information. You can keep product costs confidential by assigning a code to product prices. Only persons who understand the code will be able to decipher it.

Printing the Product Price List. To print the Product Price List, follow these steps:

1. Highlight the Reports menu from the Opening menu. Press Enter.
2. Press 3 to select the Inventory Reports submenu.
3. Press 2 to select the Product Price List option.

The screen in Figure 6-39 will appear.

The cursor should be positioned at the first Enter Your Selection field.

To sort the Product Price List by Vendor:

Figure 6-39. The Product Price Listing Screen

```
07/01/88                    Product Price Listing                       LHP
10:26 AM            Dr. Humane's Small Animal Hospital

        Sort By :                         Rank By :

        1  Inventory #                    1   Inventory #
        2  Description                    2   Description
        3  Department                     3   Sales Units
        4  Bin                            4   Sales Dollars
        5  Vendor                         5   Last Sales Date
                                          6   Purchase Units
        Enter Your Selection :            7   Purchase Dollars
                                          8   Last Purchase Date
                                          9   On Hand Units
                                          10  On Hand Dollars
                                          11  Profit
                                          12  Turns
                                          13  Gross Profit

                                          Enter Your Selection :
```

4. Type 5 and press Enter.

To print all product prices sorted by Vendor:

5. Press Enter twice.

DacEasy will automatically enter the words *First Record* at the From field and *Last Record* at the To field.

The screen will look like the one in Figure 6-40.

The cursor will then move to the second Enter Your Selection field.

To rank the Product Price List by Inventory #:

6. Type 1 and press Enter.

To print all product prices ranked by Inventory #:

7. Press Enter twice.

DacEasy automatically enters the words *First Record* at the From field and *Last Record* at the To field. The system will also display a cost code field as shown in Figure 6-41.

If you want to keep product prices confidential, enter a code in this field. If you don't, press Enter. The report will start printing.

8. Type the Code Name and press Enter.

The Product Price List will start printing.

Figure 6-40. The Screen Prepared to Sort by Vendor

```
07/01/88                Product Price Listing                    LHP
10:26 AM           Dr. Humane's Small Animal Hospital
═══════════════════════════════════════════════════════════════════

                                    Rank By :

      Sorted by : Vendor            1   Inventory #
                                    2   Description
      From : (First Record)         3   Sales Units
      To   : (Last Record)          4   Sales Dollars
                                    5   Last Sales Date
                                    6   Purchase Units
                                    7   Purchase Dollars
                                    8   Last Purchase Date
                                    9   On Hand Units
                                    10  On Hand Dollars
                                    11  Profit
                                    12  Turns
                                    13  Gross Profit

                                    Enter Your Selection :

```

F1-Help F4-Change Date   ESC-Exit

Figure 6-41. Screen Inquiring Whether to Enter Cost Code

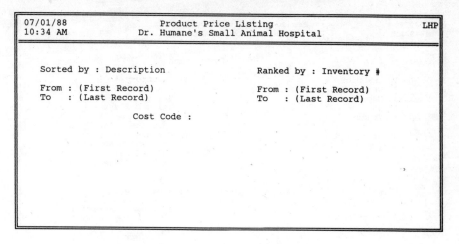

```
07/01/88                    Product Price Listing                    LHP
10:34 AM              Dr. Humane's Small Animal Hospital


    Sorted by : Description           Ranked by : Inventory #

    From : (First Record)             From : (First Record)
    To   : (Last Record)             To   : (Last Record)

              Cost Code :
```

The Product Activity Report

The Product Activity Report provides 5 sorts and 13 rankings so
you can print information needed for the daily management of
your inventory. Some of the information available from this report include unit and fractions, unit sales, price and cost, units
on hand, purchases, and sales year-to-date in both units and dollars. It also includes the cost, profit, and gross return on your
investment. These reports can be invaluable for making financial
decisions.

   Printing the Product Activity Report. To print the Product
Activity Report, follow these steps:

1. Highlight the Reports menu from the Opening menu. Press
   Enter.
2. Press 3 to select the Inventory Reports submenu.
3. Press 3 to select the Product Activity Report option.
      The screen in Figure 6-42 will appear.

   The cursor should be positioned at the first Enter Your Selection field.
   To sort the Product Activity Report by Vendor:

4. Type 5 and press Enter.
      To print only the product activity for some vendors, type
   the vendor's code as follows:

207

Figure 6-42. The Product Activity Screen

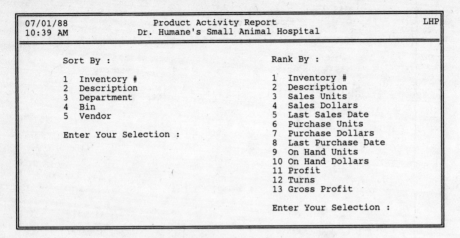

```
07/01/88                  Product Activity Report              LHP
10:39 AM              Dr. Humane's Small Animal Hospital


     Sort By :                        Rank By :

     1  Inventory #                   1  Inventory #
     2  Description                   2  Description
     3  Department                    3  Sales Units
     4  Bin                           4  Sales Dollars
     5  Vendor                        5  Last Sales Date
                                      6  Purchase Units
     Enter Your Selection :           7  Purchase Dollars
                                      8  Last Purchase Date
                                      9  On Hand Units
                                     10  On Hand Dollars
                                     11  Profit
                                     12  Turns
                                     13  Gross Profit

                                      Enter Your Selection :
```

5. Type A001 at the From field. Press Enter.
6. Type G015 at the To field. Press Enter.

 The screen will look like the one in Figure 6-43.

 The cursor will move to the second Enter Your Selection field.

 To rank the Product Activity Report by Description:

7. Type 2 and press Enter.

 To print all products (for the vendors sorted) ranked by Description:

Figure 6-43. The Screen Prepared to Sort by Vendor

```
07/01/88                  Product Activity Report              LHP
10:39 AM              Dr. Humane's Small Animal Hospital

                                      Rank By :

     Sorted by : Vendor               1  Inventory #
                                      2  Description
     From : A001                      3  Sales Units
     To   : G015                      4  Sales Dollars
                                      5  Last Sales Date
                                      6  Purchase Units
                                      7  Purchase Dollars
                                      8  Last Purchase Date
                                      9  On Hand Units
                                     10  On Hand Dollars
                                     11  Profit
                                     12  Turns
                                     13  Gross Profit

                                      Enter Your Selection :
```

8. Press Enter twice.

   DacEasy will automatically enter the words *First Record* at the From field and *Last Record* at the To field.

   The Product Activity Report will start printing.

The Product Alert Report

DacEasy's Product Alert Report also provides 5 sorts and 13 rankings so you can print a report describing the products that need to be purchased and in what quantity. This report alleviates sending duplicate orders to vendors by providing the option of printing the amount of product currently on order.

Printing the Product Alert Report. To print the Product Alert Report, follow these steps:

1. Highlight the Reports menu from the Opening menu. Press Enter.
2. Press 3 to select the Inventory Report submenu.
3. Press 4 to select the Product Alert Report option.

   The screen in Figure 6-44 will appear.

   The cursor should be positioned at the first Enter Your Selection field.

   To sort the Product Alert Report by Inventory #:

4. Type 1 and press Enter.

   To print all products that need to be reordered:

Figure 6-44. The Product Alert Report Screen

```
07/01/88                    Product Alert Report                        LHP
10:49 AM             Dr. Humane's Small Animal Hospital

        Sort By :                            Rank By :

        1  Inventory #                       1  Inventory #
        2  Description                       2  Description
        3  Department                        3  Sales Units
        4  Bin                               4  Sales Dollars
        5  Vendor                            5  Last Sales Date
                                             6  Purchase Units
        Enter Your Selection :               7  Purchase Dollars
                                             8  Last Purchase Date
                                             9  On Hand Units
                                            10  On Hand Dollars
                                            11  Profit
                                            12  Turns
                                            13  Gross Profit

                                            Enter Your Selection :
```

Figure 6-45. The Screen Prepared to Sort by Inventory #

```
07/01/88                 Product Alert Report                          LHP
10:55 AM             Dr. Humane's Small Animal Hospital


                                         Rank By :

       Sorted by : Inventory #           1  Inventory #
                                         2  Description
       From : (First Record)             3  Sales Units
       To   : (Last Record)              4  Sales Dollars
                                         5  Last Sales Date
                                         6  Purchase Units
                                         7  Purchase Dollars
                                         8  Last Purchase Date
                                         9  On Hand Units
                                         10 On Hand Dollars
                                         11 Profit
                                         12 Turns
                                         13 Gross Profit

                                         Enter Your Selection :
```

5. Press Enter twice.

   DacEasy will automatically enter the words *First Record* at the From field and *Last Record* at the To field.

   The screen will look like the one in Figure 6-45.

   The cursor will move to the second Enter Your Selection field.

   To rank the Product Alert Report by Description:

6. Type 2 and press Enter.

   To print all products that need to be reordered by Description:

7. Press Enter twice.

   DacEasy will automatically enter the words *First Record* at the From field and *Last Record* at the To field.

   The Product Alert Report will start printing.

The Service Report

DacEasy's Service Report provides three sorts and five rankings so you can print a report that analyzes your service billing. This report can serve two functions:

- It shows which products are the largest or smallest income producers.
- It can be used as a directory.

Printing the Service Report. To print the Service Report, follow these steps:

1. Highlight the Reports menu from the Opening menu. Press Enter.
2. Press 3 to select the Inventory Reports submenu.
3. Press 5 to select the Service Report option.
    The screen in Figure 6-46 will appear.

The cursor should be positioned at the first Enter Your Selection field.
To sort the Service Report by Service #:

4. Type 1 and press Enter.
    To print all services sorted by Service #:
5. Press Enter twice.
    DacEasy automatically enters the words *First Record* at the From field and *Last Record* at the To field.
    The cursor will move to the second Enter Your Selection field.
    To rank the Service Report by Description:
6. Type 2 and press Enter.
    To print all services ranked by Description:
7. Press Enter twice.
    DacEasy automatically enters the words *First Record* at the From field and *Last Record* at the To field. The system will then display the message shown in Figure 6-47.

Figure 6-46. The Service Report Screen

```
07/01/88                      Service Report                          LHP
10:56 AM          Dr. Humane's Small Animal Hospital
═════════════════════════════════════════════════════════════════════════

     Sort By :                          Rank By :

     1  Service #                       1  Service #
     2  Description                     2  Description
     3  Department                      3  Sales Units
                                        4  Sales Dollars
     Enter Your Selection :             5  Last Sales Date

                                        Enter Your Selection :
```

Figure 6-47. The Screen Asking Whether to Include Sales Information

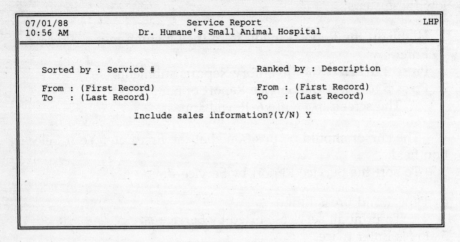

```
07/01/88                    Service Report                      LHP
10:56 AM            Dr. Humane's Small Animal Hospital
═══════════════════════════════════════════════════════════════════

    Sorted by : Service #             Ranked by : Description

    From : (First Record)             From : (First Record)
    To   : (Last Record)             To   : (Last Record)

                 Include sales information?(Y/N) Y
```

If you want to include sales information in the Service Report, type *Y*, then press Enter. If you don't, press Enter to accept the default.

8. Type *Y* and press Enter.
   The Service Report will start printing.

The Count Sheet Operation

DacEasy's Print Count Sheets option provides 5 sorts and 13 rankings so you can print inventory count sheets. Before you can enter inventory, count sheets should be printed. Count sheets are forms used to record all inventory on hand. When you or your employees perform periodic inventories, the actual count of the number of units on hand is written on these count sheets.

Printing Count Sheets. Note: If you've completed the tutorials in Chapter 4, you'll be familiar with this operation. For sample purposes only, however, a different sort and rank option is used here.

To print count sheets, follow these steps:

1. Highlight the Reports menu from the Opening menu. Press Enter.
2. Press 3 to select the Inventory Report submenu.
3. Press 6 to select the Print Count Sheets option.
   The screen in Figure 6-48 will appear.

Figure 6-48. The Count Sheets Screen

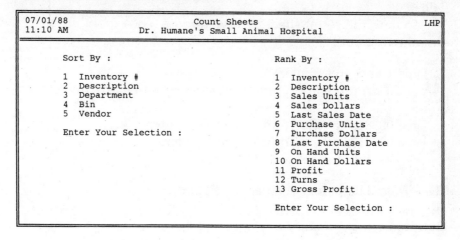

```
07/01/88                         Count Sheets                        LHP
11:10 AM              Dr. Humane's Small Animal Hospital


      Sort By :                          Rank By :

      1  Inventory #                     1  Inventory #
      2  Description                     2  Description
      3  Department                      3  Sales Units
      4  Bin                             4  Sales Dollars
      5  Vendor                          5  Last Sales Date
                                         6  Purchase Units
      Enter Your Selection :             7  Purchase Dollars
                                         8  Last Purchase Date
                                         9  On Hand Units
                                         10 On Hand Dollars
                                         11 Profit
                                         12 Turns
                                         13 Gross Profit

                                         Enter Your Selection :
```

The cursor should be positioned at the first Enter Your Selection field.

To sort count sheets by Bin:

4. Type 4 and press Enter.

   To print a count sheet for only the first bin:

5. Type 0001 at the From field. Press Enter.
6. Type 0001 at the To field. Press Enter.

   The screen will look like the one in Figure 6-49.

Figure 6-49. The Screen Prepared to Sort by Bin

```
07/01/88                         Count Sheets                        LHP
11:24 AM              Dr. Humane's Small Animal Hospital

                                         Rank By :

     Sorted by : Bin                     1  Inventory #
                                         2  Description
     From : 0001                         3  Sales Units
     To   : 0001                         4  Sales Dollars
                                         5  Last Sales Date
                                         6  Purchase Units
                                         7  Purchase Dollars
                                         8  Last Purchase Date
                                         9  On Hand Units
                                         10 On Hand Dollars
                                         11 Profit
                                         12 Turns
                                         13 Gross Profit

                                         Enter Your Selection :
```

The cursor will move to the second Enter Your Selection field.

To rank the count sheet by Inventory # (corresponding to only the first bin):

7. Type 1 and press Enter.

To print the appropriate count sheet ranked by Inventory #:

8. Type 0038188 at the From field. Press Enter.
9. Type 0038188 at the To field. Press Enter.

The count sheet will start printing.

The Physical Perpetual Comparison Report

DacEasy's Physical Perpetual Comparison Report provides 5 sorts and 13 rankings so you can print a comparative report between the products you entered in the Enter Physical Inventory operation and those products *DacEasy* continually maintains within its accounting system. For easier comparison, it's suggested that you use the same sort and rank criteria for both this report and the Print Count Sheets operation.

Printing the Physical-Perpetual Comparison Report. To print the Physical-Perpetual Comparison Report, follow these steps:

1. Highlight the Reports menu from the Opening menu. Press Enter.
2. Press 3 to select the Inventory Reports submenu.
3. Press 7 to select the Physical-Perpetual Comparison option.

The screen in Figure 6-50 will appear.

Figure 6-50. The Physical-Perpetual Comparison Report Screen

```
07/01/88          Physical-Perpetual Comparison Report          LHP
11:31 AM            Dr. Humane's Small Animal Hospital

     Sort By :                        Rank By :

     1  Inventory #                   1  Inventory #
     2  Description                   2  Description
     3  Department                    3  Sales Units
     4  Bin                           4  Sales Dollars
     5  Vendor                        5  Last Sales Date
                                      6  Purchase Units
     Enter Your Selection :           7  Purchase Dollars
                                      8  Last Purchase Date
                                      9  On Hand Units
                                     10  On Hand Dollars
                                     11  Profit
                                     12  Turns
                                     13  Gross Profit

                                     Enter Your Selection :
```

Figure 6-51. The Screen Prepared to Sort by Bin

```
07/01/88 ·          Physical-Perpetual Comparison Report          LHP
11:31 AM              Dr. Humane's Small Animal Hospital


   Sorted by : Bin                       Rank By :

   From : 0001                          1  Inventory #
   To   : 0001                          2  Description
                                        3  Sales Units
                                        4  Sales Dollars
                                        5  Last Sales Date
                                        6  Purchase Units
                                        7  Purchase Dollars
                                        8  Last Purchase Date
                                        9  On Hand Units
                                        10 On Hand Dollars
                                        11 Profit
                                        12 Turns
                                        13 Gross Profit

                                        Enter Your Selection :
```

The cursor should be positioned at the first Enter Your Selection field.

To sort the Physical-Perpetual Comparison Report by Bin:

4. Type 4 and press Enter.

    To print data for only the first bin:

5. Type 0001 at the From field. Press Enter.
6. Type 0001 at the To field. Press Enter.

    The screen will look like the one in Figure 6-51.

The cursor will move to the second Enter Your Selection field.

    To rank the report by Inventory #:

7. Type 1 and press Enter.

    To print only the Inventory # that corresponds with the Bin number:

8. Type 0038188 at the From field. Press Enter.
9. Type 0038188 at the To field. Press Enter.

    The Physical-Perpetual Comparison Report will start printing.

DacEasy's Financial Reports

DacEasy's Financials menu also provides several comprehensive financial reports. As with the report options described above, these reports, excluding the Chart of Accounts and the Financial

Statements Generator, must be printed after all your accounting transactions have been posted to the general ledger.

The following describes all of *DacEasy*'s financial reports.

The Chart of Accounts

A list of account titles and numbers showing the location of each account in a ledger is called a chart of accounts. *DacEasy*'s Chart of Accounts option lets you print a listing of all accounts in the General Ledger file. You can print either a partial list or a complete list, depending on your immediate needs. It's a good idea to keep a complete, updated list accessible at all times because it's an ideal reference when entering vouchers and other documents into the accounting system.

Printing the Chart of Accounts. To print the Chart of Accounts, follow these steps:

1. Highlight the Financials menu from the Opening menu. Press Enter.
2. Press 1 to select the Chart of Accounts option.
   The screen in Figure 6-52 will appear.

The cursor should be positioned at the Account Level field. You may choose any number between 1 and 5. The higher the number, the more detailed the account is.

Figure 6-52. The Chart of Accounts Screen

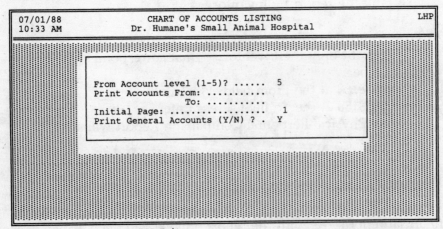

```
07/01/88                CHART OF ACCOUNTS LISTING                    LHP
10:33 AM              Dr. Humane's Small Animal Hospital



         From Account level (1-5)? ......   5
         Print Accounts From: ...........
                         To: ...........
         Initial Page: ...................   1
         Print General Accounts (Y/N) ? .   Y




F1-Help F4-Change Date   ESC-Exit
```

3. Press Enter to accept *DacEasy*'s default.
   The cursor will move to the next field. To print all of the general ledger accounts:
4. Press Enter twice.
   DacEasy automatically enters the words *First Record* at the From field and *Last Record* at the To field.
   The cursor will move to the Initial Page field.
5. Press Enter to print the Chart of Accounts starting with page 1.
   The cursor will move to the last field. To print the General Accounts:
6. Press Enter to accept *DacEasy*'s default.
   The Chart of Accounts will start printing.

For convenient reference purposes, the printed Chart of Accounts appears in Figure 6-53.

The Trial Balance

DacEasy's Trial Balance option lets you print a detailed listing of the balances in each of your General Ledger accounts. The Trial Balance proves the equality of debits and credits in the general ledger. All general ledger account titles should be listed on the Trial Balance, even if some accounts have no balances. This procedure assures that no accounts are omitted.

Printing the Trial Balance. To print the Trial Balance, follow these steps:

1. Highlight the Financials menu from the Opening menu. Press Enter.
2. Press 2 to select the Trial Balance option.
   The screen in Figure 6-54 will appear.

The cursor should be positioned at the Account Level field. You can choose how detailed you want the Trial Balance to be. The higher the number entered in this field, the more detailed your report will be.

3. Press Enter to accept *DacEasy*'s default.
   The cursor will move to the next field. To print all of the general ledger accounts:

Figure 6-53. The Printed Chart of Accounts

```
Date : 07/01/88        Dr. Humane's Small Animal Hospital        Page no. 1
Time : 10:49 AM               555 East Meadows Lane
                              San Diego, CA  92122
                               (619)555-3636

                              CHART OF ACCOUNTS
```

Acct. #	Account Name	Acct. Type	Level	Type	General
1	Assets	ASSET	1	GENERAL	
11	Current Assets	ASSET	2	GENERAL	1
1101	Petty Cash	ASSET	3	DETAIL	11
1102	Cash In Banks	ASSET	3	GENERAL	11
11021	Checking Account	ASSET	4	DETAIL	1102
11022	Payroll Account	ASSET	4	DETAIL	1102
11023	Savings Account	ASSET	4	DETAIL	1102
1103	Cash Register Fund	ASSET	3	GENERAL	11
11031	Cash Register # 1	ASSET	4	DETAIL	1103
11032	Cash Register # 2	ASSET	4	DETAIL	1103
1104	Mktable Securities	ASSET	3	GENERAL	11
11041	Cert. of Deposit	ASSET	4	DETAIL	1104
11042	US Gover. Securities	ASSET	4	DETAIL	1104
11043	Other Securities	ASSET	4	DETAIL	1104
1105	Accounts Receivable	ASSET	3	GENERAL	11
11051	Accts Rec'ble Module	ASSET	4	DETAIL	1105
11052	Allow Doubtful Accts	ASSET	4	DETAIL	1105
1106	Other Receivable	ASSET	3	GENERAL	11
11061	Affiliated Company	ASSET	4	DETAIL	1106
11062	Employee Loans	ASSET	4	DETAIL	1106
11063	Officers Loans	ASSET	4	DETAIL	1106
11064	Other Receivable	ASSET	4	DETAIL	1106
1107	Inventory	ASSET	3	GENERAL	11
11071	Inventory - Module	ASSET	4	DETAIL	1107
11072	Allow Damage/Obsol.	ASSET	4	DETAIL	1107
12	Fixed Assets	ASSET	2	GENERAL	1
1201	Autos & Trucks Net	ASSET	3	GENERAL	12
12011	Original Value	ASSET	4	DETAIL	1201
12012	Accum. Depreciation	ASSET	4	DETAIL	1201
1202	Furniture & Fixt.Net	ASSET	3	GENERAL	12
12021	Original Value	ASSET	4	DETAIL	1202
12022	Accum. Depreciation	ASSET	4	DETAIL	1202
1203	Office Equipment Net	ASSET	3	GENERAL	12
12031	Original Value	ASSET	4	DETAIL	1203
12032	Accum. Depreciation	ASSET	4	DETAIL	1203
1204	Machinery & Eq. Net	ASSET	3	GENERAL	12
12041	Original Value	ASSET	4	DETAIL	1204
12042	Accum. Depreciation	ASSET	4	DETAIL	1204
1205	Building Net	ASSET	3	GENERAL	12
12051	Original Value	ASSET	4	DETAIL	1205
12052	Accum. Depreciation	ASSET	4	DETAIL	1205
1206	Other Fixed Assets	ASSET	3	GENERAL	12
12061	Original Value	ASSET	4	DETAIL	1206
12062	Accum. Depreciation	ASSET	4	DETAIL	1206
1207	Land-Original Value	ASSET	3	DETAIL	12
13	Deferred Assets	ASSET	2	GENERAL	1
1301	Organization Expense	ASSET	3	GENERAL	13
13011	Original Value	ASSET	4	DETAIL	1301
13012	Accum. Amortization	ASSET	4	DETAIL	1301
1302	Leasehold Improv.Net	ASSET	3	GENERAL	13
13021	Original Value	ASSET	4	DETAIL	1302

Figure 6-53, *continued*

```
Date : 07/01/88        Dr. Humane's Small Animal Hospital        Page no. 2
Time : 10:49 AM              555 East Meadows Lane
                            San Diego, CA  92122
                            (619)555-3636
```

CHART OF ACCOUNTS

Acct. #	Account Name	Acct. Type	Level	Type	General
13022	Accum. Amortization	ASSET	4	DETAIL	1302
1303	Prepaid Expenses	ASSET	3	GENERAL	13
13031	Insurance	ASSET	4	DETAIL	1303
13032	Rent	ASSET	4	DETAIL	1303
13033	Interest	ASSET	4	DETAIL	1303
13034	Taxes	ASSET	4	DETAIL	1303
14	Other Assets	ASSET	2	GENERAL	1
1401	Deposits	ASSET	3	GENERAL	14
14011	Rent	ASSET	4	DETAIL	1401
14012	Leases	ASSET	4	DETAIL	1401
14013	Utilities	ASSET	4	DETAIL	1401
14014	Security	ASSET	4	DETAIL	1401
1402	Long Term Investment	ASSET	3	GENERAL	14
14021	Cert. of Deposit	ASSET	4	DETAIL	1402
14022	Other Long Term Inv.	ASSET	4	DETAIL	1402
2	Liabilities	LIAB.	1	GENERAL	
21	Short Term Liability	LIAB.	2	GENERAL	2
2101	Accts Payable-Module	LIAB.	3	DETAIL	21
2102	Notes Payable	LIAB.	3	DETAIL	21
2103	Accrued Payable	LIAB.	3	DETAIL	21
2104	Taxes Payable	LIAB.	3	GENERAL	21
21041	Payroll Taxes	LIAB.	4	GENERAL	2104
210411	Federal Income W/H	LIAB.	5	DETAIL	21041
210412	Fica W/H Employee	LIAB.	5	DETAIL	21041
210413	Fica W/H Employer	LIAB.	5	DETAIL	21041
210414	Futa	LIAB.	5	DETAIL	21041
210415	Suta	LIAB.	5	DETAIL	21041
210416	State Income W/H	LIAB.	5	DETAIL	21041
210417	City Income W/H	LIAB.	5	DETAIL	21041
210418	Disability Insurance	LIAB.	5	DETAIL	21041
21042	Sales Tax Payable	LIAB.	4	DETAIL	2104
21043	Property Tax	LIAB.	4	DETAIL	2104
21044	Franchise Tax	LIAB.	4	DETAIL	2104
21045	Foreign Tax	LIAB.	4	DETAIL	2104
21046	Income Tax Payable	LIAB.	4	GENERAL	2104
210461	Federal Income Tax	LIAB.	5	DETAIL	21046
210462	State Income Tax	LIAB.	5	DETAIL	21046
210463	City Income Tax	LIAB.	5	DETAIL	21046
21047	Other Tax Payable	LIAB.	4	DETAIL	2104
2105	Other Pyroll Payable	LIAB.	3	GENERAL	21
21051	Union Dues	LIAB.	4	DETAIL	2105
21052	Employee Charity	LIAB.	4	DETAIL	2105
21053	X'mas Fund Accrued	LIAB.	4	DETAIL	2105
2106	Dividends Payable	LIAB.	3	DETAIL	21
2107	Other Payable	LIAB.	3	DETAIL	21
22	Long Term Liability	LIAB.	2	GENERAL	2
2201	Mortgages Payable	LIAB.	3	DETAIL	22
2202	Notes Payable	LIAB.	3	DETAIL	22
2203	Current L/Term Liab.	LIAB.	3	DETAIL	22
2204	Other Long Term Liab	LIAB.	3	DETAIL	22
23	Deferred Liability	LIAB.	2	GENERAL	2

Figure 6-53, continued

CHART OF ACCOUNTS

Acct. #	Account Name	Acct. Type	Level	Type	General
2301	Commit & Contingency	LIAB.	3	DETAIL	23
2302	Deferred Income	LIAB.	3	DETAIL	23
2303	Profit/Instalm.Sales	LIAB.	3	DETAIL	23
2304	Unearned Interest	LIAB.	3	DETAIL	23
3	Stockholders Equity	CAP.	1	GENERAL	
31	Capital Stock	CAP.	2	GENERAL	3
3101	Common Stock	CAP.	3	GENERAL	31
31011	Par Value	CAP.	4	DETAIL	3101
31012	Surplus	CAP.	4	DETAIL	3101
3102	Preferred Stock	CAP.	3	GENERAL	31
31021	Par Value	CAP.	4	DETAIL	3102
31022	Surplus	CAP.	4	DETAIL	3102
3103	Treasury Stock	CAP.	3	DETAIL	31
32	Retained Earnings	CAP.	2	GENERAL	3
3283	1983 Profit/(Loss)	CAP.	3	DETAIL	32
3284	1984 Profit/(Loss)	CAP.	3	DETAIL	32
3285	1985 Profit/(Loss)	CAP.	3	DETAIL	32
3286	1986 Profit/(Loss)	CAP.	3	DETAIL	32
3287	1987 Profit/(Loss)	CAP.	3	DETAIL	32
33	Current Earnings	CAP.	2	DETAIL	3
4	Revenues	REV.	1	GENERAL	
41	Sales	REV.	2	GENERAL	4
4101	Sales Dept. 01	REV.	3	DETAIL	41
4102	Sales Dept. 02	REV.	3	DETAIL	41
42	Sales Returns	REV.	2	GENERAL	4
4201	Returns Dept. 01	REV.	3	DETAIL	42
4202	Returns Dept. 02	REV.	3	DETAIL	42
43	Shipping	REV.	2	GENERAL	4
4301	Freight	REV.	3	DETAIL	43
4302	Insurance	REV.	3	DETAIL	43
4303	Packaging	REV.	3	DETAIL	43
4304	Surcharge	REV.	3	DETAIL	43
44	Financial Income	REV.	2	GENERAL	4
4401	Ints. Investments	REV.	3	DETAIL	44
4402	Finance Charges	REV.	3	DETAIL	44
4403	Dividends	REV.	3	DETAIL	44
4404	Purchase Discounts	REV.	3	DETAIL	44
45	Other Revenues	REV.	2	GENERAL	4
4501	Recovery Bad Debt	REV.	3	DETAIL	45
4502	Gain in Sale/Assets	REV.	3	DETAIL	45
4503	Miscellaneous	REV.	3	DETAIL	45
5	Total Expenses	EXP.	1	GENERAL	
51	Cost of Goods Sold	EXP.	2	GENERAL	5
5101	COGS Dept. 01	EXP.	3	DETAIL	51
5102	COGS Dept. 02	EXP.	3	DETAIL	51
52	Gen & Admin Expenses	EXP.	2	GENERAL	5
5201	Payroll	EXP.	3	GENERAL	52
52011	Wages	EXP.	4	GENERAL	5201
520111	Salaries	EXP.	5	DETAIL	52011
520112	Hourly	EXP.	5	DETAIL	52011
520113	Commisions	EXP.	5	DETAIL	52011

Figure 6-53, continued

CHART OF ACCOUNTS

Acct. #	Account Name	Acct. Type	Level	Type	General
520114	Overtime	EXP.	5	DETAIL	52011
520115	Compensations	EXP.	5	DETAIL	52011
520116	Bonuses	EXP.	5	DETAIL	52011
520117	Other Wages	EXP.	5	DETAIL	52011
520118	Contract Labor	EXP.	5	DETAIL	52011
52012	Benefits	EXP.	4	GENERAL	5201
520121	Health Insurance	EXP.	5	DETAIL	52012
520123	Dental Insurance	EXP.	5	DETAIL	52012
520124	401(k) Plan	EXP.	5	DETAIL	52012
520125	Other Benefits	EXP.	5	DETAIL	52012
52013	Taxes	EXP.	4	GENERAL	5201
520131	Fica Employer	EXP.	5	DETAIL	52013
520132	Futa	EXP.	5	DETAIL	52013
520133	Suta	EXP.	5	DETAIL	52013
520134	Disability Insurance	EXP.	5	DETAIL	52013
520135	Other Payroll Taxes	EXP.	5	DETAIL	52013
5202	Maintenance	EXP.	3	GENERAL	52
52021	Autos & Trucks	EXP.	4	DETAIL	5202
52022	Furniture & Fixtures	EXP.	4	DETAIL	5202
52023	Office Equipment	EXP.	4	DETAIL	5202
52024	Machinery & Equip.	EXP.	4	DETAIL	5202
52025	Building	EXP.	4	DETAIL	5202
52026	Other Assets	EXP.	4	DETAIL	5202
5203	Depreciation	EXP.	3	GENERAL	52
52031	Autos & Trucks	EXP.	4	DETAIL	5203
52032	Furniture & Fixtures	EXP.	4	DETAIL	5203
52033	Office Equipment	EXP.	4	DETAIL	5203
52034	Machinery & Equip.	EXP.	4	DETAIL	5203
52035	Building	EXP.	4	DETAIL	5203
52036	Other Assets	EXP.	4	DETAIL	5203
5204	Amortization	EXP.	3	GENERAL	52
52041	Organization Expense	EXP.	4	DETAIL	5204
52042	Leasehold Improv.	EXP.	4	DETAIL	5204
5205	Rents and Leases	EXP.	3	GENERAL	52
52051	Autos & Trucks	EXP.	4	DETAIL	5205
52052	Furniture & Fixtures	EXP.	4	DETAIL	5205
52053	Office Equipment	EXP.	4	DETAIL	5205
52054	Machinery & Equip.	EXP.	4	DETAIL	5205
52055	Building	EXP.	4	DETAIL	5205
52056	Other Leases or Rent	EXP.	4	DETAIL	5205
5206	Assets Insurance	EXP.	3	GENERAL	52
52061	Autos & Trucks	EXP.	4	DETAIL	5206
52062	Furniture & Fixtures	EXP.	4	DETAIL	5206
52063	Office Equipment	EXP.	4	DETAIL	5206
52064	Machinery & Equip.	EXP.	4	DETAIL	5206
52065	Building	EXP.	4	DETAIL	5206
52066	Other Assets Insur.	EXP.	4	DETAIL	5206
5207	Travel & Entertain	EXP.	3	GENERAL	52
52071	Lodging	EXP.	4	DETAIL	5207
52072	Transportation	EXP.	4	DETAIL	5207
52073	Meals	EXP.	4	DETAIL	5207

Figure 6-53, continued

CHART OF ACCOUNTS

Acct. #	Account Name	Acct. Type	Level	Type	General
52074	Entertainment	EXP.	4	DETAIL	5207
52075	Other Travel Expense	EXP.	4	DETAIL	5207
5208	Shipping	EXP.	3	GENERAL	52
52081	Freight	EXP.	4	DETAIL	5208
52082	Insurance	EXP.	4	DETAIL	5208
52083	Packaging	EXP.	4	DETAIL	5208
52084	Duties	EXP.	4	DETAIL	5208
52085	Other Shipping Exp.	EXP.	4	DETAIL	5208
5209	Taxes (other)	EXP.	3	GENERAL	52
52091	Sales Tax/Purchases	EXP.	4	DETAIL	5209
52092	Property Tax	EXP.	4	DETAIL	5209
52093	Franchise Tax	EXP.	4	DETAIL	5209
52094	Other Taxes	EXP.	4	DETAIL	5209
5210	Consulting Fees	EXP.	3	GENERAL	52
52101	Accountants	EXP.	4	DETAIL	5210
52102	Legal	EXP.	4	DETAIL	5210
52103	Other	EXP.	4	DETAIL	5210
5211	Office Supplies	EXP.	3	DETAIL	52
5212	Telephone & Telegrph	EXP.	3	DETAIL	52
5213	Mail/Postage	EXP.	3	DETAIL	52
5214	Utilities	EXP.	3	DETAIL	52
5215	Alarms	EXP.	3	DETAIL	52
5216	Contribution/Donat.	EXP.	3	DETAIL	52
5217	Licenses/Permits	EXP.	3	DETAIL	52
5218	Memships/Dues/Subscr	EXP.	3	DETAIL	52
5219	Advertising	EXP.	3	GENERAL	52
52191	Broadcast Advert.	EXP.	4	DETAIL	5219
52192	Print Advertising	EXP.	4	DETAIL	5219
5220	Promotion	EXP.	3	GENERAL	52
52201	Catalogues	EXP.	4	DETAIL	5220
52202	Brochures	EXP.	4	DETAIL	5220
52203	Other Promotions	EXP.	4	DETAIL	5220
5221	Public Relations	EXP.	3	DETAIL	52
5222	Marketing Research	EXP.	3	DETAIL	52
5223	Bad Debt Loss	EXP.	3	DETAIL	52
5224	Inventory Losses	EXP.	3	DETAIL	52
5299	Other Expenses	EXP.	3	DETAIL	52
53	Financial Expenses	EXP.	2	GENERAL	5
5301	Credit Card Discount	EXP.	3	DETAIL	53
5302	Interest	EXP.	3	DETAIL	53
5303	Bank Charges	EXP.	3	DETAIL	53
5304	Sales Discounts	EXP.	3	DETAIL	53
5305	Agents Commisions	EXP.	3	DETAIL	53
5399	Other Financial Exp.	EXP.	3	DETAIL	53
54	Other Expenses	EXP.	2	GENERAL	5
5401	Cash Short	EXP.	3	DETAIL	54
5402	Loss on Sale/Assets	EXP.	3	DETAIL	54
5403	Miscellaneous Losses	EXP.	3	DETAIL	54
55	Income Tax	EXP.	2	GENERAL	5
5501	Federal Income Tax	EXP.	3	DETAIL	55
5502	State Income Tax	EXP.	3	DETAIL	55

Figure 6-53, continued

```
Date : 07/01/88        Dr. Humane's Small Animal Hospital      Page no. 6
Time : 10:49 AM                555 East Meadows Lane
                               San Diego, CA  92122
                                 (619)555-3636

                            CHART OF ACCOUNTS

                                            Acct.
       Acct. #  Account Name                Type   Level  Type     General
       -------  -----------------------     -----  -----  -------  --------
       5503        City Income Tax          EXP.     3    DETAIL    55
       D           Journal Difference       OTHER    1    DETAIL

        Number of Accounts printed 257
```

4. Press Enter twice.

    DacEasy will automatically enter the words *First Record* at the From field and *Last Record* at the To field.

    The cursor will move to the Initial Page field.

5. Press Enter to start the report with page 1.

    The cursor will move to the last field. To print the General Accounts:

6. Press Enter to accept *DacEasy*'s default.

    The screen will display a message as shown in Figure 6-55.

    If you want to print inactive accounts, type *Y*, then press Enter. If you don't, press Enter to accept *DacEasy*'s default.

Figure 6-54. The Print Trial Balance Screen

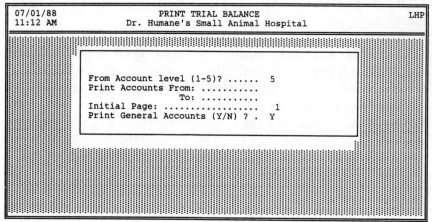

```
07/01/88                  PRINT TRIAL BALANCE                        LHP
11:12 AM             Dr. Humane's Small Animal Hospital




          From Account level (1-5)? ......   5
          Print Accounts From: ..........
                          To: ..........
          Initial Page: .................   1
          Print General Accounts (Y/N) ? .  Y



F1-Help F4-Change Date  ESC-Exit
```

Figure 6-55. The Screen Asking Whether to Include Inactive Accounts

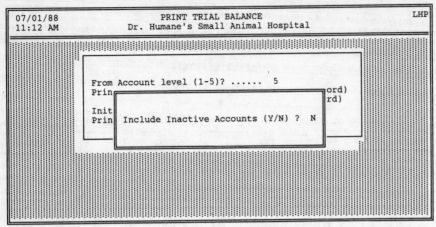

```
07/01/88                  PRINT TRIAL BALANCE                    LHP
11:12 AM              Dr. Humane's Small Animal Hospital

         From Account level (1-5)? ......  5
         Prin|                                         |ord)
             |                                         |rd)
         Init|                                         |
         Prin| Include Inactive Accounts (Y/N) ?  N   |
             |                                         |

SORTING...
```

7. Press Enter.

   The Trial Balance will start printing.

The Balance Sheet/Income Statement

DacEasy's Balance Sheet/Income Statement option lets you print the financial condition/progress of your business. Most management decisions can best be made after owners have determined the amount of assets, liabilities, and capital. The information needed can be obtained by inspecting general ledger accounts, but it's easier to use when it's organized and reported on a balance sheet.

The income statement reports the financial progress of your business. Merchandising businesses report revenue, cost of merchandise sold, gross profit on sales, expenses, and net income or net loss. You can compare current and previous income statements to determine the reasons for increases or decreases in net income. This comparison can be quite helpful in making management decisions about future business operations.

Printing the Balance Sheet/Income Statement. To print the Balance Sheet/Income Statement, follow these steps:

1. Highlight the Financials menu from the Opening menu. Press Enter.

Figure 6-56. The Print Financial Statements Screen

```
07/01/88              PRINT FINANCIAL STATEMENTS                    LHP
11:21 AM          Dr. Humane's Small Animal Hospital



        From Account level (1-5)? ......   5
        Print Accounts From: ..........
                        To: ..........
        Initial Page: ..................   1




F1-Help F4-Change Date   ESC-Exit
```

2. Press 3 to select the Balance Sheet/Income Statement option.
   The screen in Figure 6-56 will appear.

   The cursor should be positioned at the Account Level field.
You can choose how detailed you want the Balance Sheet/Income
Statement printout. The higher the number entered in this field,
the more detailed your report will be.

3. Press Enter to accept *DacEasy*'s default.
   The cursor will move to the next field. To print all of the
   general ledger accounts:
4. Press Enter twice.
   DacEasy automatically enters the words *First Record* at the
   From field and *Last Record* at the To field.
   The cursor will move to the Initial Page field.
5. Press Enter to start the report on page 1.
   The screen will display a message as shown in Figure
   6-57.

   If you want to print inactive accounts, type *Y*, then press
Enter. If you don't want to print inactive accounts, press Enter to
accept *DacEasy*'s default.

6. Press Enter.
   The Balance Sheet/Income Statement will start printing.

225

Figure 6-57. Screen Asking Whether to Include Inactive Accounts

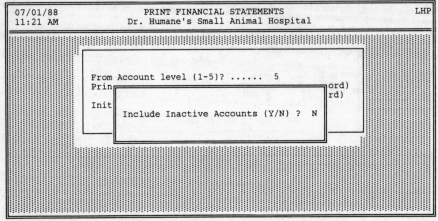

```
07/01/88              PRINT FINANCIAL STATEMENTS              LHP
11:21 AM            Dr. Humane's Small Animal Hospital


        From Account level (1-5)? ...... 5
        Prin                                        ord)
                                                    rd)
        Init
               Include Inactive Accounts (Y/N) ?  N




SORTING...
```

The Changes in Financial Conditions Report

The Changes in Financial Conditions option lets you print a report that shows the net amounts for uses and sources of money for:

- The current period
- This year
- Last year
- The year before last

Printing the Changes in Financial Conditions Report. To print the Changes in Financial Conditions Report, follow these steps:

1. Highlight the Financials menu from the Opening menu. Press Enter.
2. Press 4 to select the Changes in Financial Conditions option.
    The screen in Figure 6-58 will appear.

The cursor should be positioned at the Account Level field. You can choose how detailed you want this report printed. The higher the number entered in this field, the more detailed your report will be.

3. Press Enter to accept *DacEasy*'s default.
    The cursor will move to the next field. To print all accounts:

226

Figure 6·58. The Print Financial Statements Screen

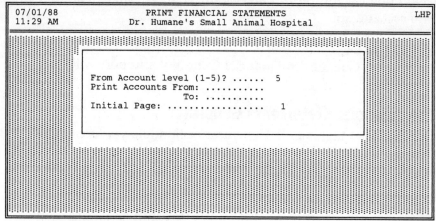

```
07/01/88              PRINT FINANCIAL STATEMENTS                    LHP
11:29 AM             Dr. Humane's Small Animal Hospital


         From Account level (1-5)? ......  5
         Print Accounts From: ..........
                        To: ..........
         Initial Page: .................  1




F1-Help F4-Change Date   ESC-Exit
```

4. Press Enter twice.

     DacEasy automatically enters the words *First Record* at the From field and *Last Record* at the To field.

     The cursor will move to the last field. To print the report starting with page 1:

5. Press Enter to accept *DacEasy*'s default.

     The screen will display a message as shown in Figure 6-59.

Figure 6·59. The Screen Asking Whether to Include Inactive Accounts

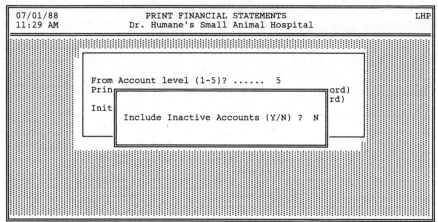

```
07/01/88              PRINT FINANCIAL STATEMENTS                    LHP
11:29 AM             Dr. Humane's Small Animal Hospital


         From Account level (1-5)? ......  5
         Prin                                              ord)
                                                           rd)
         Init
              Include Inactive Accounts (Y/N) ?  N




S O R T I N G . . .
```

If you want to print all accounts, type *Y*, then press Enter. If you don't want to print all accounts, press Enter to accept *DacEasy*'s default.

6. Press Enter.
    The Changes in Financial Conditions Report will start printing.

The Financial Statements Generator

The Financial Statements Generator option lets you create customized financial reports. All reports you create in this operation are printed using the Print Financial Reports submenu (option 2).

Creating Customized Statements

Note: If you've read through Chapter 2, you'll be familiar with this operation. For sample purposes only, however, different examples will be used here.

If you're using *DacEasy*'s built-in Chart of Accounts, a financial statements format is automatically created.

If you're not, financial statements must be created.

To create a report format, or edit an existing one:

1. Highlight the Financials menu from the Opening menu. Press Enter.
2. Press 5 to select the Financial Statement Generator option.
3. Press 1 to select the Edit Financial Reports option.
    The screen in Figure 6-60 will appear.

Virtually any type of report can be created. The data for reports are obtained from the Chart of Accounts file.

As you can see, four custom statements are available:

• Balance Sheet (BAL)
• Income Statement (INC)
• Financial Ratio Statement 1 (RA1)
• Financial Ratio Statement 2 (RA2)

The Financial Ratio Statements provide data illustrating the difference between current assets and current liabilities.

Specialized reports, such as Arithmetic and Geometric ratios, can also be created through *DacEasy*. Arithmetic ratios illustrate the correlation between the numbers by a simple amount differ-

Figure 6-60. The Financial Statements Maintenance Screen

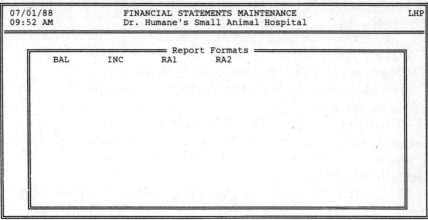

```
07/01/88                 FINANCIAL STATEMENTS MAINTENANCE                LHP
09:52 AM                 Dr. Humane's Small Animal Hospital

                    ═══════════ Report Formats ═══════════
          BAL       INC       RA1       RA2
```

F1-Help F2-Edit F3-Add F6-Delete F8-Duplicate ESC-Exit

ence calculated by subtracting one account from another. Geometric ratios illustrate the correlation as a percentage calculated by dividing one amount into another.

To edit the Financial Ratio Statement 1 format, follow these steps:

4. Press the right-arrow key twice.
5. Press the F2 (Edit) function key.

The screen in Figure 6-61 will appear.

Figure 6-61. The Financial Ratio Statement 1 Screen

```
07/01/88                                                                 LHP
09:54 AM                 Dr. Humane's Small Animal Hospital

  Enter Report Name : RA1
─────────────────────────────────────────────────────────────────────────
  Print                            Amount Amount To          Lines
  (Y/N)  Acct.# Description        From    1   2   3    %   99=pg.
  ───    ─────  ───────────        ─────  ─── ─── ───  ───  ──────
   Y            FINANCIAL RATIOS    0                          C
   Y            ANALYSIS:           0                          C
   Y                                0
   Y            Acid Test:          0                          1
   Y                                0
   Y            The ratio determines 0
   Y            the relation between 0
   Y            Cash availability   0
   Y            and Short Term Debt: 0                         1
   Y            Arithmetic Ratio:   0                          C
   Y                                0
   Y     1101   Petty Cash          99      +
```

F1-Help ALT I-Insert ALT D-Delete ALT P-Print F10-Process ESC-exit

DacEasy reports are formatted line by line and numbers can be totaled within the report. You can also add or delete a line at a later time.

To help you complete this file, a brief description of each field is explained below.

Note: Because the tutorials in this manual use *DacEasy*'s Chart of Accounts, no hands-on samples are incorporated in the following example.

Enter Report Name. This field identifies the report. You can use up to four alphanumeric characters to describe it. If you enter a code that already exists, its information will appear and can be reviewed or revised.

Print. This field gives you the option of whether you want the line you're on printed in the report. *DacEasy* automatically prints each line unless you enter an *N* in this field. Also, enter *N* if you're using the line for calculation purposes only.

Note: All calculations are still performed whether or not this line is printed.

Account #. This field is optional. Enter the appropriate account number from your Chart of Accounts, or if you don't want to use account data, skip this field by pressing Enter or the right-arrow key.

Description. This field automatically displays the account name that corresponds with the account number entered in the previous field.

Note: You can revise this field, using up to 20 characters, to describe the account. The account name in the Chart of Accounts won't be affected.

Amount From. The number 99 is automatically inserted in this field if a valid account was entered in the Account # field. The number 99 means the information to be printed on this line has an account balance. Five other special codes can also be entered within this field:

1. To print a description only, enter 0 in this field.
2. To print the total from Accumulator 1, enter 1.
3. To print the total from Accumulator 2, enter 2.
4. To print the total from Accumulator 3, enter 3.
5. To compute and print a ratio using two Accumulator columns, press / (slash).

Accumulators are columns in the Amount To field (which follows). Special codes are entered in these columns that tell the system how to compute and print financial reports. An explanation of ratios appears later in this chapter.

Amount To. This field has four columns (Accumulators) 1, 2, 3, and %. The first 3 columns are used to:

- Store information to the Accumulator
- Add to the Accumulator
- Subtract from the Accumulator
- Read from the Accumulator
- Use the Accumulator in ratio computations
- Clear the Accumulator

The following codes can be used in these columns:

+	Add the amount from the current line to the Accumulator
−	Subtract the amount from the current line from the Accumulator
0	Clear the Accumulator

If you enter a slash (/) in the Amount From column, enter one of these codes in the appropriate column:

N	Use the Accumulator as the numerator (top value) in division (ratio) computations
D	Use the Accumulator as the denominator (bottom value) in division computations

The % column (Accumulator) stores a value used as the base (root) in the computation of percentages throughout reports.

Lines 99=pg. This field allows you to enter special format instructions.

Format	Text in Lines 99=pg
Single spacing between lines	1
Double spacing between lines	2
New page	99
Single line under the amount fields	−
Double lines under amount fields	=
Center a description on the report	C

231

What is a Ratio?

A ratio is the number resulting from the division of one number by another. *DacEasy Accounting* Version 3.0 provides the capability to perform division within the report design operation. This enables you to enter information for ratio analysis.

To perform division computations, the following operations are necessary:

- The numerator (top value) for the division computation must be entered for accumulation in one of the three Amount To columns.
- The denominator (bottom value) for the division computation must be entered for accumulation in another Amount To column.
- A / (slash) must be entered in the Amount From field on the line where you want the computation executed.
- An *N* must be entered in the Amount To column holding the numerator.
- A *D* must be entered in the Amount To column holding the denominator.

To assist you in the format of reports, *DacEasy* also provides these keys:

- To add a new line at the cursor, press Alt-I.
- To delete the line at the cursor, press Alt-D.
- To print a copy of the report that's currently onscreen, press Alt-P.
- To save your work and exit the operation, press the F10 function key or the Esc key.

Exiting the format operation. To exit the Format operation, press Esc. At the exit prompt, press Enter to accept the default (*Y*).

Printing Financial Statements. To print a financial statement(s), follow these steps:

1. Highlight the Financials menu from the Opening menu. Press Enter.
2. Press 5 to select the Financial Statements Generator option.
3. Press 2 to select the Print Financial Reports option.

The screen in Figure 6-62 will appear.

Figure 6-62. The Print Financial Statements Screen

```
07/01/88                    PRINT FINANCIAL STATEMENTS                      LHP
09:57 AM                  Dr. Humane's Small Animal Hospital

                     ═══════════ Report Formats ═══════════
            BAL          INC        RA1          RA2
```

```
F1-Help F2-Select F3-Unselect F10-Print Statements ESC-Exit
```

4. Press the right- or left-arrow key and then press the F2 (Select function key) to indicate which report(s) you want printed. An asterisk will appear at each of the reports to be printed. To remove an asterisk, press the F3 (Unselect) function key.

   Once you've selected the report(s) to be printed,

5. Press F10 (Print Statements).

   The message *Include Account Numbers (Y/N)? Y* will appear on the screen. This prompt gives you the option of printing your reports with or without account numbers. Type *N* and press Enter if you don't want to include account numbers; otherwise, press Enter to accept the default.

   The report(s) you selected will start printing.

Chapter 7
DacEasy's End of Period and Forecasting Operations

DacEasy's End of Period Operations

The length of time for which a business analyzes financial information is called a *fiscal period*. A fiscal period is also known as an *accounting period*. Each business chooses a fiscal period length that meets its own needs. Your business may use a one-month fiscal period. Or it may use a three-month, six-month, or one-year fiscal period. Businesses don't use fiscal periods longer than one year because tax reports must be made at least once a year.

A fiscal period can begin on the first day of any month. For example, your business might use a one-year fiscal period that begins on January 1, 1988, and ends on December 31, 1988. Another business might use a one-year fiscal period that begins on July 1, 1988, and ends on June 30, 1989. Businesses most often choose a one-year fiscal period that ends during a period of low business activity. In this way, the end of year accounting activities don't come at a time when other business activity is heaviest.

When a fiscal period is closed out, accounting records are *zeroed out* so new fiscal period data can be entered.

DacEasy's Periodic menu lets you close your books at the end of each month and at the end of each fiscal year for the following accounting areas:

- General Ledger
- Accounts Receivable
- Accounts Payable
- Inventory

Closing Out the General Ledger

To close out the General Ledger at the end of a month, follow these steps:

Figure 7-1. The General Ledger End Month Screen

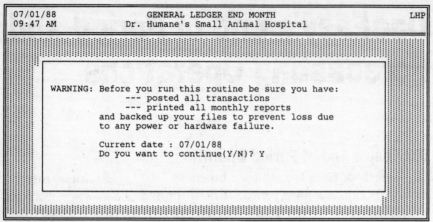

```
07/01/88              GENERAL LEDGER END MONTH              LHP
09:47 AM            Dr. Humane's Small Animal Hospital


        ┌──────────────────────────────────────────────────┐
        │                                                  │
        │   WARNING: Before you run this routine be sure you have: │
        │              --- posted all transactions         │
        │              --- printed all monthly reports      │
        │         and backed up your files to prevent loss due │
        │         to any power or hardware failure.          │
        │                                                  │
        │         Current date : 07/01/88                  │
        │         Do you want to continue(Y/N)? Y           │
        │                                                  │
        └──────────────────────────────────────────────────┘


```

F1-Help ESC-Exit

1. Highlight the Periodic menu from the Opening menu. Press
   Enter.
2. Press 1 to select the General Ledger submenu.
3. Press 1 to select the End Month operation.
     The screen in Figure 7-1 will appear.

   If you need to post any transactions, print any monthly reports, or back up your data files, type *N* and press Enter at the
prompt. You will exit this operation. To continue, press Enter.

4. Press Enter.
     The screen will display the closing date. Press Enter to
   accept this date or type the new date, then press Enter.
5. Press Enter.
     The screen in Figure 7-2 will appear.
6. Press Enter to start the closing process.
     Once the closing operation has been run, all posted trans-
   actions will be deleted from the General Ledger transaction
   file. The Current Balance from each account is transferred to
   the Previous Balance field, and the This Period field is cleared
   so new fiscal period data can be entered.

   To close out the General Ledger at the end of the fiscal year,
follow these steps:

236

Figure 7-2. Prompt to Start Closing

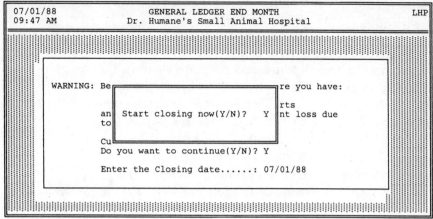

```
07/01/88                    GENERAL LEDGER END MONTH                    LHP
09:47 AM              Dr. Humane's Small Animal Hospital



             WARNING: Be┌──────────────────────────┐re you have:

                      an│  Start closing now(Y/N)?   Y │nt loss due
                      to│                          │
                      Cu└──────────────────────────┘
                      Do you want to continue(Y/N)? Y

                      Enter the Closing date......: 07/01/88
```

F1-Help ESC-Exit

1. Highlight the Periodic menu from the Opening menu. Press Enter.
2. Press 1 to select the General Ledger submenu.
3. Press 2 to select the End Year operation.
   The screen in Figure 7-3 will appear.

If you need to compute and print forecasts, print annual reports, or back up your data files, type *N* and press Enter at the prompt. You will exit this operation. To continue, press Enter.

Figure 7-3. Warning Screen When End Year Operation Is Chosen

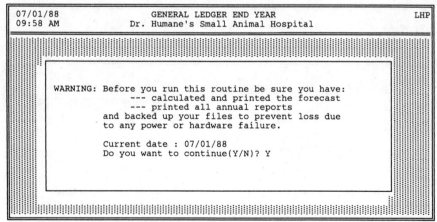

```
07/01/88                    GENERAL LEDGER END YEAR                     LHP
09:58 AM              Dr. Humane's Small Animal Hospital



        WARNING: Before you run this routine be sure you have:
                  --- calculated and printed the forecast
                  --- printed all annual reports
               and backed up your files to prevent loss due
               to any power or hardware failure.

               Current date : 07/01/88
               Do you want to continue(Y/N)? Y
```

F1-Help ESC-Exit

4. Press Enter.

A message asking you to enter the Clear to account will appear.

The *Clear to* account is the account, located in the general ledger, where the sum of the year's earnings are posted. Once all income and expense accounts are cleared, the year's net profit or net loss is posted to the Clear to account.

Note: Account # 3286 (1986 Profit/Loss) is a clear to account (see the Chart of Accounts in Chapter 6).

5. Enter the clear to account. Press Enter.

The screen in Figure 7-4 will appear.

6. Press Enter to start the closing process.

Once this closing operation has been run, all statistical data is updated for each general ledger account. The information contained in the This Year field transfers to the Last Year field. The information contained in the Last Year field transfers to the Year Before Last field, and the information contained in the This Year field is removed so the new fiscal year's data can be entered.

Closing Out the Accounts Receivable Transactions

To close out Accounts Receivable transactions at the end of a month, follow these steps:

1. Highlight the Periodic menu from the Opening menu. Press Enter.

Figure 7-4. Confirmation Screen Appears Prior to Closing

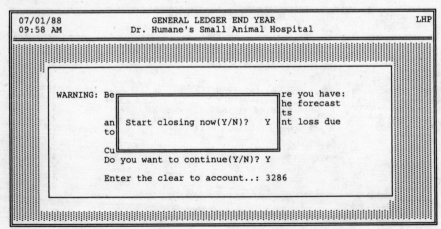

```
 07/01/88              GENERAL LEDGER END YEAR                    LHP
 09:58 AM          Dr. Humane's Small Animal Hospital



      WARNING: Be┌──────────────────────────────┐re you have:
               │                              │he forecast
            an │  Start closing now(Y/N)?   Y │ts
            to │                              │nt loss due
            Cu└──────────────────────────────┘
               Do you want to continue(Y/N)? Y

               Enter the clear to account..: 3286
```

F1-Help ESC-Exit

2. Press 2 to select the Accounts Receivable submenu.
3. Press 1 to select the End Month operation.

   The screen in Figure 7-5 will appear.

   If you need to post transactions, print monthly reports, or back up your data files, type *N* and press Enter at the prompt. You will exit this operation. To continue, press Enter.

4. Press Enter.

   The screen will display the closing date. Press Enter to accept this date or type a new date, then press Enter.
5. Press Enter.

   The cursor will move to the From field as shown in Figure 7-6. To close all appropriate accounts:
6. Press Enter twice.

   DacEasy will automatically enter the words *First Record* at the From field and *Last Record* at the To field, and the screen will change, displaying the message *Start Closing Now?*

7. Press Enter to start the closing process.

   Once the closing operation has been run, *DacEasy* removes all customer invoices with a balance of 0 from the Open Invoice file. The system also removes all *balance forward* transactions for the month. Any other invoices still in the file are not affected.

Figure 7-5. The Preliminary Screen for Closing Out Accounts Receivable

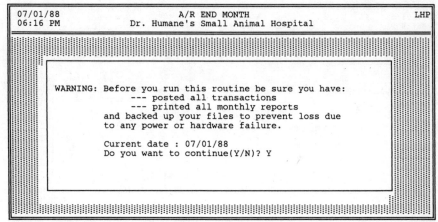

```
07/01/88                          A/R END MONTH                          LHP
06:16 PM                Dr. Humane's Small Animal Hospital


        WARNING: Before you run this routine be sure you have:
                 --- posted all transactions
                 --- printed all monthly reports
                 and backed up your files to prevent loss due
                 to any power or hardware failure.

                 Current date : 07/01/88
                 Do you want to continue(Y/N)? Y




F1-Help ESC-Exit
```

Figure 7-6. The Accounts Receivable End Month Screen

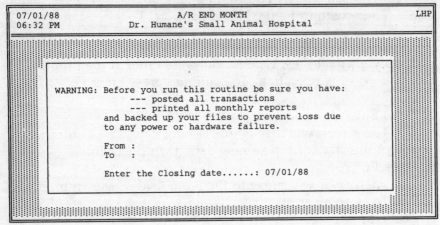

```
07/01/88                    A/R END MONTH                        LHP
06:32 PM              Dr. Humane's Small Animal Hospital


        WARNING: Before you run this routine be sure you have:
                 --- posted all transactions
                 --- printed all monthly reports
                 and backed up your files to prevent loss due
                 to any power or hardware failure.

                 From :
                 To   :

                 Enter the Closing date......: 07/01/88
```

F1-Help ESC-Exit

To close out Accounts Receivable transactions at the end of the fiscal year, follow these steps:

1. Highlight the Periodic menu from the Opening menu. Press Enter.
2. Press 2 to select the Accounts Receivable submenu.
3. Press 2 to select the End Year operation.
    The screen in Figure 7-7 will appear.

Figure 7-7. End Year Close Out of Accounts Receivable

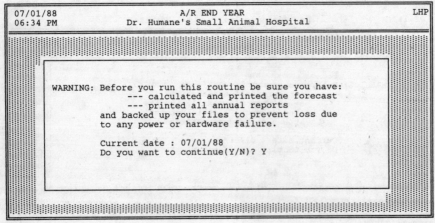

```
07/01/88                    A/R END YEAR                         LHP
06:34 PM              Dr. Humane's Small Animal Hospital


          WARNING: Before you run this routine be sure you have:
                   --- calculated and printed the forecast
                   --- printed all annual reports
                   and backed up your files to prevent loss due
                   to any power or hardware failure.

                   Current date : 07/01/88
                   Do you want to continue(Y/N)? Y
```

F1-Help ESC-Exit

If you need to compute and print forecasts, print annual reports, or back up your data files, type *N* and press Enter at the prompt. You will exit this operation. To continue, press Enter.

4. Press Enter.

The screen will display the message *Start Closing Now?*

5. Press Enter to start the closing process.

Once this closing operation has been run, statistical data for each customer is updated. The information contained in the This Year field transfers to the Last Year field. The information contained in the Last Year field transfers to the Year Before Last field, and the information contained in the This Year field is removed so the new fiscal year's data can be entered.

Generating Accounts Receivable Finance Charges

DacEasy's Accounts Receivable Generate Finance Charges operation automatically computes finance charges for your customers by applying the finance charge rate contained in the customer's file to the customer's aging. A summary general ledger transaction is also generated through this operation.

To generate any applicable finance charges, follow these steps:

1. Highlight the Periodic menu from the Opening menu. Press Enter.
2. Press 2 to select the Accounts Receivable submenu.
3. Press 4 to select the Generate Finance Charges operation.

The screen in Figure 7-8 will appear.

If you need to enter and post any invoices and transactions or back up your data files, type *N* and press Enter at the prompt. You'll exit this operation. To continue, press Enter.

4. Press Enter.

The screen in Figure 7-9 will appear.

5. Press Enter to start generating finance charges.

Closing Out Accounts Payable Transactions

To close out Accounts Payable transactions at the end of the month, follow these steps:

Figure 7-8. The Finance Charges Screen

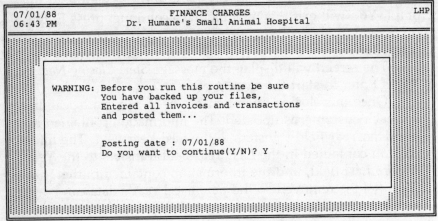

```
07/01/88                    FINANCE CHARGES                      LHP
06:43 PM             Dr. Humane's Small Animal Hospital



        WARNING: Before you run this routine be sure
                 You have backed up your files,
                 Entered all invoices and transactions
                 and posted them...


                 Posting date : 07/01/88
                 Do you want to continue(Y/N)? Y




F1-Help ESC-Exit
```

1. Highlight the Periodic menu from the Opening menu. Press Enter.
2. Press 3 to select the Accounts Payable submenu.
3. Press 1 to select the End Month operation.

   The screen in Figure 7-10 will appear.

If you need to post transactions, print monthly reports, or back up your data files, type *N* and press Enter at the prompt. You will exit this operation. To continue, press Enter.

Figure 7-9. Screen Awaiting Confirmation to Continue

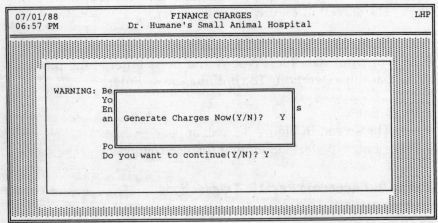

```
07/01/88                    FINANCE CHARGES                      LHP
06:57 PM             Dr. Humane's Small Animal Hospital



        WARNING: Be
                 Yo
                 En    Generate Charges Now(Y/N)?     Y        s
                 an


                 Po
                 Do you want to continue(Y/N)? Y




F1-Help ESC-Exit
```

Figure 7·10. The Accounts Payable End Month Screen

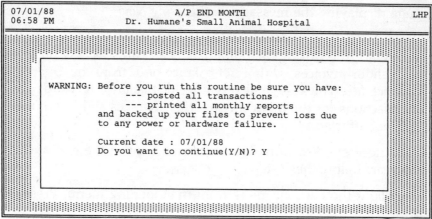

```
07/01/88                      A/P  END MONTH                        LHP
06:58 PM              Dr. Humane's Small Animal Hospital



        WARNING: Before you run this routine be sure you have:
                  --- posted all transactions
                  --- printed all monthly reports
                and backed up your files to prevent loss due
                to any power or hardware failure.

                Current date : 07/01/88
                Do you want to continue(Y/N)? Y




F1-Help ESC-Exit
```

4. Press Enter.

   The screen will display the closing date. Press Enter to accept this date or type a new date, then press Enter.
5. Press Enter.

   The cursor will move to the From field as shown in Figure 7-11. To close all appropriate accounts,
6. Press Enter twice.

Figure 7·11. Accounts Payable Screen Awaiting First and Last Record Entry

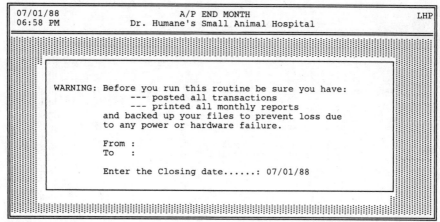

```
07/01/88                      A/P  END MONTH                        LHP
06:58 PM              Dr. Humane's Small Animal Hospital




        WARNING: Before you run this routine be sure you have:
                  --- posted all transactions
                  --- printed all monthly reports
                and backed up your files to prevent loss due
                to any power or hardware failure.

                From :
                To   :

                Enter the Closing date......: 07/01/88


F1-Help ESC-Exit
```

DacEasy will automatically enter the words *First Record* at the From field and *Last Record* at the To field, and the screen will change displaying the message *Start Closing Now?*

7. Press Enter to start the closing process.

Once the closing operation has been run, *DacEasy* removes all vendor invoices, with a net balance of 0, from the Open Invoice file. The system also removes all balance forward transactions for the month. Any other invoices still in the file are not affected.

To close out Accounts Payable transactions at the end of the fiscal year, follow these steps:

1. Highlight the Periodic menu from the Opening menu. Press Enter.
2. Press 3 to select the Accounts Payable submenu.
3. Press 2 to select the End Year operation.

The screen in Figure 7-12 will appear.

If you need to compute and print forecasts, print annual reports, or back up your data files, type *N* and press Enter at the prompt. You will exit this operation. To continue, press Enter.

4. Press Enter.

The screen will display the message *Start Closing Now?*
5. Press Enter to start the closing process.

Figure 7-12. The Accounts Payable End Year Screen

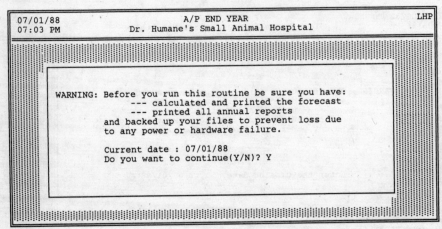

```
07/01/88                    A/P END YEAR                      LHP
07:03 PM            Dr. Humane's Small Animal Hospital



        WARNING: Before you run this routine be sure you have:
        ---          --- calculated and printed the forecast
                     --- printed all annual reports
                and backed up your files to prevent loss due
                to any power or hardware failure.

                Current date : 07/01/88
                Do you want to continue(Y/N)? Y




F1-Help ESC-Exit
```

Once this closing operation has been run, statistical data for each vendor is updated. The information contained in the This Year field transfers to the Last Year field. The information contained in the Last Year field transfers to the Year Before Last field, and the information contained in the This Year field is removed so the new fiscal year's data can be entered.

Closing Out Inventory Transactions

To close out Inventory transactions at the end of the fiscal year, follow these steps:

1. Highlight the Periodic menu from the Opening menu. Press Enter.
2. Press 4 to select the Inventory submenu.
3. Press 1 to select the End Year operation.
   The screen in Figure 7-13 will appear.

If you need to compute and print forecasts, print annual reports, or back up your data files, type *N* and press Enter at the prompt. You will exit this operation. To continue, press Enter.

4. Press Enter.
   The screen will display the message *Start Closing Now?*
5. Press Enter to start the closing process.
   Once this closing operation has been run, statistical information regarding inventory and services is updated. The infor-

Figure 7-13. The Inventory End Year Screen

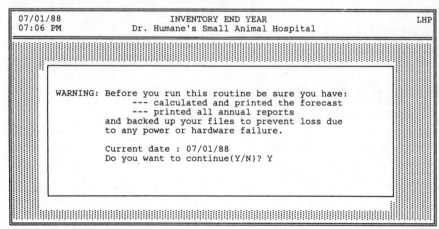

```
07/01/88                     INVENTORY END YEAR                      LHP
07:06 PM               Dr. Humane's Small Animal Hospital



        WARNING: Before you run this routine be sure you have:
                 --- calculated and printed the forecast
                 --- printed all annual reports
                 and backed up your files to prevent loss due
                 to any power or hardware failure.

                 Current date : 07/01/88
                 Do you want to continue(Y/N)? Y




F1-Help ESC-Exit
```

mation contained in the This Year field transfers to the Last Year field. The information contained in the Last Year field transfers to the Year Before Last field, and the information contained in the This Year field is removed so the new fiscal year's data can be entered.

DacEasy's Forecasting Operations

The ability to forecast the future performance of your business can be very valuable. In the past, before the use of computer accounting programs like *DacEasy Accounting*, projecting future trends was extremely time-consuming because only paper, a pencil, and a calculator were available. Calculating the effects of changes took hours.

This disadvantage probably lead many companies to go out of business because they didn't want to take the time to perform these projections by hand. These companies had no idea what the future held for them or what it was going to take to run a successful business.

Fortunately for you, *DacEasy* provides a Forecasting Module that automatically updates and maintains all statistical and balance information. Up to three years of historical statistics are maintained for the general ledger, customer, vendor, product, and services files. *DacEasy* uses information in these files to project the future performance of your business.

DacEasy provides four forecasting methods:

- previous year
- percent
- trend
- least square

This allows you to forecast trends from different perspectives.

Forecasting Operations

DacEasy provides three forecasting operations:

1. Automatic Calculations
2. Print Forecast
3. Print Statistical YTD (Year to Date)
    All three of these operations can be performed from within the General Ledger, Accounts Receivable, Accounts Payable, and Inventory Periodic submenu.

Figure 7-14. The General Ledger Forecast Calculation Screen

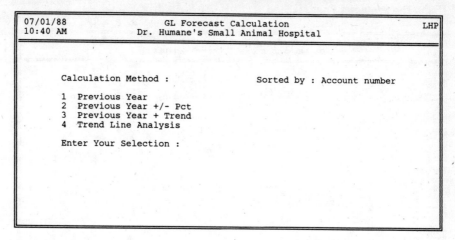

```
07/01/88                    GL Forecast Calculation                      LHP
10:40 AM                Dr. Humane's Small Animal Hospital


         Calculation Method :              Sorted by : Account number

         1  Previous Year
         2  Previous Year +/- Pct
         3  Previous Year + Trend
         4  Trend Line Analysis

         Enter Your Selection :
```

The General Ledger Automatic Calculations Operation

To perform forecast calculations for the general ledger, follow these steps:

1. Highlight the Periodic menu from the Opening menu. Press Enter.
2. Press 1 to select the General Ledger submenu.
3. Press 3 to select the Forecast submenu.
4. Press 1 to select the Automatic Calculations operation.
   The screen in Figure 7-14 will appear.

To perform the Previous Year calculation method:

5. Type 1 and press Enter.
   The screen in Figure 7-15 will appear.

To calculate all general ledger accounts:

6. Press Enter twice.
   DacEasy will automatically enter the words *First Record* at the From field and *Last Record* at the To field. Then the system will begin the calculation process.
   Once completed, you'll return to the Periodic menu.

**Figure 7-15. Screen Prepared to Perform a Forecast
Using the Previous Year Method**

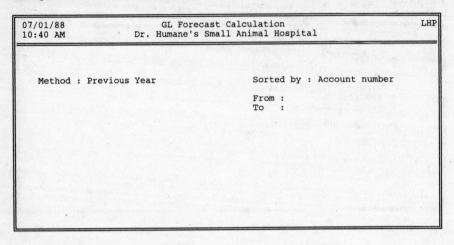

```
07/01/88              GL Forecast Calculation              LHP
10:40 AM           Dr. Humane's Small Animal Hospital


    Method : Previous Year          Sorted by : Account number

                                    From :
                                    To   :
```

The Accounts Receivable Automatic Forecast Calculations Operation

To perform automatic calculations for Accounts Receivable, follow these steps:

1. Highlight the Periodic menu from the Opening menu. Press Enter.
2. Press 2 to select the Accounts Receivable submenu.
3. Press 3 to select the Forecast submenu.
4. Press 1 to select the Automatic Calculations operation.
     The screen in Figure 7-16 will appear.

     The cursor should be positioned at the first Enter Your Selection field.
     To perform the Trend Line Analysis calculation method:

5. Type 4 and press Enter.
     The cursor will move to the second Enter Your Selection field.
     To sort the calculations by Code,
6. Type 1 and press Enter.
     To calculate all Accounts Receivable by Code:
7. Press Enter twice.

Figure 7-16. The Accounts Receivable Automatic Forecast Calculations Operation Screen

```
┌─────────────────────────────────────────────────────────────────────┐
│ 07/01/88              AR Forecast Calculation                  LHP   │
│ 09:43 AM         Dr. Humane's Small Animal Hospital                  │
│                                                                       │
│                                                                       │
│     Calculation Method :                  Sort By :                  │
│                                                                       │
│     1  Previous Year                      1  Code                    │
│     2  Previous Year +/- Pct              2  Department              │
│     3  Previous Year + Trend              3  Sales Person           │
│     4  Trend Line Analysis                                           │
│                                           Enter Your Selection :     │
│     Enter Your Selection :                                           │
│                                                                       │
│                                                                       │
│                                                                       │
│                                                                       │
└─────────────────────────────────────────────────────────────────────┘
```

DacEasy will automatically enter the words *First Record* at the From field and *Last Record* at the To field. Then the system will begin the automatic calculations process.

Once completed, you'll return to the Periodic menu.

The Accounts Payable Automatic Forecast Calculations Operation

To perform automatic calculations for Accounts Payable, follow these steps:

1. Highlight the Periodic menu from the Opening menu. Press Enter.
2. Press 3 to select the Accounts Payable submenu.
3. Press 3 to select the Forecast submenu.
4. Press 1 to select the Automatic Calculations operation.

   The screen in Figure 7-17 will appear.

The cursor should be positioned at the first Enter Your Selection field.

To perform the Previous Year + Trend calculation method:

5. Type 3 and press Enter.

   The cursor will move to the second Enter Your Selection field.

   To sort the calculations by Type:

Figure 7-17. The Accounts Payable Forecast Calculation Screen

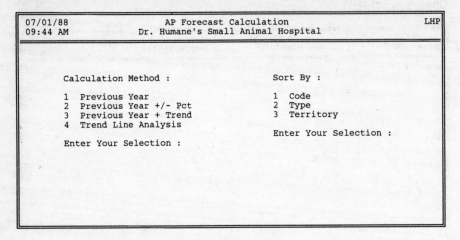

```
07/01/88              AP Forecast Calculation              LHP
09:44 AM         Dr. Humane's Small Animal Hospital


        Calculation Method :              Sort By :

        1  Previous Year                  1  Code
        2  Previous Year +/- Pct          2  Type
        3  Previous Year + Trend          3  Territory
        4  Trend Line Analysis
                                          Enter Your Selection :
        Enter Your Selection :
```

6. Type 2 and press Enter.

   To calculate all Accounts Payable by Type:
7. Press Enter twice.

   DacEasy will automatically enter the words *First Record* at the From field and *Last Record* at the To field. Then the system will begin the calculation process.

   Once completed, you'll return to the Periodic menu.

The Inventory Automatic Forecast Calculations Operation

Note: This operation lets you calculate both the inventory and service areas of your accounting system.

   To perform automatic calculations for Inventory, follow these steps:

1. Highlight the Periodic menu from the Opening menu. Press Enter.
2. Press 4 to select the Inventory submenu.
3. Press 2 to select the Forecast submenu.
4. Press 1 to select the Automatic Calculations operation.

   The screen in Figure 7-18 will appear.

   To perform calculations for Services,

5. Type *S* and press Enter.

   The screen in Figure 7-19 will appear.

Figure 7-18. Screen Asking Whether to Calculate Inventory or Service

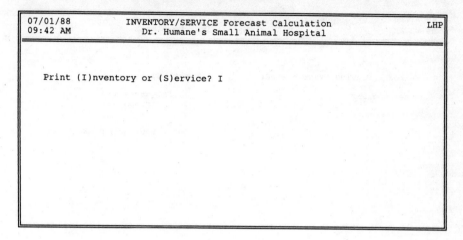

```
07/01/88              INVENTORY/SERVICE Forecast Calculation         LHP
09:42 AM                  Dr. Humane's Small Animal Hospital
══════════════════════════════════════════════════════════════════════


    Print (I)nventory or (S)ervice? I




```

The cursor should be positioned at the first *Enter Your Selection* field.

To perform the Previous Year +/− Pct. calculation method:

6. Type 2 and press Enter.
   The screen in Figure 7-20 will appear.
7. Enter 5 as the desired percent. Press Enter.

Figure 7-19. The Inventory Automatic Forecast Calculations Operation Screen for Services

```
07/01/88              INVENTORY/SERVICE Forecast Calculation         LHP
09:45 AM                  Dr. Humane's Small Animal Hospital
══════════════════════════════════════════════════════════════════════


        Calculation Method :              Sort By :

        1  Previous Year                  1  Inventory #
        2  Previous Year +/- Pct          2  Department
        3  Previous Year + Trend
        4  Trend Line Analysis
                                          Enter Your Selection :
        Enter Your Selection :


```

Figure 7-20. Prompt to Enter Percent

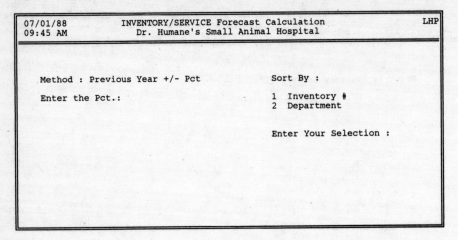

```
07/01/88          INVENTORY/SERVICE Forecast Calculation          LHP
09:45 AM              Dr. Humane's Small Animal Hospital


    Method : Previous Year +/- Pct          Sort By :

    Enter the Pct.:                         1  Inventory #
                                            2  Department


                                            Enter Your Selection :
```

The cursor will move to the second Enter Your Selection field.

To sort the calculations by Inventory # (Service #):

8. Type 1 and press Enter.

To calculate all Service files by Inventory # (Service #):

9. Press Enter twice.

DacEasy will automatically enter the words *First Record* at the From field and *Last Record* at the To field. Then the system will begin the calculations process.

Once completed, you'll return to the Periodic menu.

Printing Forecasts

To print the General Ledger Forecast Report, follow these steps:

1. Highlight the Periodic menu from the Opening menu. Press Enter.
2. Press 1 to select the General Ledger submenu.
3. Press 3 to select the Forecast submenu.
4. Press 2 to select the Print Forecast operation.

The screen in Figure 7-21 will appear.

To sort all general ledger account numbers:

5. Press Enter twice.

Figure 7-21. The Print General Ledger Forecast Screen

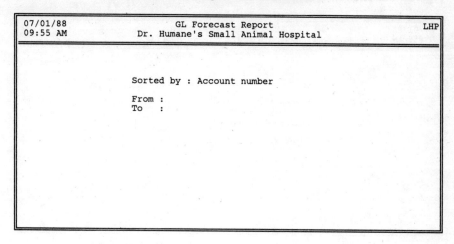

```
07/01/88                        GL Forecast Report                          LHP
09:55 AM               Dr. Humane's Small Animal Hospital


                Sorted by : Account number

                From :
                To   :
```

DacEasy will automatically enter the words *First Record* at the From field and *Last Record* at the To field.

The General Ledger Forecast Report will start printing.

To print the Accounts Receivable Forecast Report, follow these steps:

1. Highlight the Periodic menu from the Opening menu. Press Enter.
2. Press 2 to select the Accounts Receivable submenu.
3. Press 3 to select the Forecast submenu.
4. Press 2 to select the Print Forecast operation.

    The screen in Figure 7-22 will appear.

To sort this report by Code:

5. Type 1 and press Enter.

    To print all Accounts Receivable sorted by Code:
6. Press Enter twice.

    DacEasy will automatically enter the words *First Record* at the From field and *Last Record* at the To field.

    The screen in Figure 7-23 will appear.

If you want to include cost/profit in this report, press Enter. If you don't, type *N*, then press Enter.

Figure 7-22. The Print Accounts Receivable Forecast Screen

```
07/01/88                    AR Forecast Report                    LHP
09:55 AM            Dr. Humane's Small Animal Hospital


                    Sort By :

                    1   Code
                    2   Department
                    3   Sales Person

                    Enter Your Selection :
```

7. Press Enter.

   The Accounts Receivable Forecast Report will start printing.

   To print the Accounts Payable Forecast Report, follow these steps:

1. Highlight the Periodic menu from the Opening menu. Press Enter.

Figure 7-23. The Prompt to Choose Whether to Include Cost/Profit in Report

```
07/01/88                    AR Forecast Report                    LHP
09:59 AM            Dr. Humane's Small Animal Hospital


                    Sorted By : Code

                    From : (First Record)
                    To   : (Last Record)

                    Include cost/profit in report (Y/N)? Y
```

Figure 7-24. The Print Accounts Payable Forecast Screen

```
07/01/88                    AP Forecast Report                        LHP
10:07 AM              Dr. Humane's Small Animal Hospital



                   Sort By :

                   1  Code
                   2  Type
                   3  Territory

                   Enter Your Selection :




```

2. Press 3 to select the Accounts Payable submenu.
3. Press 3 to select the Forecast submenu.
4. Press 2 to select the Print Forecast operation.
     The screen in Figure 7-24 will appear.

To sort this report by Code:

5. Type 1 and press Enter.
     To print all Accounts Payable sorted by Code:
6. Press Enter twice.
     DacEasy automatically enters the words *First Record* at the
  From field and *Last Record* at the To field.
     The Accounts Payable Forecast Report will start printing.

To print the Inventory Forecast Report, follow these steps:
Note: This operation lets you print either the Inventory or
Service Forecast Report.

1. Highlight the Periodic menu from the Opening menu. Press
   Enter.
2. Press 4 to select the Inventory submenu.
3. Press 2 to select the Forecast submenu.
4. Press 2 to select the Print Forecast operation.
     The screen in Figure 7-25 will appear.

Figure 7-25. The Inventory/Service Forecast Screen

```
┌─────────────────────────────────────────────────────────────┐
│ 07/01/88          INVENTORY/SERVICE Forecast Report      LHP  │
│ 10:08 AM          Dr. Humane's Small Animal Hospital          │
│───────────────────────────────────────────────────────────── │
│                                                               │
│                                                               │
│          Print (I)nventory or (S)ervice? I                    │
│                                                               │
│                                                               │
│                                                               │
│                                                               │
│                                                               │
│                                                               │
│                                                               │
│                                                               │
│                                                               │
│                                                               │
└─────────────────────────────────────────────────────────────┘
```

To print the Service Forecast Report:

5. Type *S* and press Enter.
   The screen in Figure 7-26 will appear.

   To sort this report by Inventory # (Service #):

6. Type 1 and press Enter.
   To print all services sorted by Inventory # (Service #):
7. Press Enter twice.

Figure 7-26. Prompt to Choose Inventory #

```
┌─────────────────────────────────────────────────────────────┐
│ 07/01/88          INVENTORY/SERVICE Forecast Report      LHP  │
│ 10:08 AM          Dr. Humane's Small Animal Hospital          │
│───────────────────────────────────────────────────────────── │
│                                                               │
│              Sort By :                                        │
│                                                               │
│              1  Inventory #                                   │
│              2  Department                                    │
│                                                               │
│              Enter Your Selection :                           │
│                                                               │
│                                                               │
│                                                               │
│                                                               │
└─────────────────────────────────────────────────────────────┘
```

256

DacEasy will automatically enter the words *First Record* at the From field and *Last Record* at the To field.

The Inventory Forecast Report will start printing.

Printing the Statistical YTD (Year to Date) Report

Note: When you print the Statistical YTD reports, select the same sorting options you used when you created the forecast.

To print the General Ledger Statistical YTD Report, follow these steps:

1. Highlight the Periodic menu from the Opening menu. Press Enter.
2. Press 1 to select the General Ledger submenu.
3. Press 3 to select the Forecast submenu.
4. Press 3 to select the Print Statistical YTD operation.
   The screen in Figure 7-27 will appear.

To print this report sorted by all general ledger account numbers:

5. Press Enter twice.
   DacEasy will automatically enter the words *First Record* at the From field and *Last Record* at the To field.
   The General Ledger Statistical YTD Report will start printing.

Figure 7-27. The Print Statistical Year to Date Screen

```
 07/01/88                    GL Statistical YTD Report                   LHP
 10:13 AM              Dr. Humane's Small Animal Hospital



                    Sorted by : Account number

                    From :
                    To   :






F1-Help F4-Change Date   ESC-Exit
```

257

To print the Accounts Receivable Statistical YTD Report, follow these steps:

1. Highlight the Periodic menu from the Opening menu. Press Enter.
2. Press 2 to select the Accounts Receivable submenu.
3. Press 3 to select the Forecast submenu.
4. Press 3 to select the Print Statistical YTD operation.
   The screen in Figure 7-28 will appear.

To sort this report by Code:

5. Type 1 and press Enter.
   To print all Accounts Receivable sorted by Code:
6. Press Enter twice.
   DacEasy will automatically enter the words *First Record* at the From field and *Last Record* at the To field.
   A message will appear on the screen asking if you want to include cost/profit in this report. If you do, press Enter. If you don't want to include this information, type *N*, then press Enter.
7. Press Enter.
   The Accounts Receivable Statistical YTD Report will start printing.

Figure 7-28. The Print Accounts Receivable Statistical YTD Screen

```
07/01/88                    AR Statistical YTD Report              LHP
10:13 AM               Dr. Humane's Small Animal Hospital




             Sort By :

             1  Code
             2  Department
             3  Sales Person

             Enter Your Selection :




```

Figure 7-29. The Print Accounts Payable Statistical YTD Screen

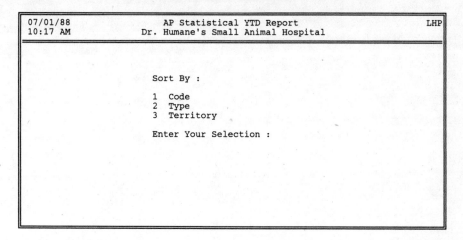

```
07/01/88                    AP Statistical YTD Report                    LHP
10:17 AM              Dr. Humane's Small Animal Hospital



                        Sort By :

                        1   Code
                        2   Type
                        3   Territory

                        Enter Your Selection :
```

To print the Accounts Payable Statistical YTD Report, follow these steps:

1. Highlight the Periodic menu from the Opening menu. Press Enter.
2. Press 3 to select the Accounts Payable submenu.
3. Press 3 to select the Forecast submenu.
4. Press 3 to select the Print Statistical YTD operation.
   The screen in Figure 7-29 will appear.

To sort this report by Code:

5. Type 1 and press Enter.
   To print all Accounts Payable sorted by Code:
6. Press Enter twice.
   DacEasy will automatically enter the words *First Record* at the From field and *Last Record* at the To field.
   The Accounts Payable Statistical YTD Report will start printing.

Chapter 8
DacEasy's Menus

DacEasy's operations are accessed through eight opening menu options:

- File
- Transaction
- Journals
- Posting
- Reports
- Financials
- Periodic
- Options

The following describes each menu option and the operations that are processed through them.

The File Menu
The options located in the File Menu are used to create customer, vendor, inventory, and service files, as well as special billing and purchase order codes and statement messages (Figure 8-1).

The Accounts File
The Accounts File is used to create your own chart of accounts or to add, change, or delete accounts within *DacEasy's* existing chart of accounts.

The Customers File
The Customers File is used to enter information and account balances for customers, notes receivables, employee receivables, and so on.

The Vendors File
The Vendors File is used to enter information and balances for vendors, notes payable, utilities, and so forth.

Figure 8-1. The Options on the File Menu

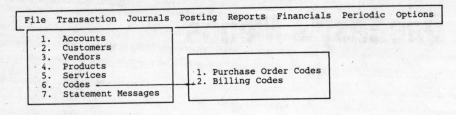

The Products File

The Products File lets you incorporate inventory into your accounting files.

The Services File

The Services File lets you create a file to control any services your business may offer.

The Codes Option

The Codes option lets you create special billing and purchase order codes such as freight, packaging, and insurance. These non-inventory items must be accounted for within your accounting system. You can create up to 20 billing codes and 20 purchase order codes. These codes must be set up before you try to use them in either the Purchase Order or Billing operations.

Statement Messages Option

This feature lets you print tailored messages on your customer's monthly statements based on their present balance and the age of the balance. There are five categories for which statement messages can be used:

1. Inactive
2. Current Balance
3. Late 1–30 Days
4. Late 31–60 Days
5. Late Over 60 Days

The Transaction Menu

The options located in the Transaction menu are used to enter or print all transaction data. The options available are seen in Figure 8-2.

Figure 8-2. The Options on the Transaction Menu

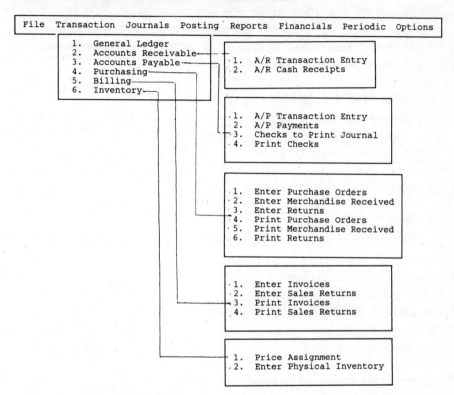

```
File  Transaction  Journals  Posting  Reports  Financials  Periodic  Options
        1.  General Ledger
        2.  Accounts Receivable        1.  A/R Transaction Entry
        3.  Accounts Payable           2.  A/R Cash Receipts
        4.  Purchasing
        5.  Billing
        6.  Inventory
                                       1.  A/P Transaction Entry
                                       2.  A/P Payments
                                       3.  Checks to Print Journal
                                       4.  Print Checks


                                       1.  Enter Purchase Orders
                                       2.  Enter Merchandise Received
                                       3.  Enter Returns
                                       4.  Print Purchase Orders
                                       5.  Print Merchandise Received
                                       6.  Print Returns


                                       1.  Enter Invoices
                                       2.  Enter Sales Returns
                                       3.  Print Invoices
                                       4.  Print Sales Returns


                                       1.  Price Assignment
                                       2.  Enter Physical Inventory
```

The General Ledger option

This operation is used to enter transactions such as bank charges, employee loans, payroll, account balances, and so on.

The Accounts Receivable Transaction Entry Operation

This operation lets you enter transactions such as special discounts or late charges. You can also enter invoices through this operation if you're not utilizing *DacEasy*'s Billing module.

The Accounts Receivable Cash Receipts Operation

This operation lets you enter transactions involving the receipt of cash or credit card sales. You can also enter any payments or advances received from your customers.

The Accounts Payable Transaction Entry Operation

This operation lets you enter transactions not purchased through the purchase order system, such as telephone bills, utilities, rent, credit cards, bank loans.

The Accounts Payable Payments Operation

The Payments operation gives you several options. You can enter partial payments or withhold payments using this operation. Transfers and advances made to your vendors may also be entered as well as any necessary adjustments.

The Checks to Print Journal

This journal lets you review and edit any checks to print before the figures are transferred to a preprinted checks. This journal is advantageous because it allows you to decrease a payment or payments due to your current bank balance or reprint checks if necessary.

The Print Checks Operation

This operation is used to make payments for selected invoices. In order to align the checks with your printer properly, *DacEasy* always voids the first check.

The Enter Purchase Orders Operation

The Enter Purchase Orders operation lets you enter purchase orders for your vendors.

The Enter Merchandise Received Operation

The Enter Merchandise Received operation lets you enter the product you received. Note: You don't have to have a purchase order on file to receive merchandise.

The Enter Returns Operation

This operation lets you enter any product returned to your vendor (that is, a product inferior in quality or damaged upon receipt). Once entered, *DacEasy* automatically reverses entries made to the product and general ledger files.

The Print Purchase Orders Operation

This operation allows you to print any purchase orders you've created through the Enter Purchase Orders operation.

The Print Merchandise Received Operation

This operation allows you to print any merchandise-received transactions you entered through the Enter Merchandise Received operation.

The Print Returns Operation

This operation allows you to print any merchandise-returned transactions you entered through the Enter Returns operation.

The Enter Invoices Operation

The Enter Invoices operation lets you enter customer invoices, thus notifying your customer of monies owed.

The Enter Sales Returns Operation

This operation lets you enter any merchandise returned by your customer (that is, a product that is inferior in quality or damaged). Once entered, *DacEasy* automatically reverses entries made to the Customer, Product, and General Ledger files.

The Print Invoices Operation

This operation allows you to print invoices entered through the Enter Invoices operation.

The Print Sales Returns Operation

This operation allows you to print sales returns entered through the Enter Sales Returns operation.

The Price Assignment Operation

The Price Assignment operation lets you enter criteria on your inventory through several sorting options so product prices can be analyzed from a variety of perspectives.

The Enter Physical Inventory Operation

This operation lets you enter products that are recorded on count sheets during a physical inventory.

The Journals Menu

The options located in the Journals menu are used to print and review your accounting transactions before they're posted to the general ledger. The options available are seen in Figure 8-3.

The General Ledger Journal Option

The General Ledger Journal option lets you print any of the journals created in the general ledger. This journal sorts information transaction by transaction for a given period.

Figure 8-3. The Options on the Journal Menu

```
File  Transaction  Journals  Posting  Reports  Financials  Periodic  Options
                   ┌─────────────────────────┐
                   │ 1.  G/L Journal         │
                   │ 2.  G/L Activity        │
                   │ 3.  A/R Transactions    │
                   │ 4.  A/R Cash Receipts   │
                   │ 5.  A/P Transactions    │
                   │ 6.  A/P Payments        │
                   │ 7.  Purchase Journal    │
                   │ 8.  P.O. Status Report  │
                   │ 9.  Sales Journal       │
                   └─────────────────────────┘
```

The General Ledger Activity Option

The General Ledger Activity option is similar to the General Ledger Journal; however, it lets you print a detailed report sorted by account.

The Accounts Receivable Transactions Option

The Accounts Receivable Transactions option lets you print a journal containing all accounts receivable transactions not recorded in *DacEasy*'s Billing system (that is, adjustments).

The Accounts Receivable Cash Receipts Option

The Accounts Receivable Cash Receipts option lets you print a journal containing all transactions involving the receipt of cash.

The Accounts Payable Transactions Option

The Accounts Payable Transactions option lets you print a journal containing all transactions involving vendors not controlled through the Purchase Order system (that is, telephone, utilities, rent, temporary personnel services), as well as petty cash transactions.

The Accounts Payable Payments Option

The Accounts Payable Payments option lets you print a journal containing a list of all printed checks, whether they're printed by the computer, handwritten, voided, electronic transfers, or automatic charges to your bank.

The Purchase Journal

The Purchase Journal option lets you print a journal containing all merchandise received or returned.

The Purchase Order Status Report

The Purchase Order Status Report option lets you print a journal containing all purchase orders still pending and all products ordered.

The Sales Journal

The Sales Journal option lets you print a journal containing all invoice and sales returns transactions.

The Posting Menu

The options located in the Posting menu are used to post all accounting entries. The options available are seen in Figure 8-4.

The General Ledger Option

The General Ledger Posting option is used to update general ledger account balances with entries recorded in the transaction file. It's important to back up your *DacEasy* data files before running this operation.

The Accounts Receivable Option

The Accounts Receivable Posting option is used to update customer balances. This operation also provides summary transactions for the general ledger. Back up your data files before running this operation.

The Accounts Payable Option

The Accounts Payable Posting option is used to update vendor balances. This operation also prepares the check register for your checking accounts and provides summary transactions for the general ledger. Back up your data files before running this operation.

Figure 8-4. The Options on the Posting Menu

```
┌─────────────────────────────────────────────────────────────────────────┐
│ File  Transaction  Journals  Posting  Reports  Financials  Periodic  Options │
└──────────────────────────────┬──────────────────────────┬────────────────┘
                               │ 1.  General Ledger       │
                               │ 2.  Accounts Receivable  │
                               │ 3.  Accounts Payable     │
                               │ 4.  Purchase Orders      │
                               │ 5.  Billing              │
                               │ 6.  Physical Inventory   │
                               └──────────────────────────┘
```

The Purchase Orders Option

The Purchase Order Posting option is used to update the statistical history in both your product and vendor files. This operation also updates the general ledger.

The Billing Option

The Billing Posting option is used to update the statistical history in both your product and customer files. The general ledger is also updated.

The Physical Inventory Option

The Physical Inventory Posting option is used to post the differences (adjustments). Make sure you've entered the physical inventory count accurately before running this operation. After you've run this posting operation, the Inventory and Cost of Goods Sold accounts (indicated in the General Ledger Interface table) will receive the adjustments.

The Reports Menu

The options located in the Reports menu are used to print a variety of Accounts Receivable, Accounts Payable, and Inventory reports. The options available are seen in Figure 8-5.

The Accounts Receivable Statements Report

The Statements Report option provides five sorts and ten rankings you can select when printing statements.

Figure 8-5. The Options Available on the Reports Menu

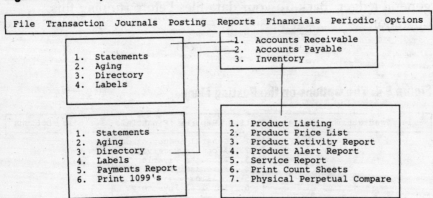

```
File  Transaction  Journals  Posting  Reports  Financials  Periodic  Options

                                           1.  Accounts Receivable
                                           2.  Accounts Payable
                                           3.  Inventory
              1.  Statements
              2.  Aging
              3.  Directory
              4.  Labels


              1.  Statements           1.  Product Listing
              2.  Aging                2.  Product Price List
              3.  Directory            3.  Product Activity Report
              4.  Labels               4.  Product Alert Report
              5.  Payments Report      5.  Service Report
              6.  Print 1099's         6.  Print Count Sheets
                                       7.  Physical Perpetual Compare
```

The Accounts Receivable Aging Report

The Aging Report option provides five sorts and ten rankings you can select when printing this report.

The Accounts Receivable Directory Option

The Accounts Receivable Directory option provides five sorts and ten rankings so you can print customer directories.

The Accounts Receivable Labels Option

The Accounts Receivable Labels option provides five sorts and ten rankings so you can print labels for mailings, phone/address cards, and so forth.

The Accounts Payable Statements Report

The Accounts Payable Statements Report option provides five sorts and nine rankings so you can print statements reminding vendors of invoices that are still open.

The Accounts Payable Aging Report

The Aging Report option provides five sorts and nine rankings you can select when printing this report.

The Accounts Payable Directory Option

The Accounts Payable Directory option provides five sorts and nine rankings so you can print vendor directories.

The Accounts Payable Labels Option

The Accounts Payable Labels option provides five sorts and nine rankings so you can print labels for mailings, phone/address cards, and so on.

The Accounts Payable Payments Report

The Accounts Payable Payments Report option lets you generate a report listing all invoices, when they're due, and any applicable discounts. Two sorting options are available when you print this report. It can be subtotaled by:

• Date
• Vendor

The Print 1099s Option

The Print 1099s option lets you print a listing of all vendors who must receive federal form 1099 from you at the end of the calendar year. You must enter both the vendor's Tax Id. Number and the minimum payment amount before printing this report.

The Inventory Product Listing Option

The Product Listing option provides 5 sorts and 13 rankings so you can print a product catalog.

The Inventory Product Price List Option

The Product Price List option provides 5 sorts and 13 rankings so you can print a comprehensive report displaying the product name, unit of measure and fractions per unit, department, location (bin), vendor code, and tax information. You can keep product cost confidential by assigning a code to product prices.

The Inventory Product Activity Report

The Product Activity Report provides 5 sorts and 13 rankings so you can print information needed for the daily management of your inventory.

The Inventory Product Alert Report

The Product Alert Report provides 5 sorts and 13 rankings so you can print a report describing what products need to be purchased and in what quantity.

The Service Report

The Service Report provides three sorts and five rankings so you can print a report that analyzes your service billing.

The Inventory Print Count Sheets Option

The Print Count Sheets option provides 5 sorts and 13 rankings so you can print inventory count sheets.

The Inventory Physical-Perpetual Compare Option

The Physical-Perpetual Compare option provides 5 sorts and 13 rankings so you can print a comparative report between the products you entered in the Enter Physical Inventory operation and

Figure 8-6. The Options on the Financials Menu

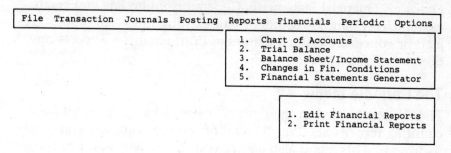

```
File  Transaction  Journals  Posting  Reports  Financials  Periodic  Options
                                               ┌──────────────────────────────────┐
                                               │ 1.  Chart of Accounts             │
                                               │ 2.  Trial Balance                 │
                                               │ 3.  Balance Sheet/Income Statement│
                                               │ 4.  Changes in Fin. Conditions    │
                                               │ 5.  Financial Statements Generator│
                                               └──────────────────────────────────┘

                                                    ┌────────────────────────────┐
                                                    │ 1. Edit Financial Reports  │
                                                    │ 2. Print Financial Reports │
                                                    └────────────────────────────┘
```

those products *DacEasy* continually maintains within its accounting system.

The Financials Menu

The options located in the Financials menu are used to create, edit, or print various financial reports. The options available are seen in Figure 8-6.

The Chart of Accounts

DacEasy's Chart of Accounts option lets you print a listing of all accounts in the General Ledger file. You can print either a partial list or a complete list, depending on your immediate needs.

The Trial Balance

DacEasy's Trial Balance option lets you print a detailed listing of the balances in each of your general ledger accounts.

The Balance Sheet/Income Statement

DacEasy's Balance Sheet/Income Statement option lets you print the financial condition/progress of your business.

The Changes in Financial Conditions Report

DacEasy's Changes in Financial Conditions option lets you print a report that shows the net amounts for uses and sources of money for:

- The current period
- This year
- Last year
- The year before last

The Financial Statements Generator

DacEasy's Financial Statements Generator option lets you create customized financial reports or edit existing ones. All reports created or edited are printed using the Print Financial Reports option.

The Periodic menu

The options located in the Periodic menu let you close out accounting records at either the end of the month or the end of the fiscal year. This menu also allows you to calculate and print forecasts for the General Ledger, Accounts Receivable, Accounts Payable, and Inventory files. The options available in the menu are seen in Figure 8-7.

The End of Month Operations

These operations let you close the books at the end of the month for the General Ledger, Accounts Receivable, and Accounts Payable files only (not the Inventory files).

The End of Year Operations

These operations let you close the books at the end of the year for the General Ledger, Accounts Receivable, Accounts Payable, and Inventory files only (not the Inventory files).

Figure 8-7. The Options Available on the Periodic Menu

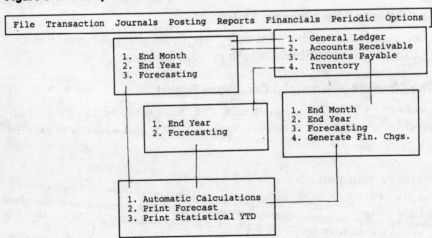

The Accounts Receivable Generate Finance Charges Operation

DacEasy's Accounts Receivable Generate Finance Charges operation automatically computes finance charges for your customers by applying the finance charge rate contained in the customer's file to the customer's aging. A summary general ledger transaction is also generated through this operation.

The Automatic Forecast Calculations Operations

DacEasy provides four forecasting methods for the General Ledger, Accounts Receivable, Accounts Payable, and Inventory files:

- Previous year
- Percent
- Trend
- Least square

The Print Forecast Operation

The Print Forecast Operation lets you print the forecasts you've calculated for each of the General Ledger, Accounts Receivable, Accounts Payable, and Inventory files.

The Print Statistical YTD Operation

This operation prints statistical year-to-date information for the General Ledger, Accounts Receivable, Accounts Payable, and Inventory files.

The Options Menu

The options located in the Options menu are used to specify various settings within your accounting system. The options available in this menu are seen in Figure 8-8.

The Interface Option

The General Ledger Interface table is used to control the integration between *DacEasy's* modules. If you're using your own chart of accounts, this chart must be created before entering this operation. This option lets you assign account numbers the various modules will use when the general ledger is posted.

Figure 8-8. The Selections Available on the Options Menu

```
┌─────────────────────────────────────────────────────────────────┐
│ File Transaction Journals Posting Reports Financials Periodic Options │
└─────────────────────────────────────────────────────────────────┘
                                              ┌──────────────────────┐
                                              │ 1.  Interface        │
                                              │ 2.  Company Id.      │
                                              │ 3.  Tax Table        │
                                              │ 4.  Status           │
                                              │ 5.  Rehash           │
                                              │ 6.  Password         │
                                              │ 7.  Defaults         │
                                              └──────────────────────┘
                                         ┌────────────────────────┐
                                         │ 1. Cost System         │
                                         │ 2. Invoice/P.O. No.    │
                                         │ 3. Printer Codes       │
                                         │ 4. Colors              │
                                         │ 5. Messages            │
                                         └────────────────────────┘
```

The Company Id. Option

DacEasy's Company Id. option lets you enter your company's name, address, and telephone number so it will appear on all documents.

The Tax Table Option

The Tax Table option lets you enter up to ten different sales tax rates that are connected to the Accounts Receivable files through the sales tax rate field. This feature comes in handy for businesses that sell to customers who are located in geographic areas where sales tax rates differ.

The Status Option

The File Status option is accessed to display a listing of your accounting data files, the numbers of records defined, and the numbers of records used in each file. This operation can be reviewed, but not modified.

The Rehash Option

The File Rehash operation is accessed so the sizes of your files can be changed.

The Password Option

DacEasy's Password option lets you assign up to five passwords with a maximum of eight characters each. Before a file with a password can be retrieved, the correct password must be supplied.

The Cost System

DacEasy's Cost System option lets you choose three costing methods:

- Average Cost
- Last Purchase Price
- Standard Cost

DacEasy automatically chooses the Average Cost method if you don't select one yourself.

The Invoice/P.O. No. Option

DacEasy's Invoice/P.O. No. option lets you begin an automated numbering system by entering the next available number from your manual system. Any numbers from 00001 to 99999 can be entered. When the number 99999 is reached, *DacEasy* starts the numbering from the beginning again.

The Printer Codes Option

The Printer Codes option lets you set up parameters for your printer.

The Colors Option

The Colors option lets you define or edit the colors displayed by the program. (You must have a computer with a color monitor to use this operation.)

The Message File

DacEasy provides a special message file where you can store up to 40 messages. Once messages have been created and stored, they can easily be assigned to both customer and vendor files.

Chapter 9
DacEasy's File Utilities

This chapter briefly summarizes *DacEasy's* File Utilities. These utilities are accessed by highlighting the Options Opening Menu.
The Options Menu contains four utilities operations:

• Status
• Rehash
• Printer Codes
• Colors

File Status

To display a list of your accounting data files, the number of records defined, and the number of records used in each file, press 4 from the Options Menu to select the File Status operation.

The screen in Figure 9-1 will appear. This operation can be reviewed, but not modified. The numbers (records) in the Defined column are obtained during the installation procedures discussed in Chapter 1. The numbers (records) in the Used column are updated every time a file is activated (that is, through transaction entries or deletions).

Note: Your Defined and Used columns will display different numbers than Figure 9-1 because your screen is defining the files you've used.

If after reviewing the Status File you realize that too few records were defined during the installation procedure (due to underestimating), the next operation, File Rehash, lets you change your file size definitions.

Press any key to return to the Options Menu.

File Rehash

To change the sizes of your files, press 5 from the Options Menu to select the File Rehash operation. The screen in Figure 9-2 will appear.

Figure 9-1. The File Status Screen

```
07/01/88                    FILE STATUS                         LHP
09:01 AM              Dr. Humane's Small Animal Hospital

        File                  Defined      Used
        --------------------  ---------  ---------
        Accounts                275        257
        Customers               600        4
        Vendors                 12         3
        Products                100        8
        AR Open Invoices        1800       8
        AR Transactions         600        4
        AP Open Invoices        36         8
        AP Transactions         12         6
        GL Transactions         775        30
        Invoices                195        21
        Purchase Orders         100        21
        Physical Inventory      100        0
```

Press any key to continue...

This fully automated operation is used when space for a particular file is diminishing. While working in your accounting system, *DacEasy* alerts you if a particular file is running out of space and informs you to rehash your file size. It's important that you immediately enlarge the file before attempting to enter more transactions. If you're in the middle of a posting process and a warning message appears, *DacEasy* automatically and temporarily creates the required space needed to finish the posting process.

Figure 9-2. The File Rehash Screen

```
07/01/88                    FILE REHASH                         LHP
09:03 AM              Dr. Humane's Small Animal Hospital

        File                  Defined      Used
        --------------------  ---------  ---------
        Accounts                275        257
        Customers               600        4
        Vendors                 12         3
        Products                100        8
        AR Open Invoices        1800       8
        AR Transactions         600        4
        AP Open Invoices        36         8
        AP Transactions         12         6
        GL Transactions         775        30
        Invoices                195        21
        Purchase Orders         100        21
        Physical Inventory      100        0
```

F1-Help F10-Process   ESC-Exit

Once completed, go directly to the File Rehash operation to change the size of the appropriate file.

Note: Before attempting to rehash any file, it's extremely important to create backup files. These backups are the only way to restore all files if a hardware or power failure occurs during the rehash operation.

To rehash a file, follow these steps:

1. Choose the file that needs to be rehashed by moving to it with the down-arrow or Enter key.
2. Enter the new number of records.
3. Press the F10 (Process) function key.

After *DacEasy* has rehashed the appropriate file(s), the screen in Figure 9-3 will appear.

Usually floppy disk systems are more likely to receive a File Rehash Message. However, hard disk systems sometimes run out of space as well.

If your floppy system doesn't have enough disk space for the new file size, you have two options:

• You can rehash other files that have plenty of space and assign them a smaller file size.
• You can upgrade your floppy system to a hard disk system.

If your hard disk system doesn't have enough disk space for the new file size, you have three options:

Figure 9-3. The Screen that Informs You of a Successful Rehash

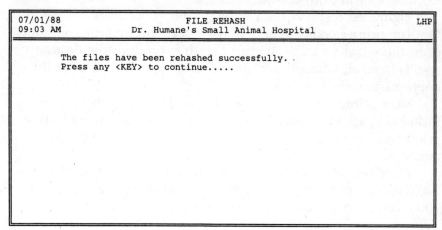

```
07/01/88                    FILE REHASH                              LHP
09:03 AM          Dr. Humane's Small Animal Hospital

         The files have been rehashed successfully.
         Press any <KEY> to continue.....
```

- You can rehash other files that have plenty of space and assign them a smaller file size.
- You can delete other programs from the hard disk.
- You can upgrade your system by getting a larger hard disk.

Setup Printer Parameters

DacEasy prints the following operations in condensed mode (16.7 characters per inch):

- Invoices
- Purchase orders
- Statements
- Reports

DacEasy prints the following operations in normal mode (10 characters per inch):

- Labels
- Checks
- The General Ledger Chart of Accounts

To set up parameters for your printer, press 7 from the Options Menu to select the Defaults Submenu. Next, press 3 to select the Printer Codes operation. This operation is used to define normal and condensed codes for your printer so the appropriate documents will print correctly.

Figure 9-4 displays the Define Printer Parameters operation.

The printer codes 18 and 15 have been entered for you. However, these codes can be modified so they produce the desired results (consult your printer manual or computer dealer for the appropriate codes).

Most printers use one or two codes. *DacEasy*, however, has included space for twelve codes because future advancements in printer and laser technology may require additional code parameters.

After you've entered the appropriate printer codes, press the F10 (Process) function key. *DacEasy* will record these codes and you'll return to the Defaults Submenu.

Figure 9-4. The Printer Parameter Screen

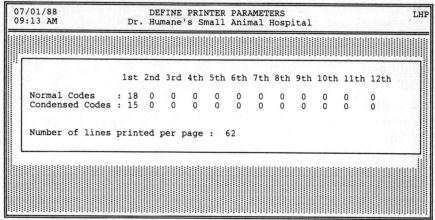

```
07/01/88                    DEFINE PRINTER PARAMETERS                    LHP
09:13 AM                Dr. Humane's Small Animal Hospital


                    1st 2nd 3rd 4th 5th 6th 7th 8th 9th 10th 11th 12th
     Normal Codes    : 18  0   0   0   0   0   0   0   0   0    0    0
     Condensed Codes : 15  0   0   0   0   0   0   0   0   0    0    0


     Number of lines printed per page :  62
```

F1-Help F10-Process ESC-Exit

Setup Color Parameters

If your computer has a color monitor, the Setup Color Parameters
operation lets you define or edit the colors displayed by the program.

To define color parameters, press 7 from the Options Menu
to select the Defaults Submenu. Next, press 4 to select the Colors
operation. The screen in Figure 9-5 will appear.

Figure 9-5. The Color Definition Screen

```
                          ══════Color Definition══════

        Horizontal Menu    Vertical Menu     Menu Selector     Background
        Window             Titles/Headers    Help Window       Prompt
        Active Field       Inactive Field    Line Status       Urgent Status

            ──────Colors──────                        ──────Examples──────


        a a a a a a a a a a a a a a a
        a a a a a a a a a a a a a a a
        a a a a a a a a a a a a a a a
        a a a a a a a a a a a a a a a
        a a a a a a a a a a a a a a a
        a a a a a a a a a a a a a a a
        a a a a a a a a a a a a a a a
        a a a a a a a a a a a a a a a
```

F1-Help F10-Process ESC-Exit

You have a choice of eight background colors:

- Black
- Dark blue
- Green
- Light blue
- Red
- Magenta
- Brown
- White

You can change the color of 12 areas of the screen:

- Horizontal Menu
- Vertical Menu
- Menu Selector
- Background
- Window
- Titles/Headers
- Help Window
- Prompt
- Active Field
- Inactive Field
- Line Status
- Urgent Message

The same color options are available for text, but with two intensities. The left half of the screen holds the low intensity text option and the right half of the screen holds the high intensity text option.

To change colors, use the arrow keys to move the light blue highlight bar to the field you want to change. Press Enter. A white box will appear around the color currently assigned to the field. Use the arrow keys to move the box to the new color. Press Enter. The field will change, exhibiting the new color. Press the F10 (Process) function key once all desired color changes are made. Note: If you're using a floppy drive system, *DacEasy* prompts you to change disks during this operation because the DEA COL file on this disk must have the new color parameters written to it.

Chapter 10

Organizing Your DOS Directories

The disk operating system (DOS) is software that organizes data input and output between the computer and disk drives. And, as you're managing your files, it helps to understand how DOS works and what it does. DOS comes in several PC versions:

- MS-DOS by Microsoft
- PC-DOS by IBM
- Others not as well known

Common DOS Commands

DOS is loaded into the computer when you turn it on and then manages all of your computer activity. It's the system that directs the interactions between your computer hardware, software, and your input without your even knowing it. DOS asks you for information using prompts such as A>, B>, and C>. The letter references the currently active disk drive. For instance, if you are currently using the disk in drive A:, the prompt will read A>. To switch to drive B:, just type *B:* and press the Enter (or Return) key.

DEL

When communicating with DOS it doesn't matter whether you type in uppercase or lowercase letters. However, you do need to enter spaces and punctuation correctly. For instance, you can't substitute *B* or *B;* for *B:* when changing drives. You need the colon. Commonly used DOS commands are DEL which means delete the following file. For example,

DEL B:DACDOCS/BUSINESS tells DOS to delete the file called Business in the DacDocs directory on the disk in drive B:.

DIR

The DIR command requests DOS to show you a list of files on the current disk and directory. For instance, if you're in drive A: and you type DIR, you'll see a list of all files on the disk in drive A:. To see the list on the disk in drive B: while you're in A:, just type DIR B:.

FORMAT

The FORMAT command tells DOS to prepare a new disk for use. You can also format a used disk; however, any files stored on it will be erased.

To format a disk, make sure the DOS A> (floppy drive system) or C> (hard drive system) prompt appears on the screen. Type

FORMAT B:

and press Enter.

Insert the disk you want to format in drive B:, then press any key to start formatting.

Important note: It's important not to open the load lever and remove the disk until formatting is complete. The red drive light will go out when the format is finished.

Once formatting is complete, the DOS prompt, *Format another (Y/N)?* will appear. Type *Y* to format another disk or type *N* to return to the DOS A> or C> prompt. Then remove the formatted disk from drive B:.

COPY

You'll also often use the COPY command to copy files from one disk to another. You already used this in Chapter 1 to make backup copies of your *DacEasy* disks and to copy the *DacEasy* files to your hard disk. For instance, to copy the Business file from the disk in drive A: to the disk in drive B:, type

COPY A:BUSINESS B:.

To copy everything on the disk in drive A: to the disk in drive B, type COPY A:*.* B:.

Data Disks

The disks on which you store the accounting files and other documents created with *DacEasy* are called *data disks*. You can also store documents on your hard disk, but it's wise to back them up on floppy disks, in case your hard disk is damaged. When you create a document, you save it as a *file*.

Files and Directories

Think of a file as if it were a piece of paper. A blank file is similar to a blank sheet of paper and once you save a document (such as a transaction) in the file, it's like a typed sheet of paper.

You save your files by copying them onto the data disks. And, although you could just store all files onto disks without any order, it's best to organize your data by creating *directories*.

Think of directories as if they were manila file folders. The directories are folders and the files are sheets of paper inside them. The folders (directories) themselves are kept inside a cabinet: the data disk. For instance, suppose you have a disk with a directory called *Business* on it. If you keep all business-related documents in that directory you'll always know where to find them. You can also create smaller directories (called *subdirectories*) within the main directory.

Getting Organized

If you have a dual-drive system, it's always a good idea to organize your disks so each contains similar data. For example, the disk labeled *DacEasy Program* contains the *DacEasy* program files and the *DacEasy Data Disk* contains the accounting files. Your data disk contains your working documents, but you may want to subdivide them even further to separate your personal accounts from your business accounts, for example, or to separate the accounts of your various enterprises. You can place these files on separately labeled disks or you can create subdirectories on one disk (an organizing scheme that is explained below).

With a hard disk system, you start with one directory—C:/. This one directory (called the *root directory*) contains all *DacEasy* system files, Help files, printer setup files, and document files you've created, and any other applications (such as your word processor) and their data files. You may become confused in the future if you can't remember the name of a document and you have to search a long list of filenames from different applications on a single directory.

All disks (floppy or hard) have a root directory, denoted by a backslash (\) following the drive letter. This directory is automatically created after the disk formatting takes place. You can create subdirectories from this root directory (using any alphanumeric name, up to eight characters in length) by entering the command MKDIR at the DOS prompt.

For example, if you're using a hard disk, it would be a good idea to create a *DacEasy* and *DacEasy* documents subdirectory at the root directory. (For a floppy-disk system, you may want to create subdirectories, such as personal and business, on your data disk. However, because of space limitations, you'll find that it often makes more sense to categorize them by using separate disks.)

Subdirectories on a Hard Disk

This discussion will specifically use a hard disk system as an example. To create subdirectories, first turn on your computer to load DOS. At the C:/ prompt, type

MKDIR DAC
and press Enter. Then, at the same prompt, type
MKDIR DACDOCS
and press Enter. Next, type
DIR
and press Enter at the C:/ prompt to list the root directory. You'll notice that you now have two additional listings:

DAC   <DIR>
DACDOCS   <DIR>

These are new subdirectories of which the root directory is the parent. The DOS directory system can be thought of as a tree, in which the root directory is the root of the tree, and subdirectories are the branches (Figure 10-1).

Now, whenever you log on to *DacEasy* and its corresponding files, all application files will be copied to the DAC subdirectory. And, when you save files you can save them all to the DacDocs subdirectory. With an application disk in drive A:, type

286

Figure 10-1. The Root, Its Subdirectories, and Their Subdirectories

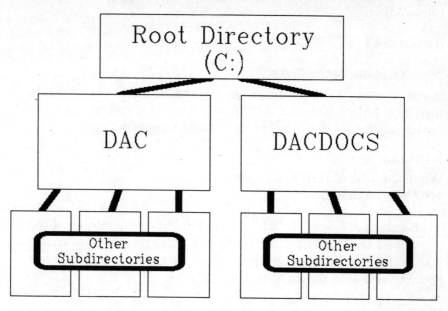

COPY A:*.* C:/DAC
at the C:/ prompt.

You'll be copying files to their specific subdirectories, as is indicated by

C:/DAC

You should also create another subdirectory at the root directory to hold your own documents. Later, you may have more than one subdirectory for specifying types of files (for example, personal or business financial files) but for now you can create one (while you are in the DAC directory) named FILES by typing

MKDIR FILES
and pressing Enter at the C:/ prompt.

If you want to call up *DacEasy*, you can't simply type *DEA* at the C:/ prompt, since it isn't in the root directory but in the subdirectory named DAC. You must first enter the full path name (the complete disk/subdirectory designation, with disk first, followed by the various levels of subdirectories) before the filename, for example,

/DAC/DEA3

Directories on Floppy Disks

If you're using a floppy drive system, create the DacDocs directory by inserting the data disk in any drive, for instance, A:, switching to that drive by typing *A:* and then typing

FORMAT A:
When the disk is formatted, type
MKDIR DACDOCS

"Sub-subdirectories." In addition to having a separate subdirectory called DacDocs for storing your *DacEasy* documents, you may want extra " sub-subdirectories" to stay organized. For instance, you might divide the subdirectory into

• Personal
• Business
• 1988
• Loans

and so on. To do this, at the C:/ prompt type
CD/DAC

Once you're in that directory, type
MKDIR BUSINESS
and press Return.

You can continue to make other directories the same way.
Whether you have a hard disk or floppy disks, you can do the same thing. Place the floppy disk in any drive—for instance, A:. Then type

A:
to move to that drive. Continue by typing
CD DACDOCS
to move to the DacDocs directory on the disk and then make other directories by typing
MKDIR BUSINESS
and so on.

In Versions 2.0 and 3.0 of *DacEasy*, *path support* is provided, in hard disk systems, for multicompany processing. This lets you create separate subdirectories for each of the businesses you're preparing without having to copy the *DacEasy* program files into each business subdirectory.

To specify the path of the business you want to access when you call *DacEasy* from DOS, type

DEA3 BUSINESS1
and press Enter.

To create a subdirectory named BUSINESS1, simply type

MKDIR/DAC/BUSINESS1
at the DOS prompt. A subdirectory named Business1 will be created within the DAC directory.

To create a subdirectory for a second business, type

MKDIR/DAC/BUSINESS2
at the DOS prompt.

Note: The subdirectory names are just examples of names you may want to use. Use any name you choose.

When a new subdirectory for a business is created, the accounting files for that business must be initialized (see Chapter 2).

Upgrading Your Dual Drive System to a Hard Disk System

Most dual drive system users will eventually want to upgrade to a hard disk system. This upgrade not only gives you greater speed and more capacity, it's also more convenient. With heated competition and recent advances in technology, the cost of hard-drive storage has come within the means of most users.

To convert your files to a hard disk system, make sure the hard disk contains DOS. (Your computer dealer can help you install DOS onto your hard disk system.) With DOS installed, follow these steps:

1. Create a directory that will contain your *DacEasy* files (see the details earlier in this Chapter on how to create DOS directories).
2. Once a directory is created, type

CD/Name of Directory

at the C> prompt and press Enter.

3. Next, insert the INSTALL disk from your *DacEasy Accounting* package into drive A:. At the C> prompt, type

A:INSTALL

and press Enter. Follow the installation procedures that appear on the screen. You may use whatever directory names you wish. For convenience, this sample will use the names suggested by *DacEasy Accounting*.

After you've completed the installation procedure, exit the program.

When the C> prompt appears:

4. Insert the disk that contains your accounting data files (the one you used in drive B: on your dual drive system) into drive A:.

5. Type:

COPY A:*.* /DEA/FILES

and press Enter.

All filenames will appear on the screen as the files are copied.

When this procedure is completed, you're ready to access *DacEasy Accounting* on your hard disk system.

Index

Products (codes)

Hematology
    CBC — cbc reagents
    COAG — COAGULATION reagents
    SERO — SEROLOGY reagents

MICROBIOLOGY
    MCB — MICRO reagents
    WAT — water bacteriology reagents & Supply

CHEMISTRY
    CHR — routine chemistry reagents (Excluding Kodak)
    KDK — Kodak reagents

IMMUNOLOGY
    RIA — Vitek Reagents
    EIA — eia reagents

SHIPPING
    PSTG postage
    FED — Fedex
    DEL — delivery charges

COMPUTER SUPPLY & OFFICE SUPPLY
    COMP — Supply
    OFFO — OFFICE SUPPLIES
    COPI — copier Supplies
    ACCT — accounting Supplies

DISPOSABLES -

- GAS - glassware (general supply)
  SECT - sectional supplies
- COL - cell collection supplies
- WDS - waste disposal supplies
- WIPE - paper towels & kimwipe

WASTE DISPOSAL

DISP - disposal fees
CONT - container supplies
DECO - DECONTAMINATION supplies

SANITORIAL

CLA - cleaning agents
BATH - bathroom supplies
JEQ - sanitorial equipment

INSTRUMENTS

RHM
REM
SER
IMM
RIA
CMP - computer
OFF - office equipment

Furniture

OFF
LAB -
CMPF